Test Prep

High School

High School Test Prep provides a complete presentation of the types of skills covered in standardized tests in a variety of formats. These formats are similar to those high school students will encounter when testing. The subject areas covered in this book include:

- **Language Arts**
- **Reading**
- **Mathematics**
- **Problem Solving**
- **Citizenship**

This workbook also includes a special section called **Cloze: Reading Comprehension Challenge** that focuses solely on advanced reading comprehension. A detailed explanation and examples of the cloze activities can be found on pages 108-115.

Developed by:
Michael Milone, Ph.D.
Richard A. Boning

Send all inquiries to: School Specialty Children's Publishing • 8720 Orion Place • Columbus, OH 43240-2111

ISBN 1-56189-752-3

3 4 5 6 7 8 9 10 PHXBK 09 08 07 06 05 04

Table of Contents

High School Test Prep

The Program That Teaches Test-Taking Achievement

For over two decades, McGraw-Hill has helped students perform their best when taking standardized achievement tests. Over the years, we have identified the skills and strategies that students need to master the challenges of taking a standardized test. Becoming familiar with the test-taking experience can help ensure your child's success.

High School Test Prep provides strategies for success

Many students need special support when preparing to take a standardized test. *High School Test Prep* gives your child the opportunity to practice and become familiar with:

- General test content
- The test format
- Listening and following standard directions
- Working in structured settings
- Maintaining a silent, sustained effort
- Using test-taking strategies

High School Test Prep is comprehensive

High School Test Prep provides a complete presentation of the types of skills covered in standardized tests in a variety of formats. These formats are similar to those your child will encounter when testing. The subject areas covered in this book include:

- **Language Arts**
- **Reading**
- **Mathematics**
- **Problem Solving**
- **Citizenship**

This workbook also includes a special section called **Cloze: Reading Comprehension Challenge** that focuses solely on reading comprehension. A detailed explanation and examples of the cloze activities can be found on pages 108-115.

High School Test Prep gives students the practice they need

Each student lesson provides several components that help develop test-taking skills:

- An Example, with directions and sample test items
- A Tips feature, that gives test-taking strategies
- A Practice section, to help students practice answering questions in each test format

Each book gives focused test practice that builds confidence:

- A **Test Yourself** lesson for each unit gives students the opportunity to apply what they have learned in the unit.
- A **Test Practice** section gives students the experience of a longer test-like situation
- A **Record of Scores** section allows students to note and track their own scores.

High School Test Prep is the first and most successful program ever developed to help students become familiar with the test-taking experience. *High School Test Prep* can help to build self-confidence, reduce test anxiety, and provide the opportunity for students to successfully show what they have learned.

Test Practice

Your child should use the answer sheet on page 106 to record the answers for the **Test Practice** section on pages 87–105.

Suggested time allotments:

Language Arts:	20–30 minutes
Reading Comprehension:	20–30 minutes
Mathematics:	20–30 minutes
Citizenship:	30 minutes

A Message to Parents and Teachers:

- **Standardized tests: the yardstick for your child's future**

  Standardized testing is one of the cornerstones of American education. From its beginning in the early part of this century, standardized testing has gradually become the yardstick by which student performance is judged. For better or worse, your child's future will be determined in great part by how well she or he performs on the standardized tests used by your school district.

- **Even good students can have trouble with testing**

  In general, standardized tests are well-designed and carefully developed to assess students' abilities in a consistent and balanced manner. However, there are many factors that can hinder the performance of an individual student when testing. These might include test anxiety, unfamiliarity with the test's format, or failing to understand the directions.

  In addition, it is rare that students are taught all of the material that appears on a standardized test. This is because the curriculum of most schools does not directly match the content of the standardized test. There will certainly be overlap between what your child learns in school and how he or she is tested, but some materials will probably be unfamiliar.

- ***High School Test Prep* will lend a helping hand**

  It is because of the shortcomings of the standardized testing process that *High School Test Prep* was developed. The lessons in the book were created after a careful analysis of the most popular achievement tests. The items, while different from those on the tests, reflect the types of materials that your child will encounter when testing. Students who use *High School Test Prep* will also become familiar with the format of the most popular achievement tests. This learning experience will reduce anxiety and give your child the opportunity to do his or her best on the next standardized test.

We urge you to review with your child the Message to Students and the feature "How to Use This Book" on pages 6–8. The information on these pages will help your child to use this book and develop important test-taking skills. We are confident that following the recommendations in this book will help your child to earn a test score that accurately reflects his or her true ability.

A Message to Students:

Frequently in school you will be asked to take a standardized achievement test. This test will show how much you know compared to other students in your grade. Your score on a standardized achievement test will help your teachers plan your education. It will also give you and your parents an idea of what your learning strengths and weaknesses are.

This book will help you do your best on a standardized achievement test. It will show you what to expect on the test and will give you a chance to practice important reading and test-taking skills. Here are some suggestions you can follow to make the best use of *High School Test Prep*.

Plan for success

- You'll do your best if you begin studying and do one or two lessons in this book each week. If you only have a little bit of time before a test is given, you can do one or two lessons each day.
- Study a little bit at a time, no more than 30 minutes a day. If you can, choose the same time each day to study in a quiet place.
- Keep a record of your score on each lesson. The charts on pp. 152–155 of this book will help you do this.

On the day of the test...

- Get a good night's sleep the night before the test. Have a light breakfast and lunch to keep from feeling drowsy during the test.
- Use the tips you learned in *High School Test Prep*. The most important tips are to skip difficult items, take the best guess when you're unsure of the answer, and try all the items.
- Don't worry if you are a little nervous when you take an achievement test. This is a natural feeling and may even help you stay alert.

How to Use This Book

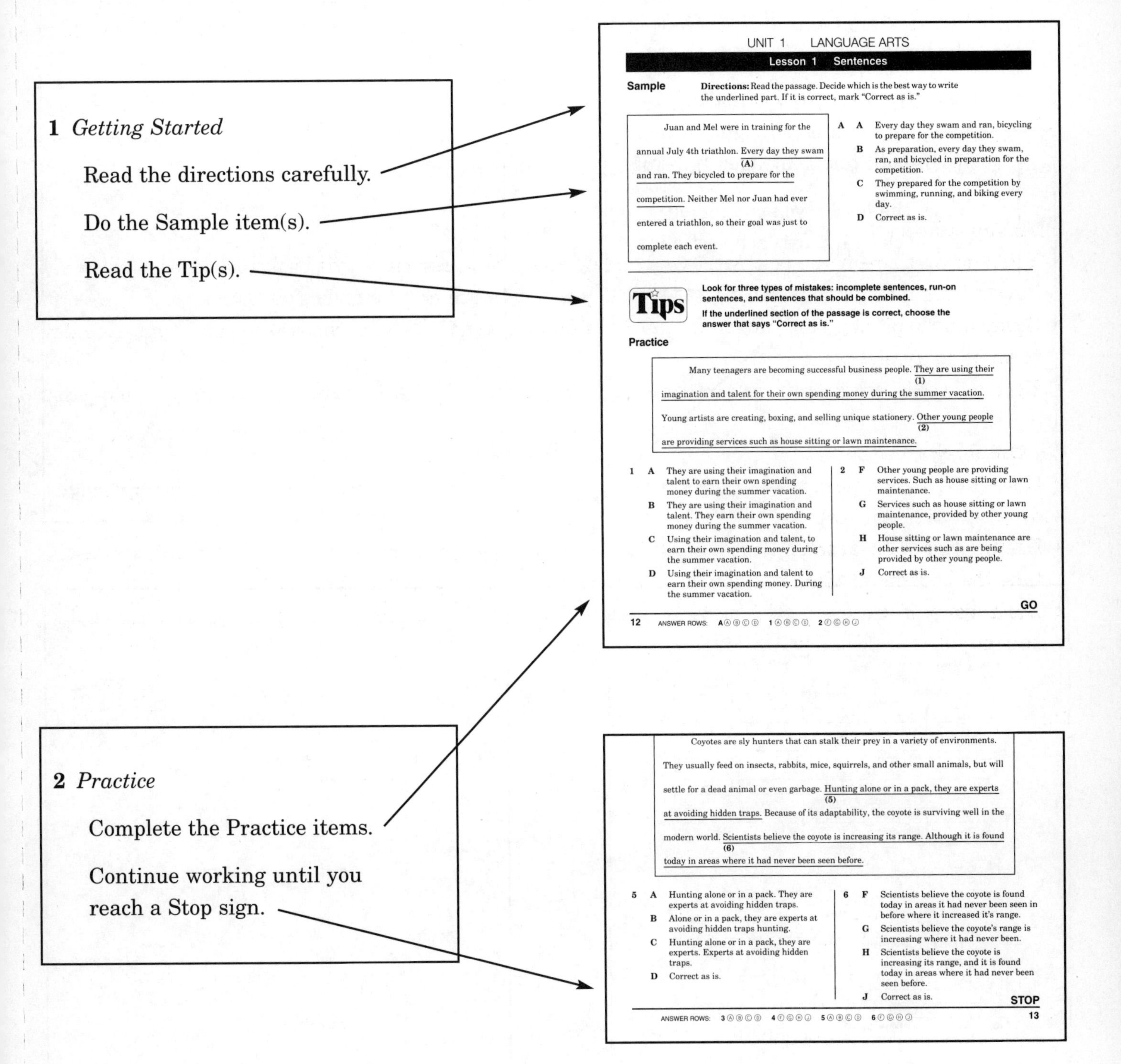

1 *Getting Started*

Read the directions carefully.

Do the Sample item(s).

Read the Tip(s).

UNIT 1 LANGUAGE ARTS

Lesson 1 Sentences

Sample **Directions:** Read the passage. Decide which is the best way to write the underlined part. If it is correct, mark "Correct as is."

Juan and Mel were in training for the annual July 4th triathlon. Every day they swam and ran. They bicycled to prepare for the competition. (A) Neither Mel nor Juan had ever entered a triathlon, so their goal was just to complete each event.

A
- A Every day they swam and ran, bicycling to prepare for the competition.
- B As preparation, every day they swam, ran, and bicycled in preparation for the competition.
- C They prepared for the competition by swimming, running, and biking every day.
- D Correct as is.

Tips

Look for three types of mistakes: incomplete sentences, run-on sentences, and sentences that should be combined.

If the underlined section of the passage is correct, choose the answer that says "Correct as is."

Practice

Many teenagers are becoming successful business people. They are using their imagination and talent for their own spending money during the summer vacation. (1) Young artists are creating, boxing, and selling unique stationery. Other young people are providing services such as house sitting or lawn maintenance. (2)

1
- A They are using their imagination and talent to earn their own spending money during the summer vacation.
- B They are using their imagination and talent. They earn their own spending money during the summer vacation.
- C Using their imagination and talent, to earn their own spending money during the summer vacation.
- D Using their imagination and talent to earn their own spending money. During the summer vacation.

2
- F Other young people are providing services. Such as house sitting or lawn maintenance.
- G Services such as house sitting or lawn maintenance, provided by other young people.
- H House sitting or lawn maintenance are other services such as are being provided by other young people.
- J Correct as is.

GO

12 ANSWER ROWS: A Ⓐ Ⓑ Ⓒ Ⓓ 1 Ⓐ Ⓑ Ⓒ Ⓓ 2 Ⓕ Ⓖ Ⓗ Ⓙ

2 *Practice*

Complete the Practice items.

Continue working until you reach a Stop sign.

Coyotes are sly hunters that can stalk their prey in a variety of environments. They usually feed on insects, rabbits, mice, squirrels, and other small animals, but will settle for a dead animal or even garbage. Hunting alone or in a pack, they are experts at avoiding hidden traps. (5) Because of its adaptability, the coyote is surviving well in the modern world. Scientists believe the coyote is increasing its range. Although it is found today in areas where it had never been seen before. (6)

5
- A Hunting alone or in a pack. They are experts at avoiding hidden traps.
- B Alone or in a pack, they are experts at avoiding hidden traps hunting.
- C Hunting alone or in a pack, they are experts. Experts at avoiding hidden traps.
- D Correct as is.

6
- F Scientists believe the coyote is found today in areas it had never been seen in before where it increased it's range.
- G Scientists believe the coyote's range is increasing where it had never been.
- H Scientists believe the coyote is increasing its range, and it is found today in areas where it had never been seen before.
- J Correct as is.

STOP

ANSWER ROWS: 3 Ⓐ Ⓑ Ⓒ Ⓓ 4 Ⓕ Ⓖ Ⓗ Ⓙ 5 Ⓐ Ⓑ Ⓒ Ⓓ 6 Ⓕ Ⓖ Ⓗ Ⓙ 13

3 *Check It Out*

Check your answers by turning to the Answer Key at the back of the book.

Keep track of how you're doing by marking the number right on the Record of Scores on pages 152–155.

Mark the lesson you completed on the checklist for each section.

Answer Key

Unit 1/Language Arts
Lesson 1 Sentences
Pages 12-13
A. C
1. A
2. J
3. C
4. F
5. D
6. H
Lesson 2 Usage
Pages 14-15
A. B
B. H
1. D
2. H
3. A
4. F
5. C
6. G
7. C
8. F
9. B
10. J
Lesson 3 Writing Mechanics
Pages 16-17
A. C
B. J
1. C
2. F
3. C
4. J
5. C
6. G
7. A
8. H
Lessons 4-8 Writing
(To score your child's writing see the Focused Holistic Scoring Guidelines on page 156)
Lesson 9 Test Yourself
Pages 23-25
A. C
1. B
2. J
3. A
B. J
C. A
4. J
5. B
6. F
7. C
D. H
8. J
9. C
10. G
11. C
(To score your child's writing see the Focused Holistic Scoring Guidelines on page 156)

Unit 2/Reading Comprehension
Lesson 10 Vocabulary
Pages 26-27
A. C
1. D
2. F
3. B
4. J
5. C
Lesson 11 Supporting Ideas
Pages 28-29
A. D
1. B
2. F
3. D
4. H
5. D
Lesson 12 Main Idea
Pages 30-31
A. A
1. C
2. G
3. D
4. H
Lesson 13 Relationships and Outcomes
Pages 32-33
A. C
1. B
2. J
3. A
4. H
5. D
6. G
Lesson 14 Inferences and Generalizations
Pages 34-35
A. B
1. D
2. F
3. B
4. J
5. A
Lesson 15 Evaluation
Pages 36-37
A. D
1. A
2. H
3. B
4. J
5. B
Lesson 16 Test Yourself
Pages 38-41
A. B
1. C
2. F
3. C
4. G
5. D
6. G
7. C
8. H
9. C
10. J
11. A
12. G
13. C
14. J

Unit 3/Mathematics Concepts
Lesson 17 Number Concepts
Pages 43-44
A. B
B. H
1. D
2. H
3. B
4. F
5. C
6. J
7. B
8. F

147

Unit 1: Language Arts Record of Scores

Page	Lesson	Lesson Name	My Score	Total Possible Score
12	1	Sentences		6
14	2	Usage		10
16	3	Writing Mechanics		8
18	4	Descriptive Writing*		60
19	5	Informative Writing*		60
20	6	Classificatory Writing*		60
21	7	Persuasive Writing*		60
22	8	Comparative Writing*		60
23	9	Test Yourself		11
		Total Scores		**335**

*See page 156 for Focused Holistic Scoring Guidelines

Unit 2: Reading Record of Scores

Page	Lesson	Lesson Name	My Score	Total Possible Score
26	10	Vocabulary		5
28	11	Supporting Ideas		5
30	12	Main Idea		4
32	13	Relationships and Outcomes		6
34	14	Inferences and Generalizations		5
36	15	Evaluation		5
38	16	Test Yourself		14
		Total Scores		**44**

152

Cloze: Reading Comprehension Challenge Checklist

116

Skills

Language Arts

Sentences:
Identifying sentence fragments and run-ons
Recognizing sentences that should be combined
Recognizing complete sentences

Usage:
Identifying the correct part of speech
Using correct subject-verb agreement with nouns, personal pronouns, indefinite pronouns, and compound subjects
Using correct pronoun-antecedent agreement
Recognizing correct verb tense
Using the correct form of adjectives, adverbs, and pronouns
Avoiding double negatives

Writing Mechanics:
Using the fundamentals of spelling
Using appropriate capitalization
Using the fundamentals of punctuation

Descriptive Writing:
Describing an object, person, place, or situation in a written composition

Informative Writing:
Describing how to do something in a written composition

Classificatory Writing:
Classifying ideas, objects, or places in a written composition

Comparative Writing:
Discussing opposing courses and supporting one of them in a written composition

Reading

Vocabulary:
Using context clues (synonym, antonym, definition and explanation, description, or example) to determine the meaning of an unfamiliar word or a specialized/technical term
Using knowledge of prefixes and suffixes to determine word meanings

Supporting Ideas:
Identifying related details
Arranging details/events in sequential order
Following complex directions

Main Idea:
Identifying the stated or paraphrased main idea of a passage
Identifying the implied main idea of a passage
Identifying the best summary of a passage

Relationships and Outcomes:
Identifying cause and effect relationships
Predicting probable future actions and outcomes

Inferences and Generalizations:
Using graphic sources for information
Making inferences and drawing conclusions
Making generalizations
Analyzing information and making judgments
Describing plot, setting, character, and mood

Evaluation:
Recognizing the author's point of view and purpose
Recognizing propaganda and persuasive devices
Distinguishing between fact and nonfact
Comparing points of view

Mathematics

Number Concepts:
Using scientific notation
Using exponential notation
Comparing and ordering rational numbers
Rounding whole numbers and decimals
Determining relationships between and among fractions, decimals, and percents

Number Relations:
Using rational number properties and inverse operations
Determining missing elements in patterns
Identifying ordered pairs and solution sets
Applying ratio and proportion
Using exponents and their properties
Evaluating variables and expressions
Solving simple equations
Using number line representations

Geometry:
Identifying lines, rays, angles, and planes
Recognizing properties of two- and three-dimensional figures
Using right-triangle geometry with the Pythagorean theorem
Recognizing similarity, congruence, and symmetry
Recognizing basic geometric constructions

Measurement:
Using metric and customary units
Converting within the metric and customary systems
Finding perimeter, circumference, area, surface area, and volume
Recognizing precision

Probability and Statistics:
Using counting methods
Finding probability
Determining the mean, median, and mode
Using frequency distributions

Addition:
Adding rational numbers

Subtraction:
Subtracting rational numbers

Multiplication:
Multiplying rational numbers

Division:
Dividing rational numbers

Estimation:
Estimating solutions

Strategies:
Identifying strategies for solving problems
Determining strategies or solving problems using percentage, measurement, or geometry
Analyzing or solving problems using probability and statistics
Making predictions

Problem Solving:
Formulating equations or inequalities
Analyzing or interpreting graphs, charts, tables, maps, or diagrams to solve problems

Reasonable Answers:
Evaluating reasonableness

Citizenship

History and Geography:
Understanding historic documents (Northwest Ordinance, Declaration of Independence, Constitution, Bill of Rights)
Identifying national symbols
Locating significant places on a map
Reading maps

Law and Government:
Recognizing diversity
Understanding basic economic concepts
Identifying the branches of government and their functions
Recognizing the major economic systems
Understanding federalism
Differentiating among the types of government
Explaining the process of making a law
Understanding basic legal principles
Identifying the functions of political parties
Understanding the role of government officials
Recognizing the importance of voting
Making informed choices
Identifying types of civic involvement

Strategies

Considering every answer choice
Noticing the lettering of answer choices
Working methodically
Indicating that an item has no mistakes
Trying out answer choices
Using context clues
Marking the correct answer as soon as it is found
Prewriting
Focusing on a given topic
Writing with elaboration
Focusing on the steps necessary to complete a task
Writing sequentially
Considering both sides of an issue
Choosing a position
Supporting a position
Discussing opposite positions
Eliminating answer choices
Using key words to locate answers
Referring to a passage to answer questions
Taking the best guess when unsure of the answer
Reasoning from facts and evidence
Skipping difficult items and returning to them later
Using key words, numbers, and figures to answer questions
Finding the answer without computing
Using visual materials to locate information
Computing carefully
Ignoring extraneous information
Indicating the correct answer is not given
Checking answers
Reworking a problem
Rereading difficult questions

High School Test Prep Checklist

Unit 1/Language Arts

Unit 2/Reading Comprehension

Unit 3/Mathematics Concepts

Unit 4/Mathematics Operations

Unit 5/Problem Solving

Unit 6/Citizenship

Test Practice

Lesson 1 Sentences

6/5/12

Sample

Directions: Read the passage. Decide which is the best way to write the underlined part. If it is correct, mark "Correct as is."

Juan and Mel were in training for the annual July 4th triathlon. Every day they swam and ran. They bicycled to prepare for the competition. (A) Neither Mel nor Juan had ever entered a triathlon, so their goal was just to complete each event.

A
- **A** Every day they swam and ran, bicycling to prepare for the competition.
- **B** As preparation, every day they swam, ran, and bicycled in preparation for the competition.
- **C** They prepared for the competition by swimming, running, and biking every day.
- **D** Correct as is.

Look for three types of mistakes: incomplete sentences, run-on sentences, and sentences that should be combined.

If the underlined section of the passage is correct, choose the answer that says "Correct as is."

Practice

Many teenagers are becoming successful business people. They are using their imagination and talent for their own spending money during the summer vacation. (1) Young artists are creating, boxing, and selling unique stationery. Other young people are providing services such as house sitting or lawn maintenance. (2)

1
- **A** They are using their imagination and talent to earn their own spending money during the summer vacation.
- **B** They are using their imagination and talent. They earn their own spending money during the summer vacation.
- **C** Using their imagination and talent, to earn their own spending money during the summer vacation.
- **D** Using their imagination and talent to earn their own spending money. During the summer vacation.

2
- **F** Other young people are providing services. Such as house sitting or lawn maintenance.
- **G** Services such as house sitting or lawn maintenance, provided by other young people.
- **H** House sitting or lawn maintenance are other services such as are being provided by other young people.
- **J** Correct as is.

GO

ANSWER ROWS: A Ⓐ Ⓑ Ⓒ Ⓓ 1 Ⓐ Ⓑ Ⓒ Ⓓ 2 Ⓕ Ⓖ Ⓗ Ⓙ

6/5/12

Have you ever wished you could see to the bottom of the ocean, well, now you can. (3) Many resort areas have opened oceanariums—gigantic aquariums that reproduce the ocean habitat so fish and other sea animals can be observed by visitors. Only a glass wall separates visitors from fish and marine animals. A viewing area that provides a result is a perfect window on the world beneath the sea. (4)

3
- A Have you ever wished that now you can see well to the bottom of the ocean?
- B Have you ever wished you could see well? Now you can, to the bottom of the ocean?
- C Have you ever wished you could see to the bottom of the ocean? Well, now you can.
- D Now you can wish to see the bottom of the ocean.

4
- F The result is a viewing area that provides a perfect window on the world beneath the sea.
- G A viewing area that provides a perfect window on the resulting world beneath the sea.
- H The result beneath the sea is a viewing area that provides a window.
- J Correct as is.

Coyotes are sly hunters that can stalk their prey in a variety of environments. They usually feed on insects, rabbits, mice, squirrels, and other small animals, but will settle for a dead animal or even garbage. Hunting alone or in a pack, they are experts at avoiding hidden traps. (5) Because of its adaptability, the coyote is surviving well in the modern world. Scientists believe the coyote is increasing its range. Although it is found today in areas where it had never been seen before. (6)

5
- A Hunting alone or in a pack. They are experts at avoiding hidden traps.
- B Alone or in a pack, they are experts at avoiding hidden traps hunting.
- C Hunting alone or in a pack, they are experts. Experts at avoiding hidden traps.
- D Correct as is.

6
- F Scientists believe the coyote is found today in areas it had never been seen in before where it increased it's range.
- G Scientists believe the coyote's range is increasing where it had never been.
- H Scientists believe the coyote is increasing its range, and it is found today in areas where it had never been seen before.
- J Correct as is.

STOP

ANSWER ROWS: 3 Ⓐ Ⓑ Ⓒ Ⓓ 4 Ⓕ Ⓖ Ⓗ Ⓙ 5 Ⓐ Ⓑ Ⓒ Ⓓ 6 Ⓕ Ⓖ Ⓗ Ⓙ

Samples

Directions: Read the passage. Decide which word or group of words fits best in each space.

It was Judy's first time horseback riding, so the instructor __(A)__ a gentle animal for her. At first, things went well. We walked along a scenic trail until we came to a spot where two streams joined. Then, for some unknown reason, Judy's horse decided to return to the barn. No matter what Judy tried to do, the horse would not be turned. He galloped __(B)__ for the stable through some trees with low branches.

A **A** choose
B chose
C choosed
D chosen

B **F** straightly
G more straight
H straight
J straighter

If you are unsure of the answer, try each choice in the blank. Read the sentence with each answer choice to yourself. The correct answer is usually the one that sounds best in the sentence.

Remember, adverbs usually modify verbs, and adjectives usually modify nouns or pronouns.

Practice

You might be __(1)__ to learn that Samuel Morse, the inventor of the telegraph, was also an artist. In fact, when he was a young man, he made his living through portrait painting. Morse hoped to have an opportunity to create the huge paintings that were to decorate the Capitol's walls in Washington, DC. He became discouraged when he was not awarded the commission and turned his energies toward inventing. Today he is __(2)__ recognized as a brilliant inventor and artist.

1 **A** surprise
B surprises
C surprising
D surprised

2 **F** wide
G wider
H widely
J widest

GO

ANSWER ROWS: A Ⓐ Ⓑ Ⓒ Ⓓ B Ⓕ Ⓖ Ⓗ Ⓙ 1 Ⓐ Ⓑ Ⓒ Ⓓ 2 Ⓕ Ⓖ Ⓗ Ⓙ

The little-known animal called the slow loris is ____(3)____ named. It is a nocturnal creature that sleeps during the day and creeps along during the night ____(4)____ for food. The slow loris feeds on insects, birds' eggs, and certain varieties of fruit. It is ____(5)____ from India to Indonesia and is about the size of a squirrel. Living in trees, the loris spends most of its time inching along branches. It is a member of the primate group and ____(6)____ resembles a small monkey.

3
- A appropriately
- B appropriate
- C more appropriate
- D more appropriately

4
- F searching
- G searches
- H search
- J searched

5
- A founded
- B finding
- C found
- D find

6
- F most close
- G closely
- H close
- J closer

Without ____(7)____, a dozen British soldiers broke into the house. Marsha and her servants were locked in the kitchen, and the Redcoats set up their headquarters in the beautiful mansion. Marsha knew that if they settled in, they might not ____(8)____ leave and the house would eventually be destroyed.

With the help of her servants, ____(9)____ managed to climb out a window. She made her way into the barn, where she found and loaded several rifles. She set fire to several bales of hay and began firing the rifles. The confusion was such that the Redcoats ____(10)____ out of the house, never to return.

7
- A warn
- B warned
- C warning
- D warns

8
- F ever
- G never
- H always
- J usually

9
- A her
- B she
- C they
- D their

10
- F flee
- G fly
- H flying
- J fled

STOP

ANSWER ROWS: 3 Ⓐ Ⓑ Ⓒ Ⓓ 5 Ⓐ Ⓑ Ⓒ Ⓓ 7 Ⓐ Ⓑ Ⓒ Ⓓ 9 Ⓐ Ⓑ Ⓒ Ⓓ
4 Ⓕ Ⓖ Ⓗ Ⓙ 6 Ⓕ Ⓖ Ⓗ Ⓙ 8 Ⓕ Ⓖ Ⓗ Ⓙ 10 Ⓕ Ⓖ Ⓗ Ⓙ

Samples

Directions: Read the passage. Decide which type of mistake is in the underlined part. If it is correct, mark "No error."

Finally, Cal had a day off and the weather was great. He gathered all of his fishing equipment and set off for a relaxing day at the lake. Cal baited his hook cast (A) it into the water, and waited patiently. Suddenly, out of the corner of his eye, he caught a movement in the sand. A tiny (B) turtle popped out of the ground and began to creep toward the water.

A
- A Spelling error
- B Capitalization error
- C Punctuation error
- D No error

B
- F Spelling error
- G Capitalization error
- H Punctuation error
- J No error

For each underlined part, look for one kind of mistake at a time. Look for mistakes in spelling first. Then look for mistakes in capitalization and punctuation.

Practice

Nancy whispered quietly "Just hold still. The (1) ambulance will be here in a minute. Everything will be all right."

Her friend, Byron, was lying on the ground holding his eye. He and Nancy had been watching some friends playing war games with paint pellets. The game was usually harmless, and the players wore protective goggls. No one ever (2) dreamed a stray pellet might injure one of the spectators.

1
- A Spelling error
- B Capitalization error
- C Punctuation error
- D No error

2
- F Spelling error
- G Capitalization error
- H Punctuation error
- J No error

GO

ANSWER ROWS: A Ⓐ Ⓑ Ⓒ Ⓓ B Ⓕ Ⓖ Ⓗ Ⓙ 1 Ⓐ Ⓑ Ⓒ Ⓓ 2 Ⓕ Ⓖ Ⓗ Ⓙ

6/6/12

Dear Orlando:
(3)

Wait until you hear this. Mimi and I are going to be on television next week.
(4)
That bone we dug up by the lake wasn't a dead cow after all. It was some kind of buffalo and the professors at the university came back and looked for more things at
(5)
the spot. I'll tell you all the details next week when you get here.

Your Cousin,
(6)
Paula

3 **A** Spelling
B Capitalization
C Punctuation
D No Mistake

4 **F** Spelling
G Capitalization
H Punctuation
J No Mistake

5 **A** Spelling
B Capitalization
C Punctuation
D No Mistake

6 **F** Spelling
G Capitalization
H Punctuation
J No Mistake

Janet Guthrie became a sports-car racer in 1963. She traveled around the country racing while she continude her career as an engineer.
(7)

Guthrie's dream was to qualify for the Indianapolis 500, and in 1977 she realized her dream. Unfortunately because of mechanical problems, she couldn't
(8)
complete the race. The next year she qualified again, and despite a broken wrist, finished ninth in the race.

7 **A** Spelling
B Capitalization
C Punctuation
D No Mistake

8 **F** Spelling
G Capitalization
H Punctuation
J No Mistake

STOP

ANSWER ROWS: 3 Ⓐ Ⓑ Ⓒ Ⓓ 4 Ⓕ Ⓖ Ⓗ Ⓙ 5 Ⓐ Ⓑ Ⓒ Ⓓ 6 Ⓕ Ⓖ Ⓗ Ⓙ 7 Ⓐ Ⓑ Ⓒ Ⓓ 8 Ⓕ Ⓖ Ⓗ Ⓙ

Almost everyone has had a "mentor," a person they know who has made a difference in their lives. It can be a friend, a family member, someone you have worked with, or somebody else. Describe your mentor in detail and explain how the person has affected your life. Write the description as if it were for a feature in your school newspaper.

Prewriting: Organizing your ideas

Read the directions carefully. Be sure you understand what you are supposed to do.

"Brainstorm" by writing your ideas down on scratch paper. Don't write your composition yet. Just write short notes about a person who has been your mentor. Try to think of all the details you can.

Don't write about things that have nothing to do with the topic. Write about only the person who has been your mentor. Include things such as how you came to know the person, how the person has affected you, and anything else that comes to mind.

Drafting: Writing your composition

Read the notes you wrote for your brainstorm. Decide which ones go together.

Think about the best way to write your composition. You will probably need more than one paragraph, so keep ideas that are related in the same paragraph. Your composition should have a clear beginning, middle, and end.

Think about who will read your composition in the school paper. Write so they will have a good understanding of your mentor. Remember, the person who reads your composition might not know your mentor. Be sure to include all the details you can think of.

Begin writing your composition. Use the notes from your "brainstorm" to write your sentences. Try to express a complete thought in each sentence.

Use adjectives and adverbs to describe your mentor in detail. Use verbs to tell about what the person means to you. If it helps you, talk to yourself quietly about your mentor. Then write down what you are saying to yourself.

Take your time and write carefully. Use the best English you can, but don't worry about mistakes. The most important thing is to write clearly and completely.

STOP

Imagine that your school is part of an exchange program involving foreign students. The students have just arrived, and this week they will attend their first high school football game. You have been asked to write a composition explaining what they should do to enjoy the game. You might begin by telling them what to wear. Then continue by explaining other things that will help them enjoy their first American football game.

Prewriting: Organizing your ideas

Read the directions carefully. Be sure you understand what you are supposed to do. If necessary, read the directions twice.

Think about the steps necessary to enjoy a football game. Don't write your composition yet. Just list the steps on scratch paper. Try to remember the routine you follow when you attend a football game. You don't want to leave anything out.

Don't write about things that are not part of enjoying a football game. Tell about finding your seats, player introductions, halftime entertainment, and anything else you can think of.

Drafting: Writing your composition

Read the list you made on scratch paper. Decide which things go together. Are there any other things you should add to your list?

Think about the best way to write your composition. Be sure you write the steps in order, from pre-game activities to leaving the stadium. You will need more than one paragraph, so keep the steps that are related in the same paragraph.

Think about the exchange students who will read your composition. They have never been to an American football game, so write as much as you can so they will be able to enjoy the game. Write about how they should dress, doing a "wave", and anything else that will help them enjoy and understand the game.

Begin writing your composition. Use the steps you listed on scratch paper to write your sentences. Try to express a complete thought in each sentence.

Take your time and write carefully. Use the best English you can, but don't worry about mistakes. The most important thing is to write clearly about what is necessary to enjoy a football game. Don't forget any steps, and put them in the right order.

STOP

You have just been chosen to represent your school at a national students convention. The convention will take place during the mid-winter holiday, and it is being held in southern Florida. You will be making the trip alone by airplane. Write a composition for a friend you haven't seen in a long time in which you explain the good and bad things about attending the convention. Explain each of your points completely.

Prewriting: Organizing your ideas

Read the directions carefully. Be sure you understand what you are supposed to do.

Think about going to the students convention. Then think of some good and bad things about the trip. Don't write your composition yet. Use scratch paper to organize your thinking. Try writing a one-sentence "nutshell" that summarizes the good things about the convention. Then write another nutshell about the bad things.

Don't write about anything else, just the good and bad things about going to the convention by yourself during the winter holiday. What would be fun? What would be a problem? How would the other people in your family feel? Will you miss being home for the holidays?

Drafting: Writing your composition

Read your nutshells and the notes you wrote on scratch paper. Decide which ideas go together. Are there any other things you should add to your notes?

Think about the best way to write your composition. You will need more than one paragraph, so keep ideas that are related in the same paragraph.

Think about who will read your composition. Write so your friend will understand the good and bad things about attending the student convention. Remember, you are writing for a friend you haven't seen for a long time. The friend knows a lot about you already but might not be familiar some of the newer things or people in your life. You may have to explain these things or people.

Begin writing your composition. Use your notes to write your sentences. Try to express a complete thought in each sentence.

Take your time and write carefully. Use the best English you can, but don't worry about mistakes. The most important thing is to write clearly so your reader will understand the good and bad things about going to the student convention.

STOP

The young people your age hang out at the local park. Unfortunately, many of them litter the area when they leave. This makes the park unpleasant for other people, and some adults now want young people kept out of the park. Write a letter to the Park Commission explaining your position about this suggestion. Explain your position clearly and convincingly.

Prewriting: Organizing your ideas

Read the directions carefully. Be sure you understand what you are supposed to do. Your letter should state your position regarding the suggestion that young people be kept out of the park.

Think about what would happen if young people were kept out of the park. Is this fair? Where would they go? How would they react? Don't write your letter yet. Use scratch paper to organize your thinking. Just write your thoughts and feelings about being kept out of the park because of the actions of a few young people.

Don't write about anything else except your thoughts and feelings on being kept out of the park. What is your position on this suggestion?

Drafting: Writing your letter

Read the notes you wrote on scratch paper. Decide which ideas go together. Are there any other things you should add to your notes? Keep in mind that your letter will be read by adults on the Park Commission.

Think about the best way to organize your letter. You will need more than one paragraph, so keep ideas that are related in the same paragraph. Your letter should move logically from one idea to another.

Think about the adults on the Park Commission who will read your letter. Write so they will understand your point of view. Your job is to convince them that your position on the issue is sensible. If you do a good job, you may even convince them to agree with your point of view.

Begin writing your letter. Use your notes to write your sentences. Try to express a complete thought in each sentence.

Take your time and write carefully. Use the best English you can, but don't worry about mistakes. The most important thing is to write clearly so your reader will understand your position about keeping young people out of the park.

STOP

Because of budget cuts, your school and another school are being combined. This means that either class size will have to be doubled, or the school will have two sessions. One session will be from 7:00 AM to noon, and the other from noon to 5:00 PM. Write a letter to your local newspaper discussing both solutions. State your position on the issue and give good reasons for your position.

Prewriting: Organizing your ideas

Read the directions carefully. Be sure you understand what you are supposed to do. Your letter should discuss the two options and then state your position on the issue.

Think about the advantages and disadvantages of large classes versus a two-session school day. Which one do you think is best? Don't write your letter yet. Use scratch paper to organize your thinking. Just write your thoughts and feelings about the change.

Don't write about anything else except the two options being proposed to solve the problem and the reasons you favor one of them.

Drafting: Writing your letter

Read the notes you wrote on scratch paper. Decide which ideas go together. Are there any other things you should add to your notes? Keep in mind that your letter will appear in the newspaper and will be read by many different people.

Think about the best way to organize your letter. You will need more than one paragraph, so you should keep ideas that are related in the same paragraph. Your letter should move logically from one idea to another.

Think about who will read your letter. Write so they will understand the options being presented and the one you support. Your job is to convince them that your position on the issue is sensible. If you do a good job, you may even convince them to agree with your point of view.

Begin writing your letter. Use your notes to write your sentences. Try to express a complete thought in each sentence.

Take your time and write carefully. Use the best English you can, but don't worry about mistakes. The most important thing is to write clearly so your reader will understand your position about the proposed solutions.

STOP

Sample A

An air show will be held at the Donleyville Airport this Sunday at 1:00 PM. The airport's director, Susan Collins, has booked a number of quality acts. She has promised exciting entertainment. (A) Tickets will be available at the gate.

A
- **A** Susan Collins, promising exciting entertainment, has booked a number of quality acts as the airport director.
- **B** The airport's director, Susan Collins, has booked a number of quality acts, she has promised exciting entertainment.
- **C** The airport's director, Susan Collins, has booked a number of quality acts and has promised exciting entertainment.
- **D** Correct as is.

The swimming pool is in Peter's town. It has a good safety record for several reasons. (1) Swimmers may not run near the pool and must be experienced before they can use the diving board. Divers may not climb out on the board until the person ahead of them is out of the water. (2) Two lifeguards are always stationed in the diving area, and the "buddy" system is used with young children. The diving area, one of the most popular spots in the pool, because of these steps is also one of the safest. (3)

1
- **A** The swimming pool that is in Peter's town, it has a good safety record for several reasons.
- **B** The swimming pool in Peter's town has a good safety record for several reasons.
- **C** In Peter's town, the safety record of the pool is for several reasons.
- **D** Correct as is.

2
- **F** Divers, on the board until the person ahead of them is out of the water.
- **G** Divers ahead of them may not climb out on the board.
- **H** The person ahead of the diver on the board may not climb out of the water.
- **J** Correct as is.

3
- **A** These steps mean that the diving area, one of the most popular spots in the pool, is also one of the safest.
- **B** These steps mean that the diving area is safe. It is one of the most popular spots in the pool.
- **C** The diving area is safe. Because of these steps, it is also one of the most popular spots in the pool.
- **D** Because the diving area is safe, it is one of the most popular spots in the pool because of these steps.

STOP

ANSWER ROWS: A Ⓐ Ⓑ Ⓒ Ⓓ 1 Ⓐ Ⓑ Ⓒ Ⓓ 2 Ⓕ Ⓖ Ⓗ Ⓙ 3 Ⓐ Ⓑ Ⓒ Ⓓ

Samples

Yesterday __(B)__ the opening of the Family Home next to the medical center. The facility will provide a place to stay for the family members of children who are seriously ill. The Family Home has six bedrooms, a spacious kitchen and dining area, a __(C)__ living room, and large indoor and outdoor recreation areas. Several permanent staff members and a group of volunteers will manage the facility.

B F will mark
G marks
H mark
J marked

C A comfortable
B more comfortable
C comfortabler
D comfortably

When __(4)__ began our hike, we had no idea it was going to turn into a major adventure. We planned to follow the marked trail through the desert, a hike of about five miles. It was not going to be as easy as it sounded.

At mile marker two, I noticed a __(5)__ shaped cactus about two hundred yards from the trail. __(6)__ nothing of it, Jordan and I walked over and took a few photos. When we finished taking our pictures, we headed back toward the trail. Unfortunately, we never found it.

For the next few hours, we wandered around in the desert. Both of us were becoming frightened. The sun was low in the sky and we knew night would be here soon. Just as we were about to panic, we heard the sound of a vehicle. A park ranger, __(7)__ by Jordan's parents, drove into view. To a pair of lost hikers, they were the most welcome sight in the world.

4 F I and Jordan
G Me and Jordan
H Jordan and me
J Jordan and I

5 A curious
B curiously
C most curious
D more curious

6 F Thinking
G Thought
H Thinks
J Having thought

7 A accompany
B accompanying
C accompanied
D accompanies

STOP

 ANSWER ROWS: B Ⓕ Ⓖ Ⓗ Ⓙ C Ⓐ Ⓑ Ⓒ Ⓓ 4 Ⓕ Ⓖ Ⓗ Ⓙ 5 Ⓐ Ⓑ Ⓒ Ⓓ 6 Ⓕ Ⓖ Ⓗ Ⓙ 7 Ⓐ Ⓑ Ⓒ Ⓓ

6/11/12

Sample D

"What time is it?" asked Jacob. "Wer'e (D) due at the restaurant at 8:00, and I don't want to be late."

D F Spelling error
G Capitalization error
H Punctuation error
J No error

Emily looked at the bicycle (8) and asked, "How do you shift gears? I've never used one like this before?" (9)

"The big shifter moves the chain to a larger sprocket," Answered (10) Kuo, "and the small shifter moves it to a smaller sprocket. You'll get used to it in no time."

"Everything else makes sense. Lets (11) get going." Emily hopped on the bike and began riding away.

8 F Spelling error
G Capitalization error
H Punctuation error
J No error

9 A Spelling error
B Capitalization error
C Punctuation error
D No error

10 F Spelling error
G Capitalization error
H Punctuation error
J No error

11 A Spelling error
B Capitalization error
C Punctuation error
D No error

STOP

Your school has a chance to receive a complete video system, including a satellite dish, televisions for each room, and even a mini-studio. The only catch is that every student in the school will be required to watch a 15-minute news show each day, and there will be commercials before and after the news show. Some students want the free video equipment, while others object to being forced to watch news and commercials in school. In a letter to your school board, explain your position on this issue. Be convincing, and explain your position completely.

STOP

ANSWER ROWS: D Ⓕ Ⓖ Ⓗ Ⓙ 9 Ⓐ Ⓑ Ⓒ Ⓓ 11 Ⓐ Ⓑ Ⓒ Ⓓ
8 Ⓕ Ⓖ Ⓗ Ⓙ 10 Ⓕ Ⓖ Ⓗ Ⓙ

NUMBER RIGHT ______

Lesson 10 Vocabulary

Sample

Directions: Read the passage and the vocabulary questions. Mark the space for the answer you think is correct.

The Babe

In 1950, Mildred Didrickson was selected by the Associated Press as the outstanding woman athlete of the first half of the century. The "Babe's" athletic accomplishments were legendary, and unlike many other athletes, she distinguished herself in a number of sports.

Born in Port Arthur, Texas, Babe was named to an All-American basketball team while still in high school. At the 1932 Olympic Games, Babe won gold medals in the javelin throw and 80-meter hurdles. Several years later, she became the leading woman golfer in America and captured the title for the Women's U.S. Open three times.

A The word distinguished in this passage means the same as —

A recognized
B high class
C stood out
D noted the differences between

Be careful! The underlined word may have more than one meaning. Choose the answer that gives the meaning of the word as it is used in the passage.

Practice

6/5/12

Is a center like this available in your area?

The new sports medicine and rehabilitation center at the West Hills Hospital has recently been completed. It is a comprehensive facility that will offer a broad range of services, including diagnosis, treatment, and prevention of injuries. Construction of the center took almost a year, but came in under budget. The money saved on construction will be used to buy additional equipment.

The director of the sports medicine center, Sheri Michaels, described it as, "A dream come true. No longer will our patients have to make the two-hour trip to Hoover City for their therapy services. Our new center is equipped to meet all our patients' needs, especially those suffering from sports or occupational injuries. We are particularly proud of our work-hardening program. It will help people injured on the job return quickly and safely. In addition, we will offer a maintenance program to ensure that their physical condition remains good after their return to work."

Sports coaches at the local high schools are enthusiastic about the new center. All the local schools have established contracts with the center for pre-season conditioning and in-season athletic training. Already, the contracts have paid off. Pre-season injuries among all the student athletes are down more than fifty percent. In addition, because of the pre-season conditioning, athletes are reaching their peak earlier in the season. One coach added that, "Players are enjoying themselves more because they are in better condition and are less likely to be injured."

One of the most popular services offered by the sports medicine center is the conditioning program for recreational athletes. Pre-Ski, for

GO

example, gives skiers a chance to get ready before they hit the slopes. When they make their annual pilgrimage to New Mexico or Colorado, they will be able to ski confidently and not suffer the usual aches and pains that follow the first day on the slopes.

Orthopedic surgeon Sandy Gonzales and athletic trainer Dan Pulaski are starting a special program for senior citizens. The goal of the program is to help the golden-agers become more active physically. "Exercise is one of the best anti-aging treatments we have," commented Dr. Gonzales. "If we can help senior citizens develop the exercise habit, they will live longer and more enjoyable lives."

Many local businesses and organizations have donated equipment to the sports medicine center. The Tyrolean Ski Shop contributed a ski simulator, the First National Bank provided a treadmill, and the Sunset Country Club gave a stationary bicycle. Other businesses have pledged a rowing machine, a stair-stepper, and a whirlpool. The pledges will be fulfilled as soon as the equipment is available from the manufacturer.

One of the unique aspects of the sports medicine and rehabilitation center is its location in the Township Line Mall. This location offers several advantages. It is convenient for patients and staff, has ample parking, and cuts down on both traffic and parking problems at the hospital. Center director Michaels stated that, "We were pleased that the space for our center was available in the mall. In addition to the sports medicine center, we were able to move many of our rehabilitation services out of the hospital to the mall. Our patients love the convenience and the atmosphere, and the hospital administrators were pleased at having so much more room at the hospital for in-patient services such as intensive care, laboratories, nursing stations, and recovery rooms. Our move to the mall will allow the hospital to expand without building an addition. The money we save by not building can be used to upgrade equipment and to improve patient care."

The sports medicine and rehabilitation center is located in the Township Line Mall on the second floor. The telephone number is 555-7328. Hours are from 8:00 AM to 9:00 PM, Monday through Saturday.

1 In this passage, comprehensive means —

A understandable
B medical
C focusing on good health
D including many things

2 The term work-hardening describes an activity that —

F helps people prepare physically for their job
G makes work more difficult and harder to do
H makes a job more secure
J turns an easy job into hard work

3 What does the term pre-season mean?

A Occurring after the season
B Occurring before the season
C Happening now
D Happening later

4 From reading this passage, you learn that a pilgrimage is —

F an exercise program
G the same as skiing
H a religious ceremony
J a journey

5 Pledged means the same as —

A supported
B lent to
C promised to give
D borrowed from

STOP

ANSWER ROWS: A Ⓐ Ⓑ Ⓒ Ⓓ 1 Ⓐ Ⓑ Ⓒ Ⓓ 2 Ⓕ Ⓖ Ⓗ Ⓙ 3 Ⓐ Ⓑ Ⓒ Ⓓ 4 Ⓕ Ⓖ Ⓗ Ⓙ 5 Ⓐ Ⓑ Ⓒ Ⓓ

Sample

8/1/12

Directions: Read the passage and the questions. Mark the space for the answer you think is correct.

8/1/12

Instant Weight Loss

It was the greatest diet known to humankind, or should I say animalkind! Chipper, my dog, lost at least three pounds in two hours.

Because summer was almost here, it was time for Chipper's annual haircut. The owner of the Pet Emporium spent about half an hour working on Chipper with his electric shears. Not only was his weight reduced, but he looked years younger. Cooler and refreshed, but somewhat confused, Chipper tried in vain to shake his furry coat. Little did he realize it would be returned to him in time for the cold winter weather.

A After Chipper had been sheared at the Pet Emporium, he —

- **A** felt warmer because summer was almost here
- **B** gained a few pounds because his hair was so long
- **C** felt colder because the winter weather was just around the corner
- **D** was surprised when he tried to shake his fur

Skim the passage quickly before answering the questions.

Look for key words in the question. Then look for key words in the passage. The correct answer will often be found near key words in the passage.

Practice

How do you feel about watching other people work?

Nothing is more refreshing on a warm summer day than watching someone else work. And the harder they work, the more refreshing it seems.

Right now, for instance, I'm sitting on my porch and watching young Beth baling the big field on top of the hill. She's been haying that field for over ten years. I know: I put her on the tractor when she was just twelve years old. She was a little shaky at first, but she soon got the hang of it. By the time she was sixteen, she could work that field faster than anyone—even me—without losing more than a few bales.

She picked a great day for baling. It's not too hot, and there's a nice breeze. On Monday, when she cut the field, it was so hot I thought the corn would start popping in the field. Didn't stop her, though. She just stuck that big hat on her head, wrapped a wet handkerchief around her neck, and set to work. I remember when I would have done the same thing.

While I'm here sipping a lemonade, Beth is driving the "hay train," a tractor pulling a baler and a rickety old wagon. She steers that tractor over the rows of hay like an engineer going down the track, with the wheels of the tractor straddling each row of hay. You'd think someone her size would never be able to see over the tractor, but somehow she manages. When she's finished, her tracks are so straight you'd think she laid them out with a surveying team.

The whole time she's haying, that dog of hers is working just as hard, running along beside her like he's afraid she'll drive away without him. Not much chance of that. Smart as a whip, that dog is, and knows more about herding cattle than most cowboys. Beth sure knew what she was doing when she trained him.

GO

The way that baler works is sheer poetry. Each row is gobbled up and pushed into shape. When just enough hay is in a bale, the automatic twiner wraps it up and ties it off. A second or so later, the bale comes flying out and into the rickety old wagon. The person who invented that machine sure was some kind of genius.

That's not to say it works perfectly. Every once in a while a bale misses the mark, especially when you are turning the rig at the end of a row. That means, of course, that you have to go back and pick up those bales and toss them into the wagon. In an hour or so, just before sundown, Beth will be doing just that.

I can remember when Beth's mother was her age. She looked an awful lot like Beth does now. Some folks think they still look like sisters. Both of them have hair the color of the summer sun and more freckles than you could count, if you had a mind to. And both of them can ride a horse good as any man. Makes a man proud to see his daughter and granddaughter taking such good care of themselves.

Beth's brother, Frank, is a whole different story. That boy's never done an honest day's work in his life. Says he wants to be a musician, and all he ever does is practice, practice, practice. Must be fairly good at it. He got himself a scholarship to one of those fancy schools in New York. His mother says he's going to be a great violinist. I think he's just going to be a fiddler. Mrs. Stevens, his high school principal, thinks it's wonderful that he's going to New York, but I know she'll miss him come summer and there's no one around to play those concerts in the park. He's some kind of fiddler. But a violinist? I just don't know.

Well, I suppose I should get up and fill this glass again. Not much fun sitting here with an empty glass. I wonder if I could teach that dog to get lemonade for me?

1 Who do you think is telling this story?

A Beth's father
B Beth's grandfather
C Beth's grandmother
D Beth's mother

2 Before bales of hay are thrown into the wagon, they must be —

F wrapped with twine
G dried
H turned
J untied and separated

3 Which of these people is not mentioned in the story?

A Mrs. Stevens
B Beth's mother
C Frank
D John

4 In this story, the way Beth drives the tractor is compared to —

F a hay train
G poetry
H an engineer driving a train
J a pilot flying a plane

5 At some time in the past, the person telling this story —

A owned the tractor, baler, and wagon that Beth is using now
B bought the dog that Beth trained
C played the fiddle and taught Frank how to play
D hayed the field like Beth is doing now

STOP

ANSWER ROWS: A Ⓐ Ⓑ Ⓒ Ⓓ 1 Ⓐ Ⓑ Ⓒ Ⓓ 2 Ⓕ Ⓖ Ⓗ Ⓙ 3 Ⓐ Ⓑ Ⓒ Ⓓ 4 Ⓕ Ⓖ Ⓗ Ⓙ 5 Ⓐ Ⓑ Ⓒ Ⓓ

Sample

Directions: Read the passage and the questions. Mark the space for the answer you think is correct.

Summer Studying

Larry wanted to improve his scores on the achievement tests he would be taking in the fall. He bought a book that would help him, and promised himself that he would spend an hour a day during the summer studying it.

The promise was hard to keep. He was busy working part-time, playing summer sports, helping out at home, and spending time with his friends. He was determined, however, and kept his promise, even if it meant working very late at night or early in the morning. Happily, his hard work paid off, and when Larry took his test, his score was among the highest in the class.

A The main idea of this story is that —

- **A** studying during the summer is hard, but it is usually worth it
- **B** the best way to improve test scores is to study during the summer
- **C** school is just as important as friends, family, and sports
- **D** an hour a day of summer study will probably raise your test scores

The main idea should describe the content of the whole passage. Be careful not to choose an answer that is a detail from the passage.

Practice

A Surprising Health Problem

Do you handle stress by clenching or grinding your teeth? If you do, you may be in for an unpleasant surprise. Many people know that grinding their teeth may cause them to chip or break, but few realize that headaches, dizziness, nausea, and even backaches may be the result of this habit.

Research has revealed that grinding your teeth may damage the joints on either side of your jaw. This causes the jaw to move out of its normal position and strain the muscles holding the head in place. This tension on the neck causes spasms and other complications. And if your jaw is stiff when you wake up, you may have been grinding your teeth in your sleep.

There are dental procedures available that will solve the problem. If you think you may be a nighttime tooth grinder, or if you clench your jaw when under stress, see your dentist.

1 Which of these is the best summary of the passage?

- **A** A dentist is the best health professional to see if you grind your teeth or clench your jaw.
- **B** The muscles in your jaw can be injured if you grind your teeth.
- **C** Grinding your teeth or clenching your jaw can cause a variety of health problems.
- **D** Some people grind their teeth at night without knowing it and should see a dentist.

GO

 ANSWER ROWS: A Ⓐ Ⓑ Ⓒ Ⓓ 1 Ⓐ Ⓑ Ⓒ Ⓓ

The First Americans

There was a time long ago when a land bridge connected Asia and North America. The first settlers in North America crossed this land bridge from what is now Siberia to Alaska. The people who made this initial crossing were probably following the animals they used for food. Some people believe the animals might have been mammoths, extinct creatures that are relatives of today's elephant.

Eventually, the oceans rose and the land bridge between the continents disappeared. The settlers, who I shall call the "First Americans," could not return to their homeland. They would have to survive in the New World they had discovered.

For the next few thousand years, the First Americans migrated south and east throughout North and South America. They made the journey all the way from Alaska to the southern tip of South America, a distance of more than 10,000 miles. Along the way, they established many different civilizations.

In the far north, above the Arctic Circle, the First Americans became hunters of the ocean. They built boats of animal skins and hunted or fished for their food. In the brief summer, they gathered berries and other plants. In the winter, they stayed in lodges much of the time preparing for the next summer. It was a hard life, but they learned to survive in these harsh conditions.

Farther south, in what is now Arizona, Utah, Colorado, and New Mexico, the First Americans became cliff dwellers. They began by living in caves that already existed in the cliffs. They discovered how to add to the caves by building structures of wood and stone. The dwellings they constructed in many ways resembled today's apartment buildings.

The First Americans of the Southwest learned to irrigate the desert. They built a system of dams and canals so they could store and use water almost any time of year. They were so successful they could raise fruits and vegetables that were not found naturally in the desert.

In Mexico and South America, the First Americans founded civilizations that were among the greatest in the world. They built huge pyramids, lived in fabulous cities, and made great advances in science and mathematics long before the Europeans arrived. They also discovered foods like corn and potatoes that became important sources of nutrition for the rest of the world.

2 What is the best summary of this passage?

- **F** People in North and South America established a variety of cultures.
- **G** People from Asia crossed a land bridge and settled North and South America, establishing many different cultures.
- **H** The land bridge that once connected North and South America has now disappeared, but it allowed the settlement of the New World.
- **J** European settlers did not realize that the New World had many rich cultures.

3 If you had to choose another title for this passage, which of these would be best?

- **A** Trapped in the New World
- **B** The Cultures of the New World
- **C** Wanderers from Asia and Their Cultures
- **D** The Earliest Settlers in the New World

4 Implied in this story is the idea that —

- **F** the original settlers of the New World had little to offer European explorers
- **G** European explorers were surprised to find so many rich and different cultures in the new world
- **H** Europeans were not the first to discover or establish advanced civilizations in the New World
- **J** elephants traveled from the New World to India and Asia

STOP

ANSWER ROWS: 2 Ⓕ Ⓖ Ⓗ Ⓙ 3 Ⓐ Ⓑ Ⓒ Ⓓ 4 Ⓕ Ⓖ Ⓗ Ⓙ

Sample

Directions: Read the passage and the questions. Mark the space for the answer you think is correct.

Preparing for a Vacation

Before leaving on vacation, arrange to have your mail and newspapers picked up. Set timers on lights and radios so they will come on at specific times each day. A home that is dark and quiet all day and night is an open invitation.

It is also helpful to move valuables away from windows where they might be seen from the street. Criminals often choose houses where there are a number of valuable objects in clear view.

Finally, let your neighbors know where you will be and when you are expected to return. If possible, leave an emergency phone number with them. If a problem ever arises, they will be able to reach you at once.

A Why would burglars be more likely to break into a house where valuables are visible through a window?

A It will be easier to remove them through the window.

B Burglars prefer working where the light is good.

C They will be certain that they will find objects worth stealing.

D They will have an easier time selling valuables if they see them first.

Skim the passage, then read the question and the answer choices carefully. Reread the part of the passage that will help you choose the right answer.

Take your best guess if you are unsure of the answer.

Practice

How do you think this camping trip affected the writer?

Monday: Here I am, in the middle of nowhere. his camping trip idea is not getting off to a very od start. It's raining, the tent leaks, and we're ten les from the nearest electricity and running v r. The hike in seemed to take forever, and I st n't understand how it could all have been up hil y did I ever let my brother talk me into this? Whe get home—if we ever get home—he's going t to do something fabulous to get back on my g ide. Maybe he should sponsor a shopping sp t the mall!

Tuesday: Things looking up. The sun came out today, so we were a to leave the tents and dry out. We're camped at e edge of a small lake that I couldn't see before b use of the rain and fog. The mountains are all a nd us, and the forest is absolutely beautiful. We ent most of the day dragging everything out of r backpacks or tents and putting it where the sun could dry it out. After lunch we headed down to the lake for a swim. Later in the afternoon we tried to catch fish for dinner, but the fish were smarter than we were. At night, we built a fire, and my brother and his friend sang songs I never heard of; I'm not sure anyone ever heard of them. It definitely wasn't MTV, but it was kind of fun.

Wednesday: We hiked to the far side of the lake and climbed to the top of a small peak. From there we could see how high the other mountains were and how far the forest spread around us. On the way up we passed through a snowfield! Here it was, the middle of July, and there was still snow on the ground. One of Art's friends explained that the snowfield would last another few weeks before it melted. He said the snow on the higher mountains stayed there year-round. He called them glaciers,

6/7/12

which surprised me. I thought glaciers were only found in places like Alaska or the South Pole.

Thursday: I caught my first fish! Some of the group went to look for fossils and the rest of us followed the stream that fed the lake. After about two miles, we came to a section that Carol said looked "fishy." She had a pack rod, which comes apart into sections that can be carried in a backpack. She let me cast it, and I caught a fish on my first try. It was a cutthroat trout about 12 inches long. It got this name because it has red slashes under its gills. I put it back in the water. It was just too pretty to eat for lunch. I caught a few more and so did Carol, but they were all returned to the stream. We enjoyed freeze-dried macaroni and cheese for lunch. It actually tasted pretty good, although we were so hungry even liver would have tasted okay.

Friday: I can't believe we are going home already. It will be nice to get a hot shower, sleep in a real bed, and eat junk food, but the trip has been wonderful. We're already talking about another camping adventure next year where we canoe down a river in Maine. It's hard to believe, but I think this city girl has a little country blood in her veins.

1 The writer of this journal ended up on the camping trip because —

- **A** she enjoys camping
- **B** her brother influenced her
- **C** her sister influenced her
- **D** she wanted to be with her friends

2 Why do you think the writer's friend, Carol, had a pack rod with her?

- **F** She could not afford to buy a regular fishing rod.
- **G** She needed it because fish was their main source of food.
- **H** The writer of the journal asked her to bring it.
- **J** She expected to go fishing while they were hiking.

3 In this journal, you learn that snow and glaciers are found in some mountains in the summer. This is possible because —

- **A** the higher you go, the cooler the temperature becomes
- **B** the higher you go, the warmer the temperature becomes
- **C** the stone in the mountains keeps the ground cool
- **D** wind rarely blows in the mountains

4 In the future, it is likely that the writer of this journal will —

- **F** eat fish she catches, even if they are pretty
- **G** try to convince her brother not to go on camping trips
- **H** be more eager to go on camping trips
- **J** be less eager to go on camping trips

5 Why was there no electricity at the place they set up camp?

- **A** The campers brought batteries so they could use electric appliances.
- **B** Electricity shouldn't be used near streams or lakes.
- **C** The storm blew the power lines down.
- **D** It was too far from the main power line.

6 When the writer of this journal returns to school, she will probably —

- **F** tell her friends what a miserable time she had camping
- **G** tell her friends what a good time she had camping
- **H** convince her friends that they should come shopping with her at the mall
- **J** eat freeze-dried food rather than regular food

STOP

ANSWER ROWS: A Ⓐ Ⓑ Ⓒ Ⓓ 2 Ⓕ Ⓖ Ⓗ Ⓙ 4 Ⓕ Ⓖ Ⓗ Ⓙ 6 Ⓕ Ⓖ Ⓗ Ⓙ
1 Ⓐ Ⓑ Ⓒ Ⓓ 3 Ⓐ Ⓑ Ⓒ Ⓓ 5 Ⓐ Ⓑ Ⓒ Ⓓ

Sample

6/7/12

Directions: Read the passage and the questions. Mark the space for the answer you think is correct.

More Than Just a Barn

On the outskirts of London, England, there is a barn that would be a major tourist attraction in America. The barn is built from the remains of a ship and dates back to the eighteenth century. What makes this barn special is that historians know which ship provided the materials for it. While examining the barn, researchers also investigated the farmhouse nearby. The door of the farmhouse was made from the same wood as the barn and was decorated with small, carved, English flowers. If you have not guessed by now, the ship was the *Mayflower*, which brought the Pilgrims from England to America.

A Why do you think the barn is not a tourist attraction in England?

- **A** There are many other tourist attractions in England.
- **B** The Pilgrims are less important to the British than they are to Americans.
- **C** Not many people in England know who the Pilgrims were.
- **D** There are many old barns in England made from famous ships.

The correct answer may not be stated directly in the passage. You may have to "read between the lines." This will help you understand what the writer means and choose the correct answer.

If a question is too hard, skip it and come back to it later.

Practice

Our Solar System

The earth is part of an astronomical grouping called a solar system. At the center of the solar system is a star, which in our case is called the sun. Surrounding the sun and revolving around it are planets and other bodies. Our solar system has nine known planets, some of which have moons of their own. In addition to planets, there are smaller bodies revolving around the sun. These are called asteroids, and some people believe they are fragments of one or more planets that broke apart for an unknown reason.

Pluto is the smallest planet. It is also the farthest from the sun. Discovered in 1930, Pluto was predicted by mathematical calculations before it was actually found. Its orbit around the sun is so unusual that it can temporarily be closer to the sun than Neptune, its nearest neighbor.

The largest planet is Jupiter, with a diameter more than ten times that of the earth. It is a mysterious planet, made up chiefly of methane and ammonia, with some hydrogen and helium present. On earth, these substances are gases, but Jupiter is so cold that they can exist as solids and liquids. The frozen gases surround a rocky core that scientists believe is about the same size as the earth.

The most spectacular planet is Saturn, which is surrounded by a series of rings. At some times, these rings can be seen in the evening sky with just a low-power telescope or even binoculars. No one is quite sure what the rings are made of, but data from the space probes Voyager I and II are being analyzed by scientists in the hope of finding an answer.

Mars and Venus are the planets that are nearest the earth. Because they are so close, people in the past wondered if they might be inhabited. Scientists know this is not possible, but there is a slight chance that some form of life might exist on one or more of the planets. Both Mars and Venus have atmospheres, and their temperature range is much closer to earth's than other planets'. Even if a life form is discovered on either planet, you can be sure it will be very different from the space creatures described in science fiction.

The planet that is nearest the sun is Mercury. It is about 36 million miles from the sun, which is equal to .4 Astronomical Units.* Mercury rotates on its axis every 59 earth days, but its year is only 88 earth days. Because of its slow rotation and nearness to the sun, the surface of Mercury facing the sun is very hot, perhaps as hot as 800° Fahrenheit. The side away from the sun is much cooler, perhaps as cold as -300° F.

The earth is unique in the solar system because it can support life. The temperature range is just right, it has an atmosphere of life-supporting gases, and it is blessed with an abundance of free water. If any of these ingredients had been missing, our planet would be just as lifeless as its neighbors.

* An Astronomical Unit or A.U. is equal to the average distance between the earth and the sun. This is approximately 9.30×10^7 miles or 1.50×10^8 kilometers.

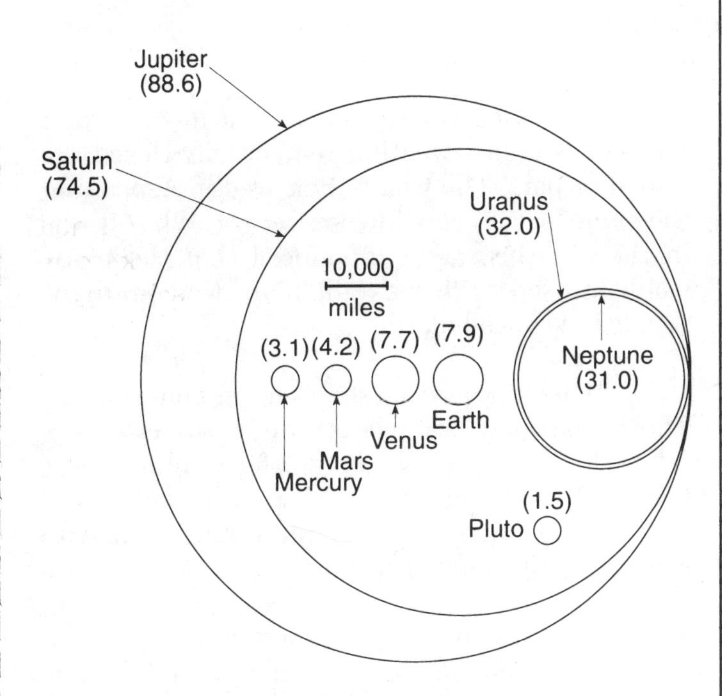

The diameters of the planets are shown in parentheses. The numbers in parentheses represent thousands of miles.

1 In what circumstances would you be most likely to measure things using Astronomical Units?

- **A** When one of the objects was the sun
- **B** When the objects were very large
- **C** When the objects were near the earth
- **D** When the distances between the objects were very great

2 Look at the chart on the left. What is the diameter of Venus?

- **F** 7700 miles
- **G** 77,000 miles
- **H** 7.7 A.U.
- **J** 7.7 times the diameter of the earth

3 Which two planets are closest in size?

- **A** Venus and Mars
- **B** Neptune and Uranus
- **C** Jupiter and Saturn
- **D** Pluto and Neptune

4 Which of these is the best definition of the term year?

- **F** 365 days
- **G** One Astronomical Unit
- **H** The time it takes a planet to rotate on its axis
- **J** The time it takes a planet to revolve around the sun

5 The average temperature on earth is —

- **A** warmer than on Jupiter
- **B** colder than on Jupiter
- **C** about the same as Pluto
- **D** warmer than Mercury

STOP

ANSWER ROWS: A Ⓐ Ⓑ Ⓒ Ⓓ 1 Ⓐ Ⓑ Ⓒ Ⓓ 2 Ⓕ Ⓖ Ⓗ Ⓙ 3 Ⓐ Ⓑ Ⓒ Ⓓ 4 Ⓕ Ⓖ Ⓗ Ⓙ 5 Ⓐ Ⓑ Ⓒ Ⓓ

Sample

Directions: Read the passage and the questions. Mark the space for the answer you think is correct.

This is a "Letter to the Editor"

Dear Editor:

Able-bodied people who park in spaces for the handicapped are both thoughtless and unfair. They don't realize how difficult it can be for a person with a disability to find a place to park and leave the car safely. The inconsiderate people who take these special places often say, "It's only for a minute." It's not just for a minute, it's for as long as it is convenient for them. And while they shop or run errands, someone who truly needs the parking spot is struggling to find one.

Eve Lang

A Why did Eve Lang write this letter to the editor?

A The letter might cause more towns to set aside parking for the disabled.

B It might encourage people to make laws about parking in spaces for the disabled.

C So disabled people will know that there are special parking spaces for them.

D Some people might feel so ashamed that they will avoid parking in spaces set aside for disabled people.

Use the information in the passage to choose the answer you think is correct. If an answer choice has nothing to do with the passage, then it is wrong and can be eliminated.

Take your best guess if you are unsure of the answer.

Practice

An Unhappy Traveler

Phyllis recently took a vacation with her family. Their airplane flights were awful, so Phyllis decided to write a letter of complaint to the airline.

To whom it may concern:

This letter describes the worst travel experience I have ever had. The problems we had were the result of poor management and thoughtless employees. Your airline should be ashamed of treating its customers so poorly.

On January 5, we arrived in Denver from Houston and checked in for our next flight. It wasn't long before the agent announced that our flight would be delayed because of a mechanical problem. The equipment was in Aspen, and they expected it to be repaired soon.

Soon shortly turned to much later, and during the delay, weather temporarily closed the Aspen airport. The weather cleared in Aspen and the plane took off very late for Denver. While it was in the air, the agent announced that the plane would be used for the next flight and that our fligh' was being cancelled.

This cancellation struck me as being un' ir. There was a mad scramble as the 50 or so passe' ,ers scheduled for our flight fought for seats or ,ater flights. When the dust settled, we were wa' listed on the 9:00 flight the next morning. W' nad to spend the night in the airport.

Coming home was no better. F ,cause of a mechanical problem, it looked like w vould miss our connection in Denver. The age assured us they would hold the Newark flight us. Needless to say, the flight to Houston taxie(ıt as we pulled

GO

into the gate. Arrangements were made for us to take the next flight, so we sat in the airport for five hours. When we finally arrived in Houston, our skis were missing. As of this writing, the skis have not been found.

Nothing you can do will make us feel better about our flights. If you are a responsible business, however, you will do what you can to see that passengers in the future are treated better.

With great displeasure,
Phyllis Dooley

This is the response Phyllis received.

Dear Ms. Dooley:

Please accept our apology for your recent inconvenience. Situations beyond our control often occur in airline travel, and unfortunately, passengers often suffer because of them.

The problem you experienced was based on a business decision. By cancelling your flight, we were able to maintain our schedule for all the remaining flights. No passengers, other than the ones on your flight, were inconvenienced. In other words, more than 500 people arrived at their destinations on time, while only 50 were late.

We checked with the supervisor on duty when your problem occurred. He informed us that several of the staff involved were new employees and were unfamiliar with our procedure for assigning seats after a cancellation. Because you checked in early, you should have been assigned seats on the next available flight ahead of many other travelers. The "mad scramble" you describe should never have happened.

Our corporate policy is that if travelers are dissatisfied, we will give them a free ticket anywhere we fly. We want to keep you and your family as customers, and we hope you will accept the enclosed tickets. We also hope that your complimentary flight is an enjoyable one.

Sincerely,
Marcia Green
Customer Relations

1 When Phyllis wrote her letter, she felt —

A annoyed
B tired
C satisfied
D responsible

2 Which of these is an OPINION?

F Weather closed the Aspen airport.
G The skis were still missing.
H There was a mad scramble for seats.
J Phyllis's family sat in the airport for five hours.

3 The purpose of the first paragraph of Marcia Green's letter is to —

A make Phyllis feel angry
B suggest the problem was not their fault
C make Phyllis feel good
D accept complete blame for the problem

4 The second paragraph of Marcia Green's letter says, in effect, that —

F the airline wanted to do the fair thing for all the passengers
G cancelling the flight was an accident
H weather was the reason for the cancellation
J the airline had a good reason for cancelling the flight

5 Phyllis Dooley and Marcia Green —

A disagree on most points
B agree that a problem occurred
C blame the weather, not the airline
D were not affected personally by the incident

STOP

ANSWER ROWS: A Ⓐ Ⓑ Ⓒ Ⓓ 1 Ⓐ Ⓑ Ⓒ Ⓓ 2 Ⓕ Ⓖ Ⓗ Ⓙ 3 Ⓐ Ⓑ Ⓒ Ⓓ 4 Ⓕ Ⓖ Ⓗ Ⓙ 5 Ⓐ Ⓑ Ⓒ Ⓓ

Sample

When Blood Won't Clot

Hemophilia is a hereditary disease that interferes with the blood's ability to form clots. Men who have the disease are in constant danger of bleeding to death from even minor injuries.

The disease is passed down from generation to generation, but it affects only males. Except in rare cases, females are the carriers but are not affected by the symptoms of the disease. In a family where the father is normal and the mother is a carrier, chances are that one out of two sons will suffer from hemophilia.

A Which of these groups is most likely to have hemophilia?

A Girls with a mother who is a carrier
B Boys with a mother who is a carrier
C Husbands whose wife is a carrier
D Wives whose husband is a carrier

6/13/12

Ski Area Debate

The Rendezvous Peak Ski Area has received final approval from the federal government to lease more than 20,000 acres of national forest land. The only hurdle that stands between the developers and their dream is next week's town referendum. The vote, which will take place on Tuesday, will determine the fate of the project. Editorials on this and the next page summarize the positions held by those opposing and supporting the Rendezvous Peak Ski Area. We urge all our subscribers to read the editorials and think carefully before making their decision in the voting booth on Tuesday.

Everybody benefits from Rendezvous Peak.

The opening of Rendezvous Peak will be a turning point for our region. It will reverse our economic downturn by providing more than a thousand jobs and bringing in hundreds of thousands of visitors a year. We desperately need this vitalizing influence.

Opponents of the ski area argue that it will hurt the environment. Phoebe Blanchard, a consultant from Environmental Designs, points out that the ski area will actually improve the environment. Rendezvous Peak is now a "lodgepole pine desert," she comments. "The dense pine forest that covers the mountain supports very few animal species and is in danger of falling victim to plant diseases. When the runs are cut for the ski area, shrubs, grasses, wildflowers, and new tree species will quickly move in. A variety of animals will thrive in this new environment, including deer, elk, bear, and small mammals. The number of song birds will increase almost at once, and the ponds used to supply artificial snowmaking equipment will attract waterfowl. In addition, the runs will act as firebreaks if a forest fire ever occurs." Blanchard's consulting firm was hired by the National Forest Service to develop an environmental impact plan.

In addition to the jobs the ski area will provide, it will become a source of tax revenue. After the area has been created, it will pay more than $2,000,000 a year in taxes. This will allow us to build the new school we need, renovate our parks and streets, and complete the low income housing project that senior citizens have been requesting. The state has promised to improve the highway if the ski area is approved. Moreover, if the ski area attracts the number of tourists that is projected, the legislature has pledged funds to improve the airport. Universal Airlines has indicated it will begin service from both coasts and from Chicago.

Everybody benefits from Rendezvous Peak. Property values will increase, store owners will see their business soar, and young people will no longer have to move away to find work. The environment will be improved, and all of us will have a recreation area to enjoy. I urge you to vote yes on Tuesday.

Cindy Koster
Marshall County Chamber of Commerce

GO

Who needs Rendezvous Peak?

Rendezvous Peak is a natural gem that should remain untouched. It is the most accessible wilderness area in the state and offers an incomparable variety of recreation opportunities. Developing the area into a ski resort will turn it into a playground for yuppies and will make it more difficult for hikers, hunters, and fishermen to use the mountain.

The lodgepole pine forest that covers the mountain is a natural wonder. It contains old-growth trees that will not be replaced for hundreds of years if they are cut down. The ski runs planned for the mountain will be scars that won't heal. Sure, they may serve as firebreaks, but how many forest fires do we have? The last major fire was in 1943, and only about 1,000 acres were affected. Besides, forest fires are nature's way of revitalizing forests. Ski runs are not.

Cutting ski runs will also remove about 5,000 acres of "oxygen engines." The mature trees cut to accommodate skiers currently remove thousands of tons of carbon dioxide a year and replace it with oxygen. This "environmentally safe" ski area will be hastening global warming.

The jobs promised by the developers will be seasonal. When spring arrives, most of the workers will be on their own until the next ski season. There is also no guarantee that local people will get the jobs. It is likely that many outsiders will come to our area seeking work as soon as jobs become available. Who's to know if these job seekers are the kind of people we want in our town?

The financial benefits to the town will be far outweighed by the costs. Most of the tax revenue generated will have to be spent on maintaining roads damaged by heavy traffic, increased police patrols, highway signs, and the like. Very few tax dollars will ever reach the citizens of town, and it is highly unlikely they will be put toward the building of a new school. And as for the new highway and larger airport, who needs them? Our town is a quiet retreat from the hustle and bustle of the world outside. A larger airport and wider highway will turn us into an upscale neighborhood in which locals can't afford to live. Who needs it?

Mark Halstead
Stop Rendezvous Coalition

1 Which statement best summarizes Cindy Koster's position?

- **A** The best way to build a new school is to develop a ski area so more taxes will be generated.
- **B** The new ski area will improve property values so people can sell their houses for more than they are worth now.
- **C** The new ski area will provide economic and recreational benefits without harming the environment.
- **D** The town is fine the way it is and doesn't need a new ski area.

2 On page 28 you learn that there will be a town <u>referendum</u>. What is a <u>referendum</u>?

- **F** An election where people have a chance to vote on an issue
- **G** A fiesta to celebrate an event such as the opening of the new ski area
- **H** A meeting in which the developers seek the approval of the federal government
- **J** A brochure describing what the ski area will look like

3 Who called Rendezvous Peak a "lodgepole pine desert"?

- **A** Cindy Koster
- **B** Mark Halstead
- **C** Phoebe Blanchard
- **D** A person who is not named

4 Which of these statements is an OPINION stated by Mark Halstead?

- **F** The state will improve the highway.
- **G** Outsiders will seek jobs at the ski area.
- **H** Cutting the ski runs will remove about 5,000 acres of trees.
- **J** Rendezvous Peak is not accessible now.

GO

ANSWER ROWS: A Ⓐ Ⓑ Ⓒ Ⓓ 2 Ⓕ Ⓖ Ⓗ Ⓙ 4 Ⓕ Ⓖ Ⓗ Ⓙ
1 Ⓐ Ⓑ Ⓒ Ⓓ 3 Ⓐ Ⓑ Ⓒ Ⓓ

5 From what you have read in this passage, you can conclude that —

A forest fires have occurred often on Rendezvous Peak

B there is no airport near the area where the ski slope is to be built

C the economy in the region where the ski slope is to be built is good

D the area where the slope is to be built is suffering through hard economic times

6 Cindy Koster quotes Phoebe Blanchard and indicates that her company, Environmental Designs, was hired by a government agency, the National Forest Service. Why do you think she presents this information?

F So readers will know their tax dollars are being spent well by the National Forest Service.

G So read s will believe the company is legitimat unbiased.

H The company h s promised to improve the road if the s i area is developed.

J Because the Fore Service will protect the environment.

7 Which of these statements is a FACT stated by Cindy Koster?

A Rendezvous Peak will be the largest ski area in the state.

B Everyone will enjoy the recreational opportunities provided by the ski area.

C The ski area will generate more than $2,000,000 in tax revenues.

D Everybody will benefit from Rendezvous Peak.

8 According to Phoebe Blanchard, the ski area will improve the environment. Which of these statements did she use to support her position?

F Lodgepole pine will quickly take over the open ski runs.

G The new plants that grow in the ski runs will be "oxygen engines."

H Cutting the runs will encourage new plant species.

J Forest fires are nature's way of revitalizing forests.

An Amazing Organ

The human eye i . truly amazing organ. It has the ability to slate reflected light from objects in the onment to signals that can be processed e brain. And what is even more astoundi , it does this by a simple yet effective proces

Light passes through the pupil or opening t ne eye. It is then focused by the lens on the ina as an upside-down image. The image received y the retina is transmitted through the optic erve to the brain where the image is "flipped" and interpreted.

The part of the eye that gives it color is called the iris. The iris, pupil, and lens are protected by a transparent covering called the cornea.

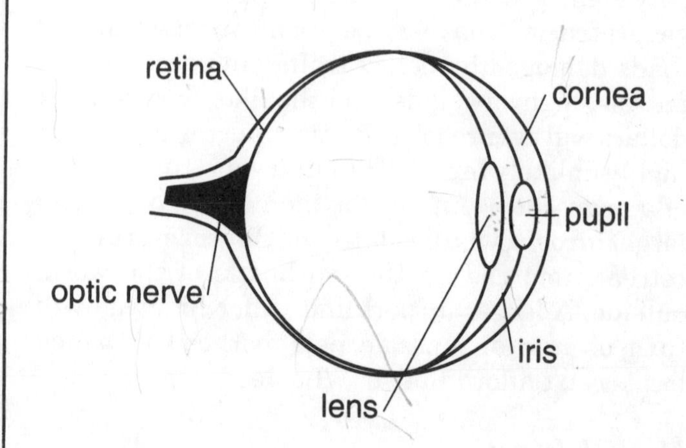

GO

Additional protection is given to the eye by the shape of the human face. The eye socket is set back slightly from the forehead and the cheekbones. As a result, injuries to the eye from large objects such as thrown balls are rare. The most obvious evidence of how well the shape of the head protects the eye is the number of "black eyes" that occur. Although painful and unsightly, a black eye is a small price to pay for an uninjured eye.

The eyelid is another layer of protection for the eye. Even though it seems flimsy, the eyelid is a tough cover that protects the eye from small and medium-sized objects like flying insects and blown dirt. The eyelid is controlled by a reflex reaction. A fast-moving object heading toward the eye will trigger the reflex and cause the eyelid to shut.

Tears are a fourth level of defense for the eye. They wash away small particles of dirt and dust that might damage the cornea. And each time you blink your eye, the eyelid lubricates the cornea with a new layer of tears that keeps the eye from drying out.

Even the pupil of the eye has a built-in safeguard. The pupil is designed to open and close according to how much light is available. If there is a sudden flash of light, for example, that might damage the retina, the pupil will quickly close as small as possible.

Scientists have studied the eye carefully in the hope of designing artificial vision systems for robots. Although they have made great strides, they are still far from developing a device that even approaches the efficiency of the human eye. Even the most sophisticated visual systems on scientific devices or advanced defense aircraft are a distant second to the human eye.

9 Signals are sent from the eye to the brain through the —

A cornea

B iris

C optic nerve

D retina

10 The word flimsy in this passage means —

F quick

G tough

H made of skin

J delicate

11 The lens is located —

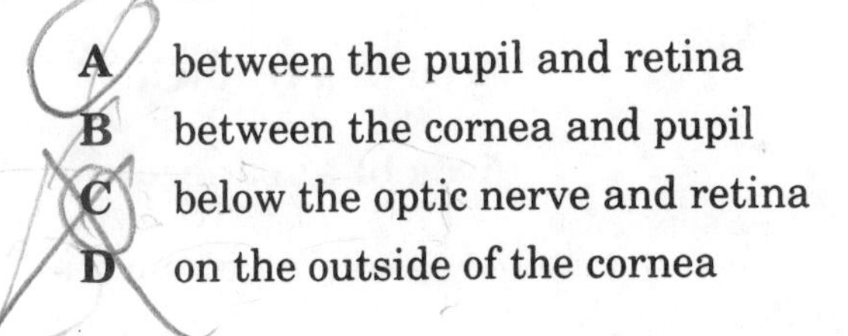

A between the pupil and retina

B between the cornea and pupil

C below the optic nerve and retina

D on the outside of the cornea

12 When a doctor shines a light in your eye, the purpose is to see how well the eye reacts. What kind of reaction would the doctor expect from a bright light shining in your eye?

F The pupil should open.

G The pupil should close.

H The lens should close.

J The iris should open.

13 Which of these injuries is probably the most serious?

A A cut eyebrow

B A black eye

C A damaged retina

D A scratch on the eyelid

14 The lens of the eye can best be compared to which of these?

F An opening that can be adjusted

G A protective covering like a fingernail

H A movie screen

J An adjustable magnifying glass

STOP

ANSWER ROWS: 9 Ⓐ Ⓑ Ⓒ Ⓓ 11 Ⓐ Ⓑ Ⓒ Ⓓ 13 Ⓐ Ⓑ Ⓒ Ⓓ
10 Ⓕ Ⓖ Ⓗ Ⓙ 12 Ⓕ Ⓖ Ⓗ Ⓙ 14 Ⓕ Ⓖ Ⓗ Ⓙ

NUMBER RIGHT ______

Formula Chart and Conversion Table

Formulas

Perimeter of a square	$P = 4s$
Perimeter of a rectangle	$P = 2(l + w)$
Circumference of a circle	$C = 2\pi r$
Area of a square	$A = s^2$
Area of a rectangle	$A = lw$ or $A = bh$
Area of a triangle	$A = \frac{bh}{2}$
Area of a trapezoid	$A = \frac{1}{2}(b_1 + b_2)h$
Area of a circle	$A = \pi r^2$
Surface area of a cube	$S = 6s^2$
Surface area of a cylinder (lateral)	$S = 2\pi rh$
Volume of a rectangular prism	$V = lwh$
Volume of a cylinder	$V = \pi r^2 h$
Volume of a cube	$V = s^3$
Pythagorean Theorem	$a^2 + b^2 = c^2$

Measurement Conversions

	METRIC	CUSTOMARY
Length	1 kilometer = 1000 meters 1 meter = 100 centimeters 1 centimeter = 10 millimeters	1 mile = 1760 yards 1 mile = 5280 feet 1 yard = 3 feet 1 foot = 12 inches
Volume and Capacity	1 liter = 1000 milliliters	1 gallon = 4 quarts 1 gallon = 128 ounces 1 quart = 2 pints 1 pint = 2 cups 1 cup = 8 ounces
Weight and Mass	1 kilogram = 1000 grams 1 gram = 1000 milligrams	1 pound = 16 ounces 1 ton = 2000 pounds
Time	1 year = 365 days 1 year = 12 months 1 year = 52 weeks 1 week = 7 days	1 day = 24 hours 1 hour = 60 minutes 1 minute = 60 seconds

GO

Lesson 17 Number Concepts

Samples

Directions: Read each mathematics problem. Mark the answer you think is correct.

A Which of the numbers below is not the same as the others?

A one-eighth

B 12.5

C 12.5%

D $\frac{1}{8}$

B Which of these numbers shows the greatest distance?

F 6×10^{-8} cm

G 8×10^{-6} cm

H 9×10^{-3} cm

J 4×10^{-3} cm

Be sure to look at key words and numbers in both the problem and the answer choices.

Practice

1 How would you express the product $2 \times 2 \times 3 \times 3 \times 3 \times 4 \times 4$ using exponential notation?

A $2^2 \times 3^2 \times 4^2$

B $2^3 \times 3^4$

C $2^2 \times 3^2 \times 4^3$

D $2^2 \times 3^3 \times 4^2$

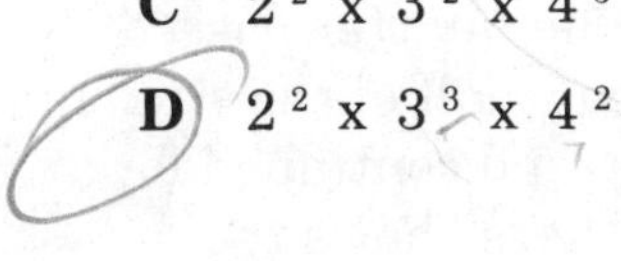

2 In a hardware store, pipe is stored in a rack with the smallest diameter on the bottom and the largest diameter on the top. Which of these would be on the top of the rack?

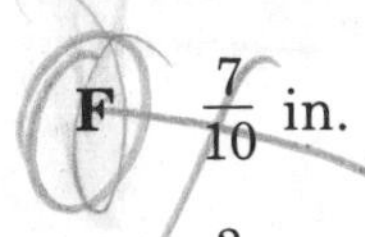

F $\frac{7}{10}$ in.

G $\frac{3}{4}$ in.

H $\frac{7}{8}$ in.

J $\frac{5}{8}$ in.

3 A map maker discovered that there was not enough room to write out a distance of 27.34 kilometers completely on a map. She decided to round the distance to the nearest tenth. Which of these distances did she use?

A 27.1 km

B 27.3 km

C 27.4 km

D 27.5 km

4 The sun is 93 million miles from the earth. How is this distance written using scientific notation?

F 9.3×10^7 miles

G 9.3×10^6 miles

H 9×10^3 miles

J 10^{93} miles

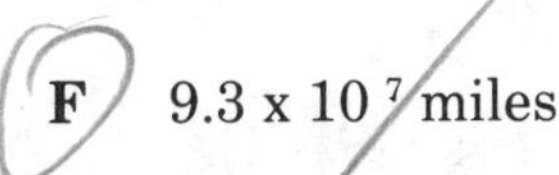

GO

5 A team of students measured the temperature of the soil in a garden at four times during the day. They discovered that the temperature increased steadily between 9:00 AM and 2:00 PM. Which of these answers shows the set of temperatures the students found?

A 84.01, 84.22, 84.19, 84.9

B 76.34, 76.2, 77.11, 77.08

C 78.01, 78.19, 78.62, 78.9

D 85.92, 85.88, 85.43, 85.12

6 The interest in Caitlin's bank account is computed at the rate of 5.58% per year. What is this rate expressed as a decimal?

F 55.8

G 5.58

H 0.558

J 0.0558

7 The diameter of the planet Jupiter is 88,640 miles. Which of these shows the diameter rounded to the nearest thousand?

A 90,000

B 89,000

C 86,000

D 80,000

8 Which of these is the same as $8^3 \cdot 3^2$?

F $8 \cdot 8 \cdot 8 \cdot 3 \cdot 3$

G $8 \cdot$ [illegible] $\cdot 3 \cdot 2$

H $8 \cdot 8 \cdot 8 \cdot 2 \cdot 2$

J $8 \cdot 3 \cdot$ [illegible] $\cdot 2 \cdot 2$

9 The price of cross-training shoes at four different stores was recently reduced. Advertisements for the stores showed how much the original price had been reduced. Which of these answers shows the greatest reduction?

A one-third

B 30%

C 0.024

D $\frac{1}{5}$

10 Which of these answer choices is closest in value to 2.3×10^{2}?

F 5.3×10^{5}

G 7.6×10^{-4}

H 9.1×10^{2}

J 2.8×10^{-2}

11 Each year, a greater proportion of students in a school pass an advanced placement test. The first year about one-quarter passed. During the second year, half of the students passed the test. The trend continued for a third year. Which of these shows the proportion of students who passed the test in the third year?

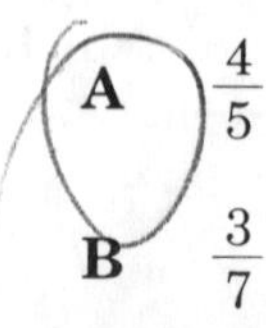

A $\frac{4}{5}$

B $\frac{3}{7}$

C $\frac{3}{8}$

D $\frac{2}{5}$

STOP

ANSWER ROWS 5 Ⓐ Ⓑ Ⓒ Ⓓ 7 Ⓐ Ⓑ Ⓒ Ⓓ 9 Ⓐ Ⓑ Ⓒ Ⓓ 11 Ⓐ Ⓑ Ⓒ Ⓓ

6 Ⓕ Ⓖ Ⓗ Ⓙ 8 Ⓕ Ⓖ Ⓗ Ⓙ 10 Ⓕ Ⓖ Ⓗ Ⓙ

Samples

Directions: Read each mathematics problem. Mark the answer you think is correct.

A What number will come next in the pattern shown below?

2, 5, 11, 23, ...

A 26

B 36

C 42

D 47

B Which answer falls within the range shown on this number line?

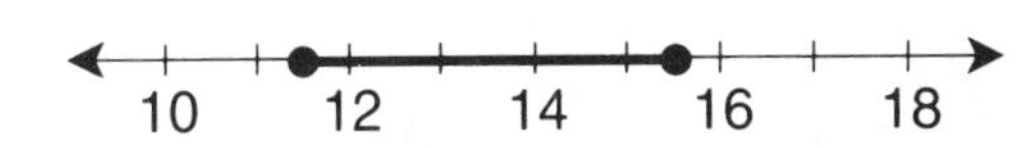

F 12.05

G 10.15

H 15.9

J 18.0

If you are not sure of the answer, take your best guess and go on to the next item.

Practice

1 What is the value of x in the expression shown below?

$6x + 10 = 46$

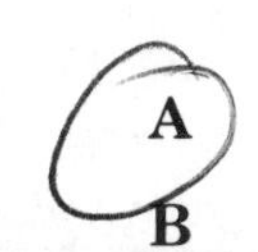

A 6

B 9

C 30

D 36

2 Which of these is equal to 5^4?

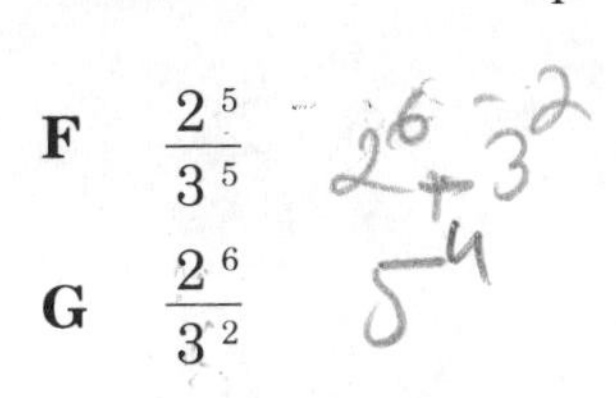

F $\frac{2^5}{3^5}$

G $\frac{2^6}{3^2}$

H $\frac{5^4}{4^5}$

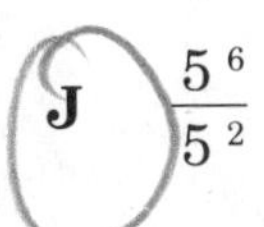

J $\frac{5^6}{5^2}$

3 Which point below is nearest (4, 5)?

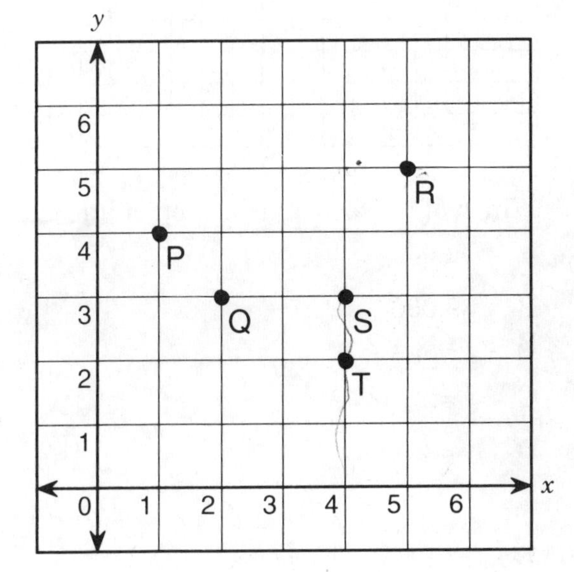

A Q

B R

C S

D T

GO

4 Which of these answers is not equal to

$$3 \times (5 - 2)$$

F (3 x 5) – (3 x 2)

G 9

H (3 x 5) – 2

J (5 – 2) x 3

Use this graph to answer questions 5 and 6.

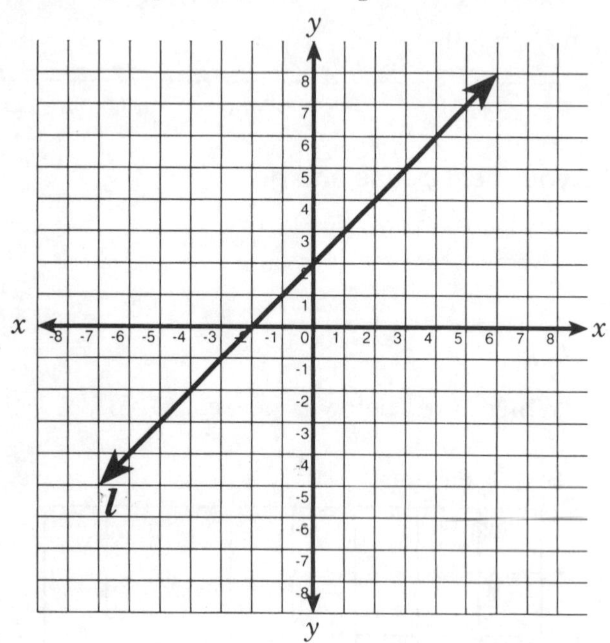

5 Which of these is an equation of line *l*?

A y = x + 3

B y = x + 2

C y = x – 2

D y = 2(x)

6 What is the value of y when x is equal to -4?

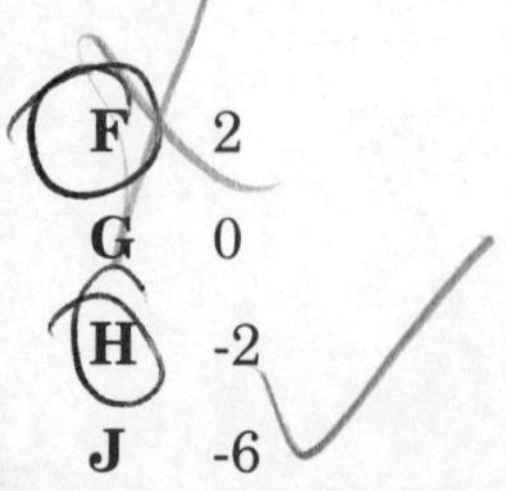

F 2

G 0

H -2

J -6

7 A research team studied a 36-acre plot of land. They found that an average of 9 hawks hunted there each day. The researchers also found an average of 81 snakes a day on the plot. What was the ratio of hawks to snakes?

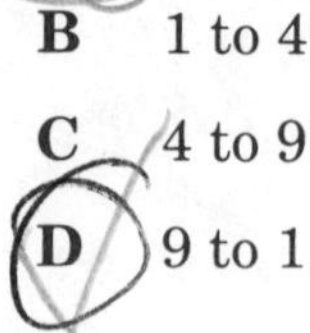

A 1 to 9

B 1 to 4

C 4 to 9

D 9 to 1

8 A car dealer determines the price she will charge for a car by using the formula:

$$P = (C \times 1.1) + T$$

where P is the price she will charge, C is the cost paid to the manufacturer, and T is a transportation fee. What will the price of a car be if it costs the dealer $12,000 and the transportation fee is $275.00?

F $13,200.00

G $13,275.00

H $13,475.00

J $13,502.50

9 In which of these is n equal to 5?

A $7n + 8 = 29$

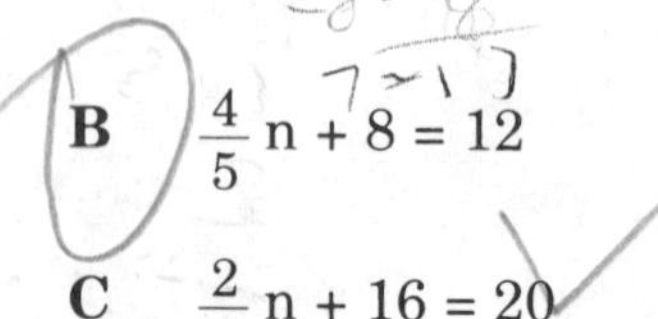

B $\frac{4}{5}n + 8 = 12$

C $\frac{2}{5}n + 16 = 20$

D $5n - 8 = 42$

STOP

Sample

Directions: Read each geometry problem. Mark the answer you think is correct.

A For which of these figures is Area = $\frac{bh}{2}$?

A

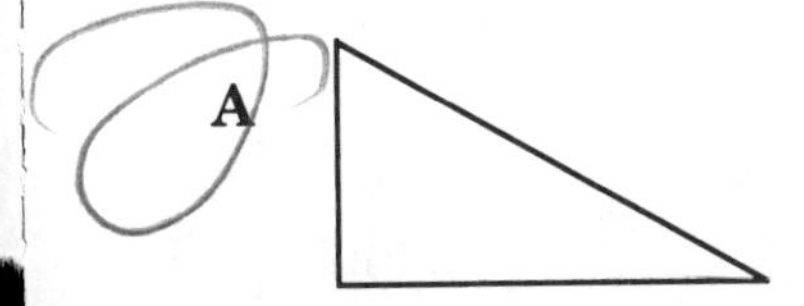

B

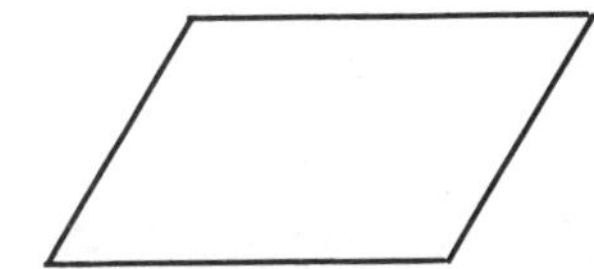

C

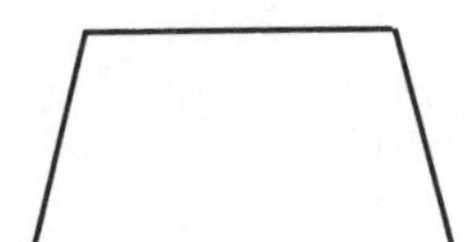

D

Look at each figure carefully and use key words in the problem to help you find the answer.

If you know which answer is correct, mark it and go on to the next item. You do not have to look at all the answer choices.

Practice

1 In the illustration below, the transformation from Figure A to Figure B involves —

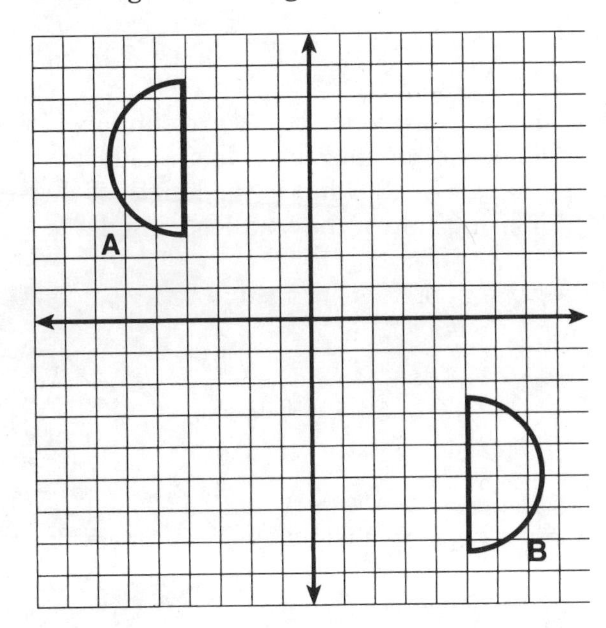

A rotation and translation

B reflection and rotation

C reflection and translation

D translation and deflection

2 Which of these statements is true?

F A polygon has five sides.

G All obtuse angles are less than 90°.

H Rotation and translation mean the same thing.

J A line of symmetry divides a figure into two identical parts.

3 Look at the answer choices below. Which of them is a ray?

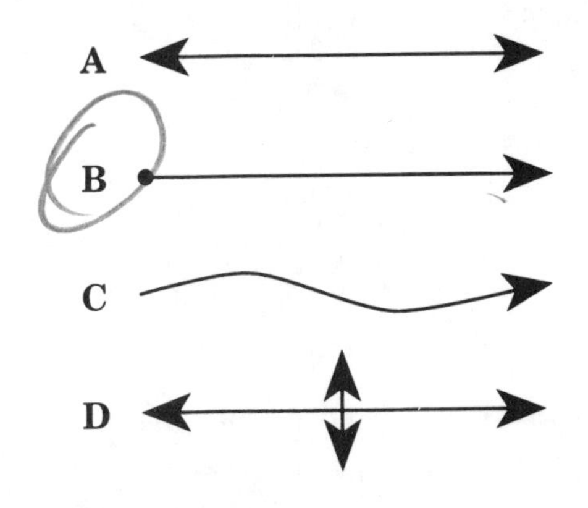

GO

ANSWER ROWS: A Ⓐ Ⓑ Ⓒ Ⓓ 1 Ⓐ Ⓑ Ⓒ Ⓓ 2 Ⓕ Ⓖ Ⓗ Ⓙ 3 Ⓐ Ⓑ Ⓒ Ⓓ

4 Look at the figure below. It shows how to —

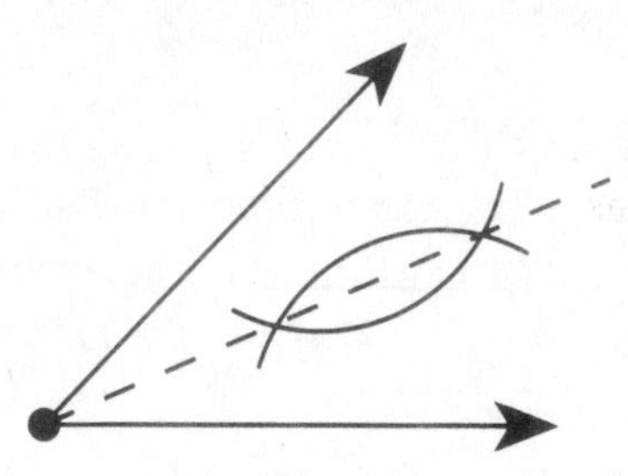

F construct an angle bisector

G determine the arc of a circle

H calculate the size of an angle

J construct a perpendicular bisector of a line segment

5 The illustration below shows the course for a triathlon. How could you find the distance of the canoe part of the race?

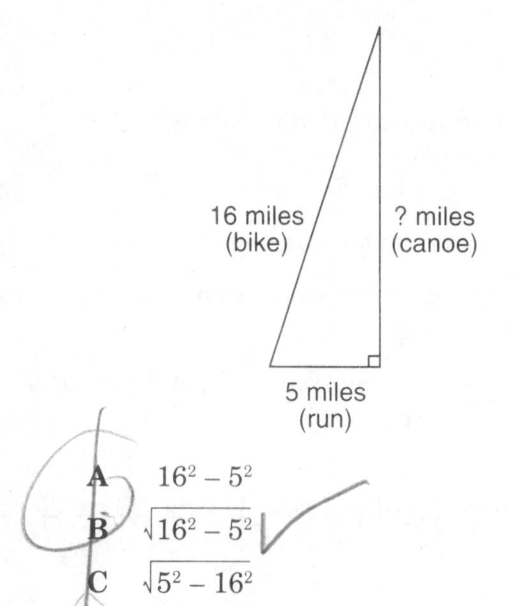

A $16^2 - 5^2$

B $\sqrt{16^2 - 5^2}$

C $\sqrt{5^2 - 16^2}$

D $\sqrt{16^2 + 5^2}$

6 Which of these statements is false?

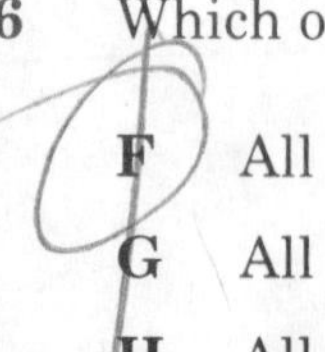

F All circles are similar.

G All squares are similar.

H All right triangles are similar.

J All equilateral triangles are similar.

7 The figure below shows a square with sides of 1 unit and a diagonal equal to the square root of 2. Based on your knowledge of squares, triangles, and the figure below, you can conclude that —

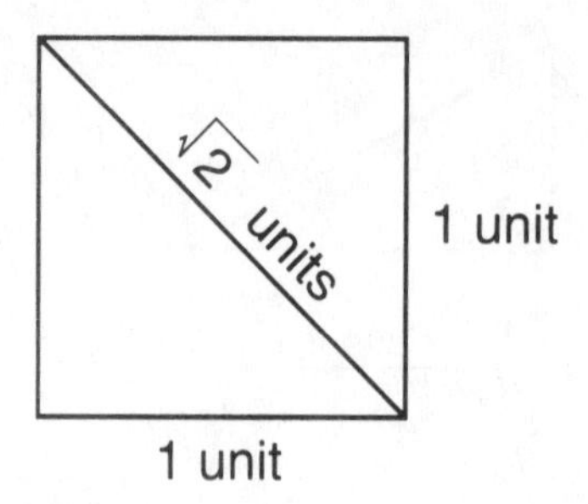

A the diagonal of any square can be found by adding the length of the sides to the square root of 2

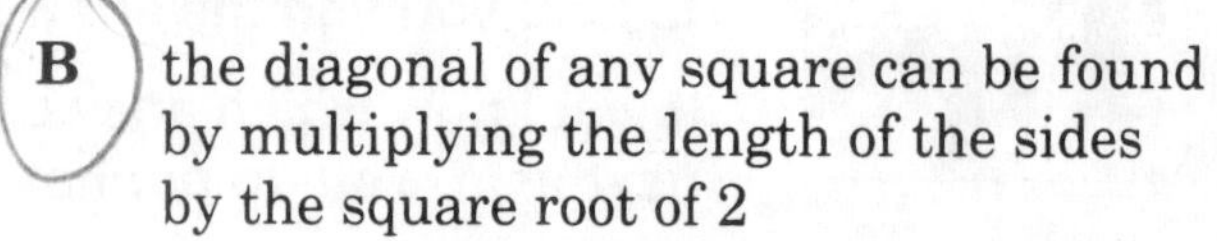

B the diagonal of any square can be found by multiplying the length of the sides by the square root of 2

C the length of the sides will be less than the square root of 2

D the diagonal will always be the square root of 2

8 The two triangles below are similar. If the length of the missing side of the larger triangle is 22, what is the length of the missing side of the smaller triangle?

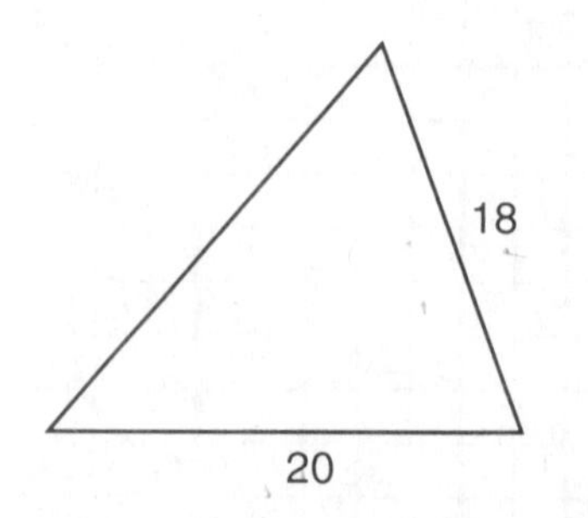

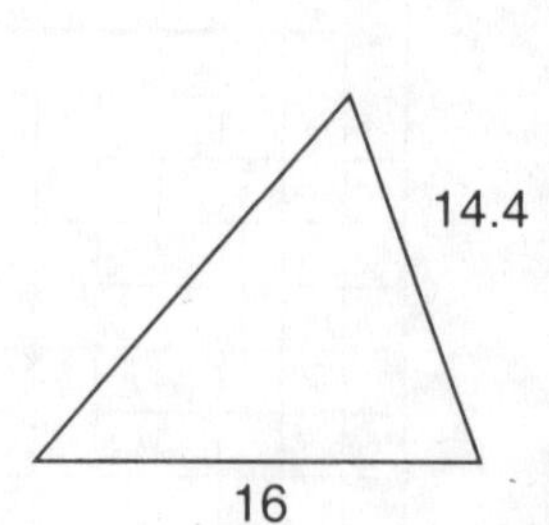

F 26.4

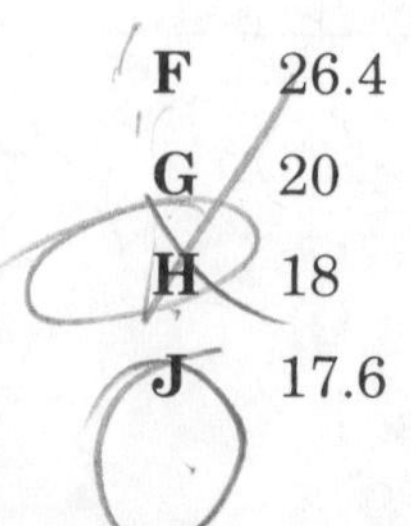

G 20

H 18

J 17.6

STOP

Sample

Directions: Read each measurement problem. Mark the answer you think is correct.

A What is the radius of this circle? Use $\pi = \frac{22}{7}$

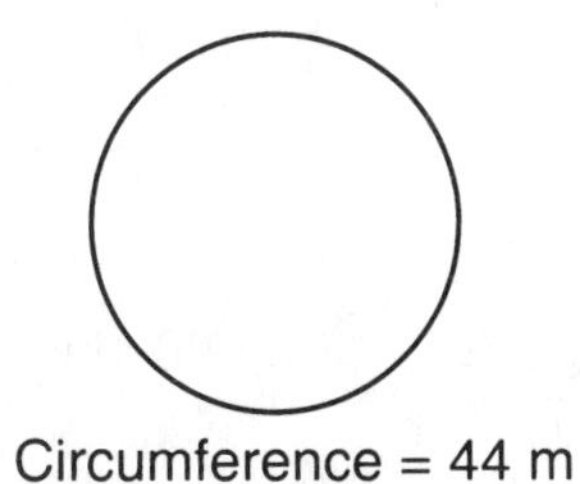
Circumference = 44 m

A 7 m

B 14 m

C 15 m

D 22 m

B A recipe that serves 4 people calls for 10 ounces of chicken. How many ***pounds*** of chicken would you need to serve 16 people?

F 1 pound

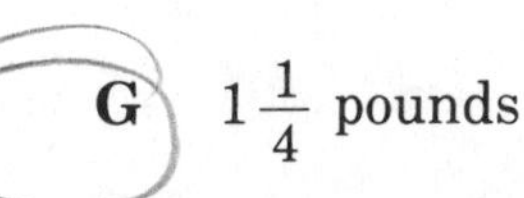

G $1\frac{1}{4}$ pounds

H $2\frac{1}{2}$ pounds

J 3 pounds

Before you try to choose an answer, be sure you know what the question is asking.

Look for key words such as *perimeter*, *circumference, area*, and *volume*.

Practice

1 A piece of wall board is 4 feet wide by 6 feet long. A carpenter cut the shape below out of a piece of wall board. What is the area of the remaining piece of wall board?

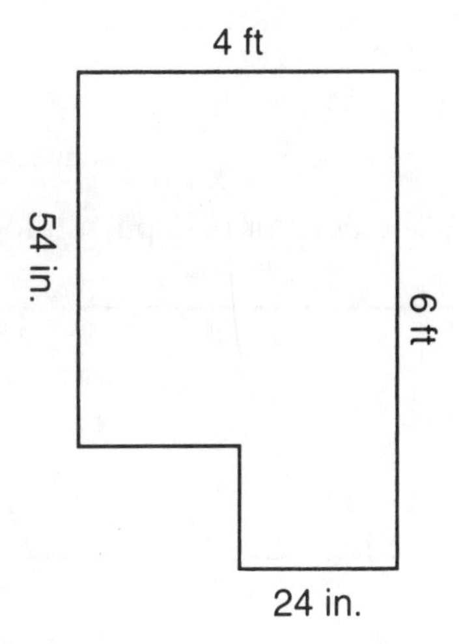

A 24 in.^{2}

B 32 in.^{2}

C 78 in.^{2}

D 432 in.^{2}

2 A standard basketball goal is about how high?

F 3 m

G 3 ft

H 300 in.

J 30 yd

3 A swimming pool is 50 yards long, 20 yards wide, and 2 yards deep. How much water will be needed to fill the pool?

A 20,000 yds ^{3}

B 2000 yds ^{3}

C 1000 yds ^{3}

D 280 yds ^{3}

GO

4 Look at the section of a ruler shown below. What is the greatest precision that can be achieved with this ruler?

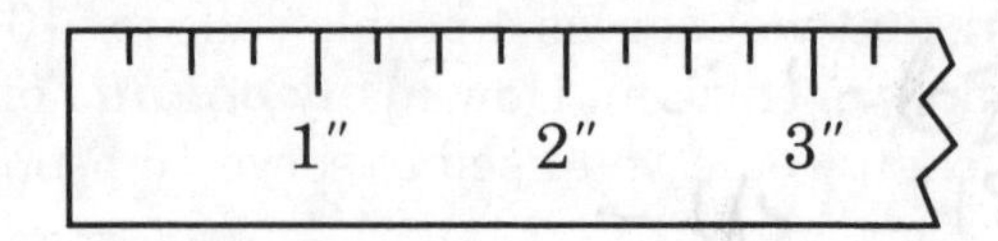

F Nearest 1 inch

G Nearest $\frac{3}{4}$ inch

H Nearest $\frac{1}{2}$ inch

J Nearest $\frac{1}{4}$ inch

5 Which of these is the greatest distance?

A 2000 feet

B 1000 yards

C $\frac{1}{4}$ mile

D 1 kilometer

6 Which statement about the figure below is true?

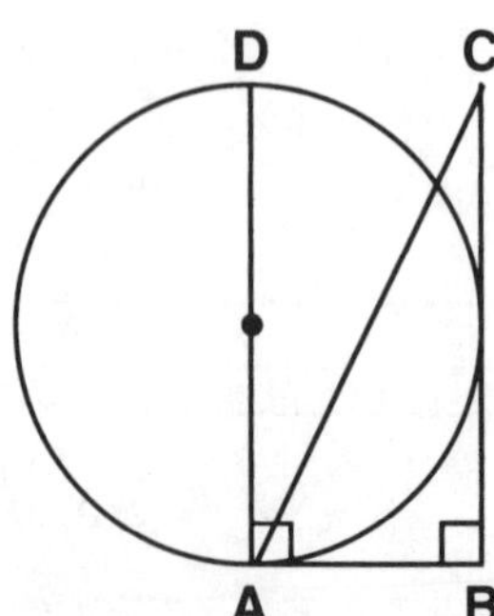

F $\overline{AD} = \overline{AC}$

G $\overline{AC} < \overline{AB}$

H $\overline{AB}$ is equal to the radius of the circle.

J $\overline{AD}$ is equal to the radius of the circle.

7 How would you find the volume of this cylinder?

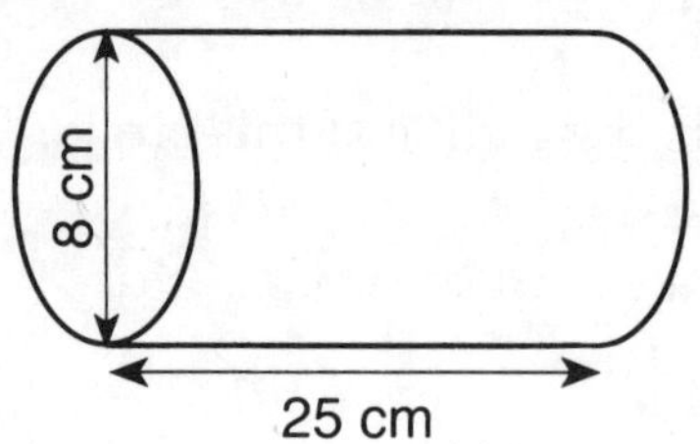

A $\frac{22}{7}$ x 400 cm ^{3}

B $\frac{22}{7}$ x 400 cm ^{3}

C $\frac{22}{7}$ x 1600 cm ^{3}

D $\frac{22}{7}$ x 6400 cm ^{3}

8 A container holds 1 liter of water. You pour 350 mL of water from the container into a glass. How much water is left in the container?

F 50 mL

G 500 mL

H 650 mL

J 750 mL

9 What is the area of this parallelogram?

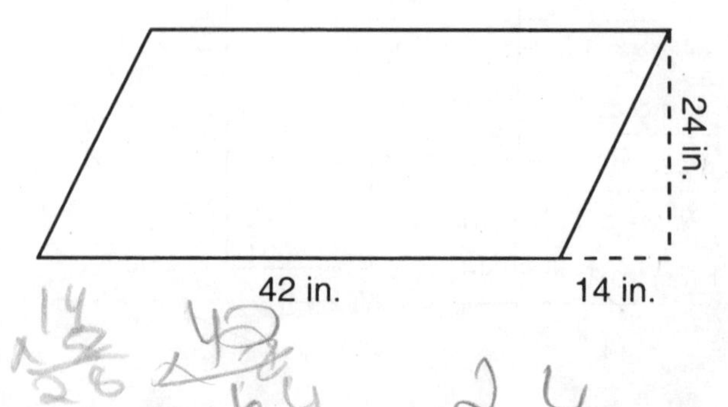

A 336 in.^{2}

B 1008 in.^{2}

C 1022 in.^{2}

D 14,112 in.^{2}

STOP

ANSWER ROWS: 4 Ⓕ Ⓖ Ⓗ Ⓙ 5 Ⓐ Ⓑ Ⓒ Ⓓ 6 Ⓕ Ⓖ Ⓗ Ⓙ 7 Ⓐ Ⓑ Ⓒ Ⓓ 8 Ⓕ Ⓖ Ⓗ Ⓙ 9 Ⓐ Ⓑ Ⓒ Ⓓ

Sample

Directions: Read each mathematics problem. Mark the answer you think is correct.

A This wheel shows 4 different prizes you can win. If you spin the wheel just once, what prize are you most likely to win?

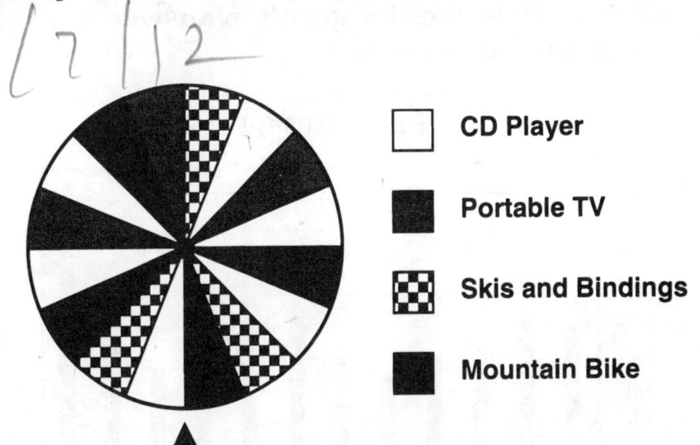

A Portable TV

B Skis and Bindings

C Mountain Bike

D CD Player

If you work on scratch paper, be sure to transfer numbers correctly from the problem to the scratch paper. Work carefully, and if the answer you find is not one of the answer choices, work the problem again.

Practice

1 Evita is planning her school schedule. She referred to the chart below and found the number of sections of math, English, and science. Each section is taught by a different teacher. She plans to take one section of each subject. How many different combinations of these three courses might she consider?

Math 1	Math 2	Math 3	
English 1	English 2	English 3	English 4
Reading 1	Reading 2	Reading 3	Reading 4
History 1	History 2	History 3	History 4
Science 1	Science 2	Science 3	
Writing 1	Writing 2	Writing 3	Writing 4

A 48

B 36

C 10

D 3

2 There are 5 pairs of gloves in a ski bag. Suppose you picked one glove at a time out of the bag without looking. How many times would you have to pick before you were sure you had a pair of gloves?

F 2 times

G 4 times

H 5 times

J 6 times

3 Raoul's scores on 4 tests were 83, 86, 80, and 81. He has one more test to take, and he wants to earn an 85 average in the class. What score must he get to have an 85 average?

A 85

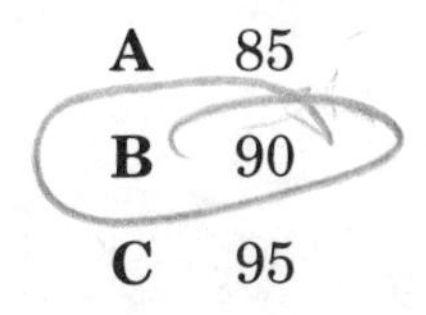

B 90

C 95

D 96

GO

This graph shows a family's monthly electric bills. Use this graph to answer questions 4 through 6.

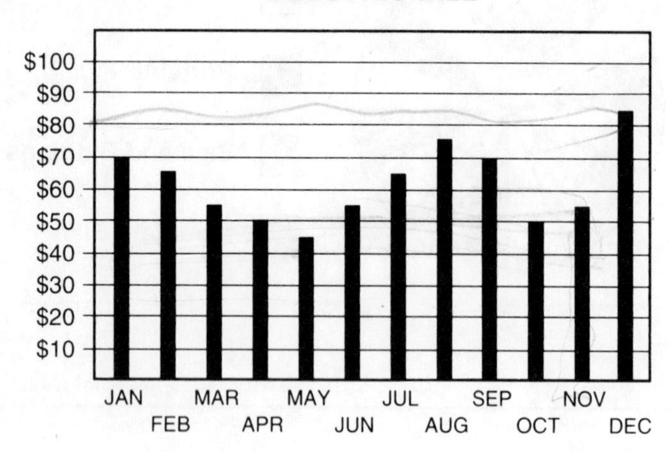

4 What is the mode of the amounts shown on the graph?

F $50

G $55

H $60

J $65

5 What is the range of the amounts shown on the graph?

A $45 to $65

B $50 to $85

C $55 to $80

D $45 to $85

6 What is the mean (average) of the amounts paid in December, January, February, and March?

F $68.75

G $68.00

H $63.75

J $63.00

7 Each month, 1 student is chosen from a class of 25 students to be the representative to student council. How would you calculate the probability of the same student being chosen as class representative for 2 months in a row?

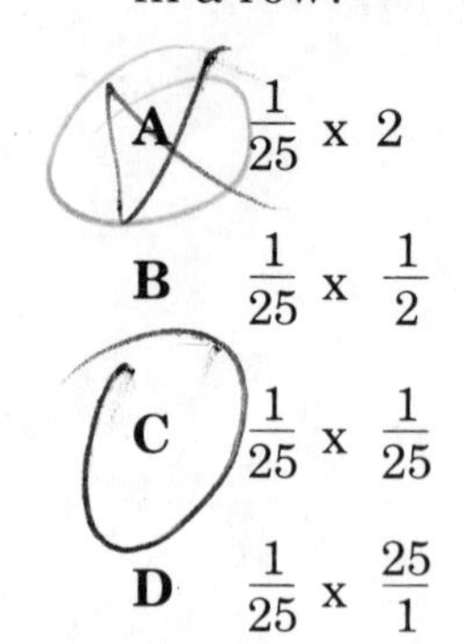

A $\frac{1}{25}$ x 2

B $\frac{1}{25}$ x $\frac{1}{2}$

C $\frac{1}{25}$ x $\frac{1}{25}$

D $\frac{1}{25}$ x $\frac{25}{1}$

This chart shows the month of birth for the students in a class. Use the chart to answer question 8.

Month of Birth	Number of Students
January	//
February	//
March	//
April	///
May	//
June	/
July	/////
August	//
September	////
October	//
November	///
December	//

8 What is the mode for this frequency distribution?

F 3

G 4

H 5

J 6

STOP

 ANSWER ROWS: 4 Ⓕ Ⓖ Ⓗ Ⓙ 5 Ⓐ Ⓑ Ⓒ Ⓓ 6 Ⓕ Ⓖ Ⓗ Ⓙ 7 Ⓐ Ⓑ Ⓒ Ⓓ 8 Ⓕ Ⓖ Ⓗ Ⓙ

Sample A

What is the area of triangle ABD?

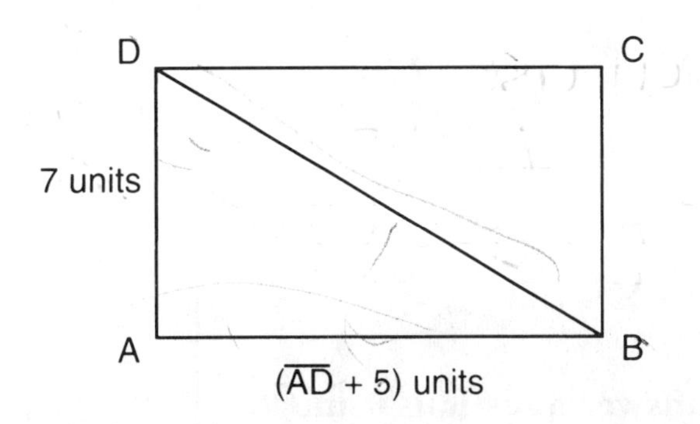

A 84 units ^{2}

B 42 units ^{2}

C 35 units ^{2}

D 17.5 units ^{2}

---

1 The picture frame below is 2 meters high by 3 meters wide. What is the perimeter of the frame in centimeters?

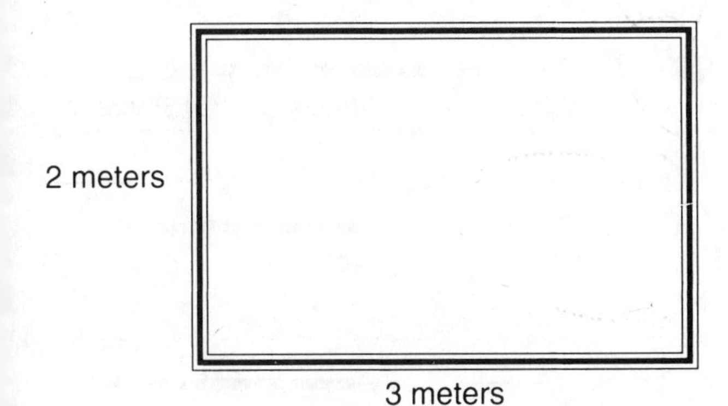

A 6 cm

B 10 cm

C 100 cm

D 1000 cm

2 A liter is equal to 0.0353 cubic feet. How would you express this number using scientific notation?

F 3.53×10^{-2} ft^3

G 35.3×10^{-4} ft^3

H 353×10^{-5} ft^3

J 3.53×10^{2} ft^3

3 Which equation is equivalent to $5T + 6 = 21$?

A $5(T + 6) = 21$

B $2(5T + 6) = 21 \div 2$

C $5T + 6 - 8 = 21 - 8$

D $3(T - 2) + 6 = 21$

4 What is the area of the circle shown below? Use $\pi = 3.14$.

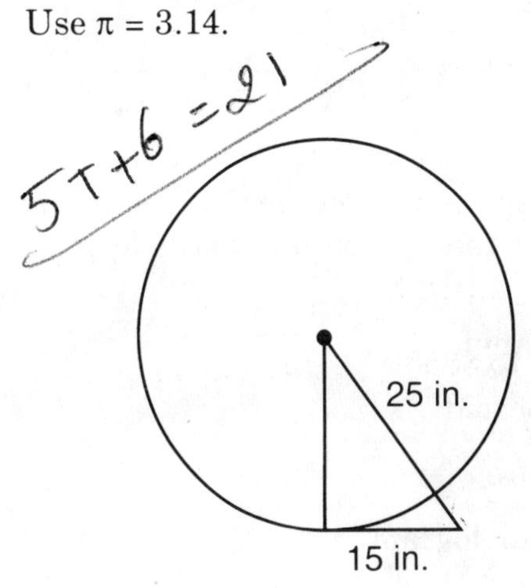

F 1962.5 units^2

G 1256 units^2

H 706.5 units^2

J 125.6 units^2

GO

ANSWER ROWS: A Ⓐ Ⓑ Ⓒ Ⓓ 1 Ⓐ Ⓑ Ⓒ Ⓓ 2 Ⓕ Ⓖ Ⓗ Ⓙ 3 Ⓐ Ⓑ Ⓒ Ⓓ 4 Ⓕ Ⓖ Ⓗ Ⓙ

5 What is the value of **a** in this equation?

$$6\,(a + 8) = 63$$

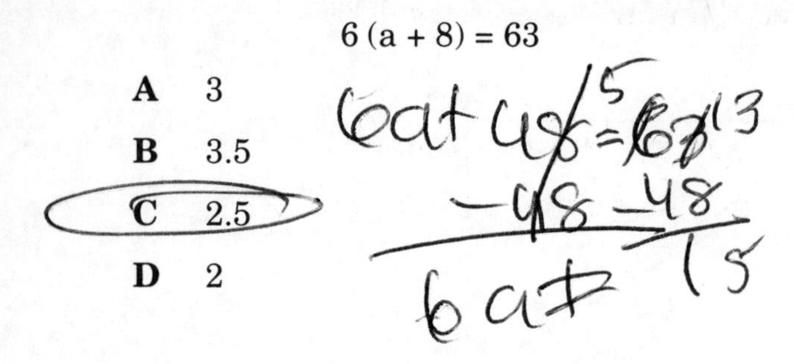

A 3

B 3.5

C 2.5

D 2

Use this figure to answer questions 6 and 7.

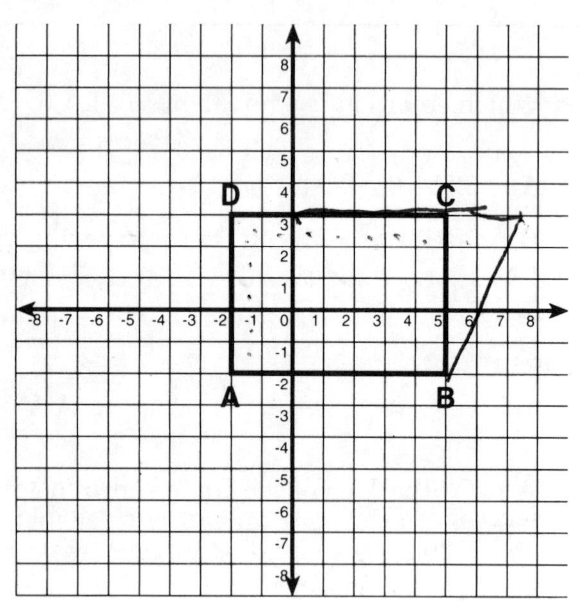

6 What shape would you have if you moved corners D and C two units to the left?

F rectangle

G trapezoid

H square

J parallelogram

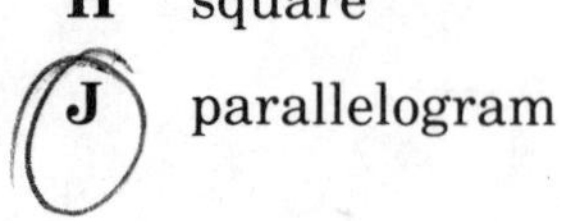

7 What is the area of the shape shown above?

A 36 units ^{2}

B 35 units ^{2}

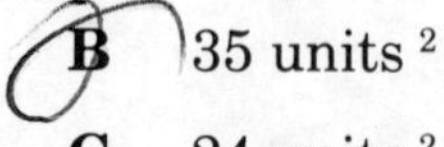

C 24 units ^{2}

D 12 units ^{2}

8 Which of these is about 0.8 yards wide?

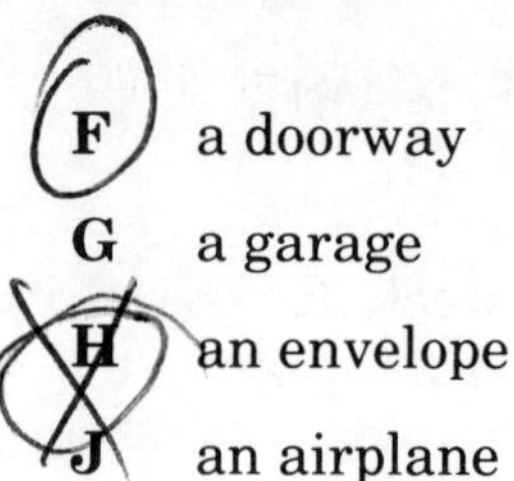

F a doorway

G a garage

H an envelope

J an airplane

9 Sue and Marty were comparison shopping for sunglasses. The most expensive glasses they found were $49.95. They found the same glasses for $11 less at a discount store. Which number line shows this range of prices?

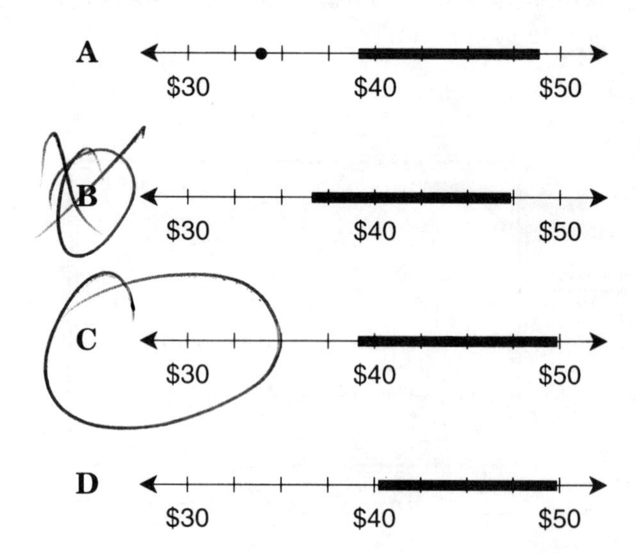

D

$30 $40 $50

10 Which number should come next in this pattern?

$$2\frac{1}{10}, 4\frac{1}{5}, 8\frac{3}{10}, \ldots$$

F $12\frac{7}{10}$

G $16\frac{2}{5}$

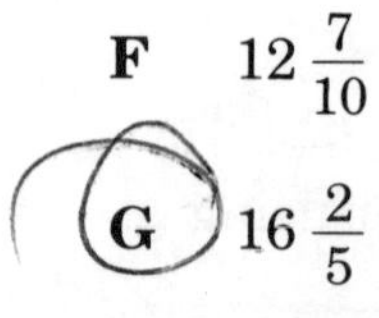

H $16\frac{7}{10}$

J $18\frac{2}{5}$

STOP

ANSWER ROWS: 5 Ⓐ Ⓑ Ⓒ Ⓓ 7 Ⓐ Ⓑ Ⓒ Ⓓ 9 Ⓐ Ⓑ Ⓒ Ⓓ
6 Ⓕ Ⓖ Ⓗ Ⓙ 8 Ⓕ Ⓖ Ⓗ Ⓙ 10 Ⓕ Ⓖ Ⓗ Ⓙ

NUMBER RIGHT ______

Lesson 23 Addition

Samples

Directions: Read each addition problem. Mark the answer you think is correct.

A Ray earns about $500 a week. He pays 15% in federal taxes, 2.6% in state taxes, and 7.5% in other taxes. He also has 5% of each paycheck transferred to a retirement account. What is the total percentage of Ray's paycheck that goes to taxes?

- **A** 15%
- **B** 22.5%
- **C** 25.7%
- **D** 27.5%
- **E** Not Here

B How long will a runway be if it is now $\frac{7}{8}$ of a mile long and you extend it by $\frac{1}{4}$ of a mile?

- **F** $1\frac{1}{8}$ miles
- **G** $1\frac{1}{4}$ miles
- **H** $1\frac{4}{7}$ miles
- **J** $1\frac{7}{8}$ miles
- **K** Not Here

When you work on scratch paper, check to be sure that digits and decimal points are lined up correctly.

If the correct answer is not shown, choose "Not Here."

Practice

1 A picture window is $8\frac{1}{3}$ feet wide. On each side of the window there is a section of drapes $2\frac{3}{4}$ feet wide. A carpenter wants to put a piece of molding above the window and both drapes. How long must the piece of molding be?

- **A** $10\frac{1}{8}$ feet
- **B** $10\frac{3}{4}$ feet
- **C** $12\frac{5}{6}$ feet
- **D** $13\frac{5}{6}$ feet
- **E** Not Here

2 A stadium currently holds 4598 fans. A new section of 2785 seats was recently added, and 6920 seats will be added next year. How many people in all will the stadium hold after next year?

- **F** 15,303
- **G** 14,303
- **H** 11,518
- **J** 7383
- **K** Not Here

3 A pumpkin weighs 15.67 kilograms. How much will it weigh if it gains 1.08 kilograms in one week and 2.2 kilograms the next?

- **A** 18.95 kg
- **B** 18.77 kg
- **C** 18.75 kg
- **D** 16.75 kg
- **E** 15.95

GO

ANSWER ROWS: A Ⓐ Ⓑ Ⓒ Ⓓ Ⓔ B Ⓕ Ⓖ Ⓗ Ⓙ Ⓚ 1 Ⓐ Ⓑ Ⓒ Ⓓ Ⓔ 2 Ⓕ Ⓖ Ⓗ Ⓙ Ⓚ 3 Ⓐ Ⓑ Ⓒ Ⓓ Ⓔ

4 The census report for a county showed that 12.88% of the adults leased automobiles and 82.9% owned them. The same report showed that 57.34% of the adults lived in a home they owned singly or jointly, and that 36.91% lived in a home they rented. What was the total percentage of adults who owned or leased automobiles?

F 84.25%

G 94.25%

H 94.78%

J 95.78%

K Not Here

5 The Kansas Turnpike is 233 miles long, the New York Thruway is 496 miles long, and the Pennsylvania Turnpike is 358 miles long. How long are these three turnpikes all together?

A 729 miles

B 854 miles

C 987 miles

D 1088 miles

E Not here

6 The members of a bicycle club are planning a trip. They will bike for $6\frac{2}{3}$ hours on the first day, 8 on the second day, $5\frac{1}{2}$ on the third day, and $3\frac{5}{6}$ on the fourth day. What is the total time they will spend biking?

F 16 hours

G $22\frac{4}{7}$ hours

H $22\frac{7}{12}$ hours

J $23\frac{5}{6}$ hours

K 24 hours

7 A business recently bought a new computer system. The computer itself cost $1845, and the software cost $679. The service contract was $180 per year, and a special backup power supply was $918. How much did the business pay for the computer, software, and power supply?

A $3622

B $3442

C $2943

D $1777

E Not Here

8 A box is $30\frac{1}{4}$ inches long, $18\frac{5}{8}$ inches wide, and $14\frac{1}{16}$ inches deep. You want to tape the box closed, but have just a little tape left. What is the shortest length of tape that will go around the box?

F $56\frac{1}{4}$ in.

G $64\frac{7}{8}$ in.

H $65\frac{3}{8}$ in.

J $98\frac{1}{4}$ in.

K Not Here

9 A space station is 1229 miles from earth. A satellite is 3387 miles from the space station. How far is the satellite from earth?

A 2158 miles

B 4616 miles

C 4618 miles

D 5616 miles

E 15,677 miles

STOP

ANSWER ROWS: 4 Ⓕ Ⓖ Ⓗ Ⓙ Ⓚ 6 Ⓕ Ⓖ Ⓗ Ⓙ Ⓚ 8 Ⓕ Ⓖ Ⓗ Ⓙ Ⓚ
5 Ⓐ Ⓑ Ⓒ Ⓓ Ⓔ 7 Ⓐ Ⓑ Ⓒ Ⓓ Ⓔ 9 Ⓐ Ⓑ Ⓒ Ⓓ Ⓔ

Samples

Directions: Read each subtraction problem. Mark the answer you think is correct.

A Kelly bought a sweater for $54.95, less a "good customer" discount of $15.29. What did she pay for the sweater?

A $39.64

B $39.66

C $49.64

D $49.66

E Not Here

B What will be left if you cut $4\frac{3}{8}$ feet off a board 12 feet long?

F $6\frac{3}{8}$ ft

G $6\frac{5}{8}$ ft

H $7\frac{5}{8}$ ft

J $16\frac{3}{8}$ ft

K Not Here

When you subtract fractions, rewrite the numbers carefully on scratch paper in a form that lets you work easily.

If you are not sure of an answer, check it by adding.

Practice

1 For three weeks, a worker earned $456.78, $399.25, and $465.66. What was the difference between the highest and lowest amounts she earned?

A $8.88

B $57.53

C $66.51

D $149.95

E Not Here

2 The barometric pressure at 8:00 AM was 29.58 in. Hg. It rose to 30.06 in. Hg by 3:00 PM. How much did the pressure rise during the day?

F 0.48 in. Hg

G 0.52 in. Hg

H 0.64 in. Hg

J 0.68 in. Hg

K Not Here

3 In order to buy a custom-made screen, Dennis had to take three measurements of the width of the door. The measurements were $30\frac{15}{16}$, $31\frac{3}{16}$, and $31\frac{1}{4}$ inches. How far apart were the two closest measurements he took?

A $\frac{1}{16}$ in.

B $\frac{1}{8}$ in.

C $\frac{1}{4}$ in.

D $1\frac{1}{16}$ in.

E $1\frac{1}{8}$ in.

GO

ANSWER ROWS: A Ⓐ Ⓑ Ⓒ Ⓓ Ⓔ B Ⓕ Ⓖ Ⓗ Ⓙ Ⓚ 1 Ⓐ Ⓑ Ⓒ Ⓓ Ⓔ 2 Ⓕ Ⓖ Ⓗ Ⓙ Ⓚ 3 Ⓐ Ⓑ Ⓒ Ⓓ Ⓔ

4 The odometer on a rental car read 6921 after a round trip to Oklahoma. The odometer at the beginning of the trip was 5077. How far was the round trip?

F 844 miles

G 1845 miles

H 1855 miles

J 1944 miles

K Not Here

5 In order to be promoted, a worker needs 15 productivity points. The worker's point total in October was $10\frac{3}{4}$ and increased in November to $12\frac{5}{16}$. How many more productivity points does the worker still need to be promoted?

A $3\frac{11}{16}$ points

B $2\frac{11}{16}$ points

C $2\frac{9}{16}$ points

D $2\frac{1}{8}$ points

E Not Here

6 Water boils at 212°F and alcohol boils at 148°F. The temperature of a container of unknown liquid is 76.55°F. How much more would you have to raise the temperature of the liquid to discover if it was alcohol?

F 71.45°F

G 71.55°F

H 72.45°F

J 72.55°F

K 135.45°F

7 The students in a school were having a fund raiser to buy a camcorder. They raised $559. The camcorder they wanted cost $799, but the store owner said she would let them have it for $50 less. How much more money did the students have to raise?

A $180

B $190

C $199

D $240

E Not Here

8 A piece of aluminum is being prepared for use in the space shuttle. It is now 0.14 mm thick, but it is only supposed to be 0.127 mm thick. How much aluminum must be ground from the piece so it is the correct thickness?

F 0.113 mm

G 0.27 mm

H 0.22 mm

J 0.12 mm

K Not Here

9 One truck carries $19\frac{5}{9}$ tons of dirt and another carries $21\frac{4}{9}$ tons. The first truck dumps its dirt into a hole but doesn't fill it. The second truck dumps $4\frac{5}{9}$ tons of dirt and fills the hole. How much dirt is left in the second truck?

A $24\frac{1}{9}$ tons

B $16\frac{8}{9}$ tons

C $16\frac{1}{9}$ tons

D 16 tons

E 15 tons

STOP

ANSWER ROWS: 4 Ⓕ Ⓖ Ⓗ Ⓙ Ⓚ 6 Ⓕ Ⓖ Ⓗ Ⓙ Ⓚ 8 Ⓕ Ⓖ Ⓗ Ⓙ Ⓚ
5 Ⓐ Ⓑ Ⓒ Ⓓ Ⓔ 7 Ⓐ Ⓑ Ⓒ Ⓓ Ⓔ 9 Ⓐ Ⓑ Ⓒ Ⓓ Ⓔ

Samples

Directions: Read each multiplication problem. Mark the answer you think is correct.

A A teacher bases students' grades on a total of 750 points. The final exam is worth 24% of a student's grade. How many points is the final exam worth?

- **A** 180
- **B** 314
- **C** 726
- **D** 774
- **E** Not Here

B Cecelia needed 25 copies of a 7 page report. The copy center charges $.08 per page, so each report will cost $.56. How much will it cost Cecelia to make 25 copies of the report?

- **F** $4.48
- **G** $5.60
- **H** $12.00
- **J** $14.00
- **K** $28.00

If necessary, work the problem on scratch paper. Be sure to copy the numbers correctly when you do.

After you have found an answer, ask yourself: "Does this answer make sense?"

Practice

1 Reggie is helping his parents build a deck. He must cut 8 boards each to a length of $6\frac{1}{3}$ feet. What will the total length of these boards be when he finishes cutting them?

- **A** 60 feet
- **B** $50\frac{2}{3}$ feet
- **C** 48 feet
- **D** $48\frac{1}{3}$ feet
- **E** Not Here

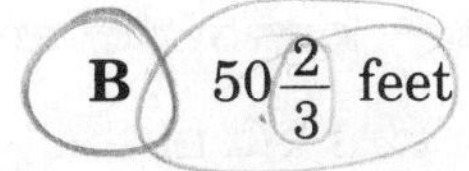

2 A round-trip plane ticket from Dallas to Phoenix costs $149. How much will it cost a college if 36 football players fly from Dallas to Phoenix and back?

- **F** $185
- **G** $4364
- **H** $5362
- **J** $5363
- **K** Not Here

3 If 1 gallon of water weighs 8.3 pounds, how much will 2.45 gallons of water weigh?

- **A** 11.75 pounds
- **B** 10.335 pounds
- **C** 19.335 pounds
- **D** 20.335 pounds
- **E** Not Here

GO

ANSWER ROWS: A Ⓐ Ⓑ Ⓒ Ⓓ Ⓔ 1 Ⓐ Ⓑ Ⓒ Ⓓ Ⓔ 3 Ⓐ Ⓑ Ⓒ Ⓓ Ⓔ
B Ⓕ Ⓖ Ⓗ Ⓙ Ⓚ 2 Ⓕ Ⓖ Ⓗ Ⓙ Ⓚ

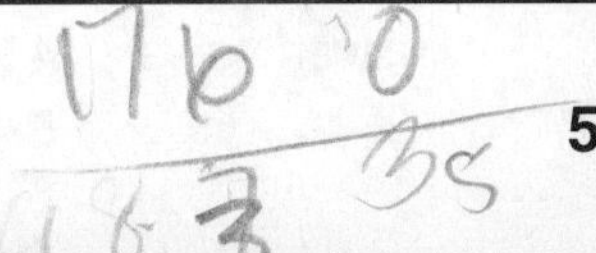

4 A company that sells books ships 175 cases of books each week. A case holds 18 books and weighs 54 pounds. How many pounds of books does the company ship in a week?

F 247 pounds
G 972 pounds
H 9540 pounds
J 9570 pounds
K Not Here

5 A truck delivered 28 pieces of pipe to a drilling site. Each piece of pipe was $22\frac{1}{4}$ feet long. How many feet of pipe were delivered by the truck?

A 623 ft
B $623\frac{1}{4}$ ft
C $672\frac{1}{4}$ ft
D 676 ft
E Not Here

6 Evaporation causes the loss of 0.39 mm of water from a lake each day. How many millimeters of water does the pond lose through evaporation in 90 days?

F 39.9 mm
G 36.1 mm
H 36.01 mm
J 35.1 mm
K 35.01 mm

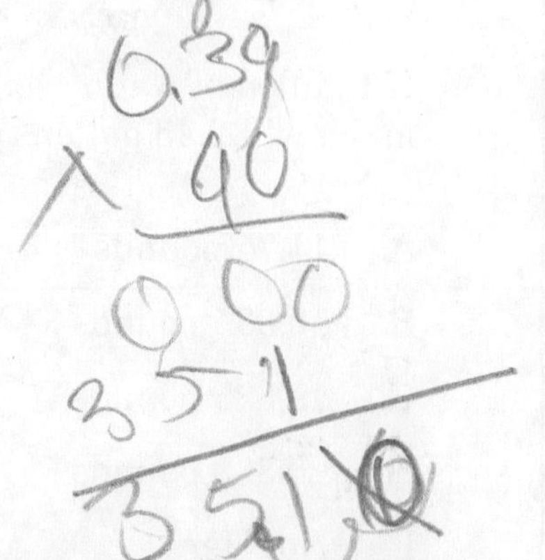

7 A ninth grade class at a local school adopted a section of highway. They pick up litter on the highway once each month. To do this, they walk an average of $5\frac{3}{8}$ miles each month. How many miles of highway do they walk in a year?

A $60\frac{3}{8}$ miles
B $64\frac{1}{2}$ miles
C $64\frac{3}{8}$ miles
D 68 miles
E Not Here

8 A container of chemicals is 0.98 meters tall. In the warehouse, the containers are normally stacked 10 high. What is the total distance from the floor of the warehouse to the top of the seventh container on the stack?

F 9.8 m
G 7.98 m
H 6.86 m
J 6.02 m
K 5.02 m

9 A garden store sells potted daisies for $3.49 each. How much will it cost to buy 16 of them?

A $39.49
B $48.49
C $54.84
D $55.84
E Not Here

STOP

ANSWER ROWS: **4** Ⓕ Ⓖ Ⓗ Ⓙ Ⓚ **6** Ⓕ Ⓖ Ⓗ Ⓙ Ⓚ **8** Ⓕ Ⓖ Ⓗ Ⓙ Ⓚ
5 Ⓐ Ⓑ Ⓒ Ⓓ Ⓔ **7** Ⓐ Ⓑ Ⓒ Ⓓ Ⓔ **9** Ⓐ Ⓑ Ⓒ Ⓓ Ⓔ

Samples

Directions: Read each division problem. Mark the answer you think is correct.

A A cantaloupe weighs 3.12 pounds. It was divided into 4 pieces. How much does each piece weigh?

- **A** 12.48 pounds
- **B** 7.12 pounds
- **C** 0.88 pounds
- **D** 0.78 pounds
- **E** Not Here

B A shipper bought 1895 pounds of potatoes for $.06 a pound. How many 50-pound bags can the shipper fill with the potatoes?

- **F** 113.7 bags
- **G** 56 bags
- **H** 50.06 bags
- **J** 39.7 bags
- **K** Not Here

Remember, you can check your answer by multiplying.

Be careful! Some problems contain numbers that are not needed to solve the problem.

Practice

1 A school library has 833 fiction books. There are an average of 17 books per shelf. How many shelves of fiction books are in the library?

- **A** 56
- **B** 49
- **C** 48.17
- **D** 39
- **E** Not Here

2 A town of 3755 has 7 doctors and 4 dentists. What is the average number of people each dentist serves, rounded to the nearest whole number?

- **F** 341
- **G** 275
- **H** 536
- **J** 839
- **K** 939

3 A box of blank video tapes costs $36.64. If one tape costs $2.29, how many tapes are in a box?

- **A** 36
- **B** 34
- **C** 17
- **D** 12
- **E** Not Here

4 A flooring tile is 9 inches on each side, so each tile has a surface area of 81 square inches. How many tiles would be needed to cover a bathroom floor that is 7776 square inches?

- **F** 90
- **G** 96
- **H** 729
- **J** 864
- **K** Not Here

GO

ANSWER ROWS: A Ⓐ Ⓑ Ⓒ Ⓓ Ⓔ 1 Ⓐ Ⓑ Ⓒ Ⓓ Ⓔ 3 Ⓐ Ⓑ Ⓒ Ⓓ Ⓔ
B Ⓕ Ⓖ Ⓗ Ⓙ Ⓚ 2 Ⓕ Ⓖ Ⓗ Ⓙ Ⓚ 4 Ⓕ Ⓖ Ⓗ Ⓙ Ⓚ

5 A homeowner burns 142.5 cubic feet of wood every 30 days. The homeowner spends about 25 minutes a day tending the fire. How much wood does the homeowner burn in one day?

A 4.7 cubic feet

B 4.75 cubic feet

C 5 cubic feet

D 5.7 cubic feet

E 5.75 cubic feet

6 An apartment building houses 250 people living in 80 apartments. The building is 10 stories tall. What is the average number of people in each apartment?

F 25

G 8

H 3.125

J 2.625

K Not Here

7 It takes $2\frac{1}{3}$ pounds of seed to fill a bird feeder. The birds empty the feeder in about 3 days. If there are 50 pounds of seed in a bag, how many times will you be able to fill a feeder from 1 bag?

A $116\frac{2}{3}$

B $116\frac{1}{3}$

C 22

D $21\frac{3}{7}$

E Not Here

8 How many 4.4-ounce bottles of glue could you fill from a container that holds 140.8 ounces?

F 32

G 32.4

H 34

J 34.4

K 35.2

9 A herd of cattle travels about $31\frac{1}{2}$ miles in a day. The cowboys who drive the cattle work 10-hour days, but the cattle walk for only 9 hours a day. How far do the cattle move in an hour?

A 4 miles

B $3\frac{1}{3}$ miles

C $2\frac{1}{2}$ miles

D 2 miles

E Not Here

10 A storage freezer has a volume of 394.4 cubic feet and an area of 49 square feet. It is filled with 68 cases of frozen fruit. Each case contains 12 packages of frozen fruit. How many cubic feet does each case hold?

F 80

G 8.04

H 6

J 5.8

K Not Here

STOP

ANSWER ROWS: 5 Ⓐ Ⓑ Ⓒ Ⓓ Ⓔ 7 Ⓐ Ⓑ Ⓒ Ⓓ Ⓔ 9 Ⓐ Ⓑ Ⓒ Ⓓ Ⓔ
6 Ⓕ Ⓖ Ⓗ Ⓙ Ⓚ 8 Ⓕ Ⓖ Ⓗ Ⓙ Ⓚ 10 Ⓕ Ⓖ Ⓗ Ⓙ Ⓚ

Sample A

Water freezes at 32°F. If the temperature is at 51°F, how far must it drop before ice forms on a pond?

A 83°F

B 32°F

C 18°F

D 16°F

E Not Here

Sample B

If a gallon of milk costs $2.25, how much will it cost to buy 18 gallons of milk for a Labor Day picnic?

F $15.75

G $20.25

H $40.50

J $42.50

K Not Here

---

1 It snowed in north Texas for 4 days in a row. The amounts were $2\frac{1}{2}$ inches, $4\frac{1}{4}$ inches, $3\frac{5}{8}$ inches, and $7\frac{1}{3}$ inches. How much snow fell in all during the 4-day period?

A $18\frac{7}{24}$ inches

B 18 inches

C $17\frac{17}{24}$ inches

D $16\frac{3}{8}$ inches

E Not Here

2 The bus route from the center of a city to the mall is 29.72 miles. The route from the mall to the airport is 32.64. How much farther is the second trip than the first?

F 62.36 miles

G 32.72 miles

H 3.92 miles

J 2.92 miles

K 2.12 miles

3 What would the total bill be if you bought a watch for $29.95, a sweater for $39.95, socks for $9.95, and a wallet for $19.95?

A $99.85

B $99.80

C $89.85

D $70.00

E $9.98

4 A mail order business calculates the percentage of its annual business for each month of the year. In September it does 4.8%, in October 5.93%, in November 14.04%, and in December 28.56%. What is the total percentage of business it does during the months of October, November, and December?

F 38.53%

G 42.6%

H 52.33%

J 53.33%

K Not here

GO

ANSWER ROWS: A Ⓐ Ⓑ Ⓒ Ⓓ Ⓔ 1 Ⓐ Ⓑ Ⓒ Ⓓ Ⓔ 3 Ⓐ Ⓑ Ⓒ Ⓓ Ⓔ

B Ⓕ Ⓖ Ⓗ Ⓙ Ⓚ 2 Ⓕ Ⓖ Ⓗ Ⓙ Ⓚ 4 Ⓕ Ⓖ Ⓗ Ⓙ Ⓚ

5 A boat is traveling at a speed of $15\frac{3}{4}$ miles an hour. Its maximum speed is 24 miles an hour. How long will it take to travel 2782 miles if it was traveling at its maximum speed?

A $16\frac{3}{4}$ hours

B $14\frac{1}{4}$ hours

C 14 hours

D $9\frac{1}{4}$ hours

E Not Here

6 In 1968, Tommie Smith won the 200-meter run in the Olympics with a time of 19.83 seconds. The Olympic winner in 1988, Jo DeLoach, won with a time of 19.75. How much faster was DeLoach's time?

F 0.08 seconds

G 0.18 seconds

H 0.19 seconds

J 39.58 seconds

K Not Here

7 A student works 2 hours a day during the summer for 21 days a month. Each day, the student earns $8.56. How much does the student earn each hour?

A $10.56

B $10.50

C $6.56

D $4.33

E $4.28

8 In a relay race, the times of the four runners on a team were 10.03 seconds, 9.98 seconds, 9.72 seconds, and 10.16 seconds. What was the total time for this team?

F 30.08 seconds

G 39.089 seconds

H 39.89 seconds

J 40.089 seconds

K 40.89 seconds

9 A chair lift at a ski area can carry 4 skiers in each chair. It takes $19\frac{4}{5}$ minutes for a chair to go from the bottom to the top and back again. How many chairs are needed to carry 296 skiers to the top of the mountain?

A $73\frac{4}{5}$

B 74

C $84\frac{1}{5}$

D 84

E Not Here

10 Roxanne runs 3.25 miles a day. She runs Monday through Friday, but not on Saturday or Sunday. How far does she run each week?

F 22.75 miles

G 22 miles

H 16.525 miles

J 16.25 miles

K 15.125 miles

STOP

ANSWER ROWS: 5 Ⓐ Ⓑ Ⓒ Ⓓ Ⓔ 7 Ⓐ Ⓑ Ⓒ Ⓓ Ⓔ 9 Ⓐ Ⓑ Ⓒ Ⓓ Ⓔ
6 Ⓕ Ⓖ Ⓗ Ⓙ Ⓚ 8 Ⓕ Ⓖ Ⓗ Ⓙ Ⓚ 10 Ⓕ Ⓖ Ⓗ Ⓙ Ⓚ

NUMBER RIGHT ________

Lesson 28 Estimation

Samples

Directions: Read each mathematics problem. Mark the answer you think is correct.

A On a baseball diamond, it is 90 feet between bases. About how far does someone run who hits a home run?

A 90 feet
B 200 feet
C between 200 and 250 feet
D between 250 and 300 feet
E between 350 and 400 feet

B Plane A travels 25% faster than plane B. If a trip takes plane B an hour, about how long will it take plane A to make the trip?

F 15 minutes
G 30 minutes
H 45 minutes
J 1 hour and 15 minutes
K 90 minutes

For some problems, there is no exact answer. If you have worked a problem on scratch paper and found an answer that is not one of the answer choices, select the answer choice that is closest to your answer.

Practice

1 Suppose that the scale on a map indicates that 1 inch = 10 miles. About how far apart would two towns be if they were 6.65 inches apart on the map?

A 6.5 miles
B 60 miles
C 65 miles
D 70 miles
E 650 miles

2 A computer technician charges $25 an hour, plus a service call charge of $15. About how much would her bill be if she spent 3 hours and 15 minutes fixing the computer in an office?

F $25
G about $40
H between $50 and $75
J about $100
K between $100 and $125

3 A pair of tennis shoes costing $50 goes on sale for 20% off the regular price. After the sale, the store raises the price 20%. About how much do the tennis shoes cost now?

A between $40 and $45
B between $45 and $50
C $50
D between $50 and $55
E $60

4 What is the total thickness of 8 boards if each board is 0.89 inches thick?

F between 1 and 2 inches
G between 2 and 6 inches
H about 6 inches
J between 6.5 and 7 inches
K about 7 inches

GO

ANSWER ROWS: A Ⓐ Ⓑ Ⓒ Ⓓ Ⓔ 1 Ⓐ Ⓑ Ⓒ Ⓓ Ⓔ 3 Ⓐ Ⓑ Ⓒ Ⓓ Ⓔ
B Ⓕ Ⓖ Ⓗ Ⓙ Ⓚ 2 Ⓕ Ⓖ Ⓗ Ⓙ Ⓚ 4 Ⓕ Ⓖ Ⓗ Ⓙ Ⓚ

5 There are 514 students in a school. Two of the students are running for student council president. Only half the students in the school voted, and of these, 106 voted for candidate A. About how many students voted for candidate B?

A less than 50

B between 50 and 90

C about 100

D between 100 and 140

E about 150

6 Freddy had $30 to spend for a picnic. He spent $17.75 on food. With the rest of the money, he bought bottles of juice. If juice costs $1.95 a bottle, about how many bottles of juice did he buy?

F 6

G 7

H 9

J 11

K 12

7 Jerry and 3 of her friends went to lunch. Each spent about $4. When they received the bill, it was for $19.86. Jerry told the waiter he had made a mistake in adding. About how far off was he from the correct amount?

A $16

B $13

C $8

D $4

E $1

8 The daily flight from El Paso to Dallas carries an average of 91 passengers. The airline reduced the price of tickets for a week and found that the average number of passengers increased by 10%. About how many more passengers flew during the 7-day week with reduced prices than during a week of regular prices?

F about 10

G about 50

H about 60

J about 600

K about 700

9 The average temperature in a city is 31° in January and 68° in May. Assume that the temperature increases about the same amount each month. What will the average temperature be in the month of March?

A about 35°

B about 40°

C about 45°

D about 50°

E about 60°

10 The monthly electric bills for a small business for 5 months were $81.25, $89.86, $86.05, $67.99, and $74.54. The owner of the business believes the bills for the rest of the year will show the same pattern. About how much will the owner of the business pay in a year for electricity?

F more than $1000

G between $900 and $1000

H between $900 and $9000

J between $700 and $8000

K less than $700

STOP

ANSWER ROWS: 5 Ⓐ Ⓑ Ⓒ Ⓓ Ⓔ 7 Ⓐ Ⓑ Ⓒ Ⓓ Ⓔ 9 Ⓐ Ⓑ Ⓒ Ⓓ Ⓔ
6 Ⓕ Ⓖ Ⓗ Ⓙ Ⓚ 8 Ⓕ Ⓖ Ⓗ Ⓙ Ⓚ 10 Ⓕ Ⓖ Ⓗ Ⓙ Ⓚ

Sample

Directions: Read each mathematics problem. Mark the answer you think is correct.

A Look at this figure. A and C are the centers of two circles. Point B is on the circumference of both circles. If AB = 2BC, what is the diameter of a circle with center A if C is on its circumference?

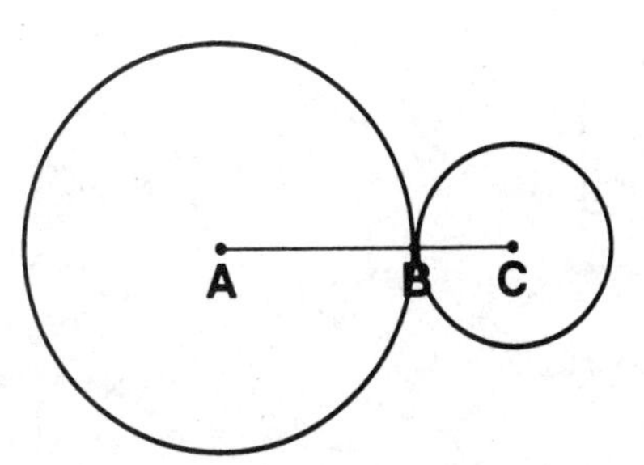

- **A** 2πAC
- **B** 2πBC
- **C** AB + BC
- **D** AC
- **E** 6BC

Read the question carefully and think about what you are supposed to do. Don't be confused by numbers or parts of figures that are not necessary to solve the problem.

Practice

1 A cord of wood is 8 feet long, 4 feet high, and 4 feet deep. How many logs are needed to make a cord if a log is 16 feet long and the surface area of a cut through the log averages 1 square foot?

- **A** 16 logs
- **B** 12.8 logs
- **C** 9 logs
- **D** 8 logs
- **E** Not Here

2 A baseball player's batting average is .250. How many hits would you expect the player to get if she comes to bat 88 times?

- **F** 25
- **G** 23
- **H** 12
- **J** 11
- **K** Not Here

3 An artist is planning to cut a mat to go around a picture. The shaded portion of the figure below shows the area of the mat. How can you calculate the area of the mat?

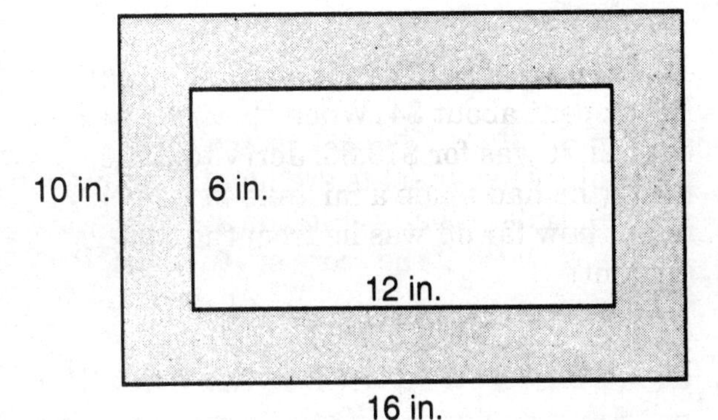

- **A** (16 x 10) – (12 x 6)
- **B** (2•10 + 2•16) – (2•6 + 2•12)
- **C** (16 x 10) + (12 x 6)
- **D** (12•16) – (6•10)
- **E** (12•16) + (6•10)

GO

ANSWER ROWS: A Ⓐ Ⓑ Ⓒ Ⓓ Ⓔ 1 Ⓐ Ⓑ Ⓒ Ⓓ Ⓔ 2 Ⓕ Ⓖ Ⓗ Ⓙ Ⓚ 3 Ⓐ Ⓑ Ⓒ Ⓓ Ⓔ

4 Suppose you tried each of these spinners just once. On which one would you most likely land on 1?

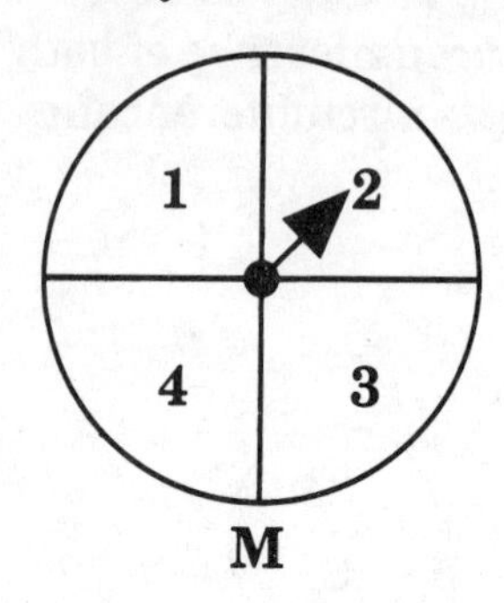

M

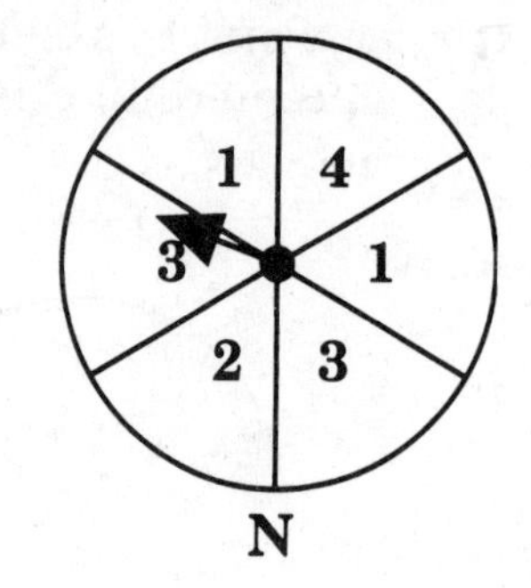

N

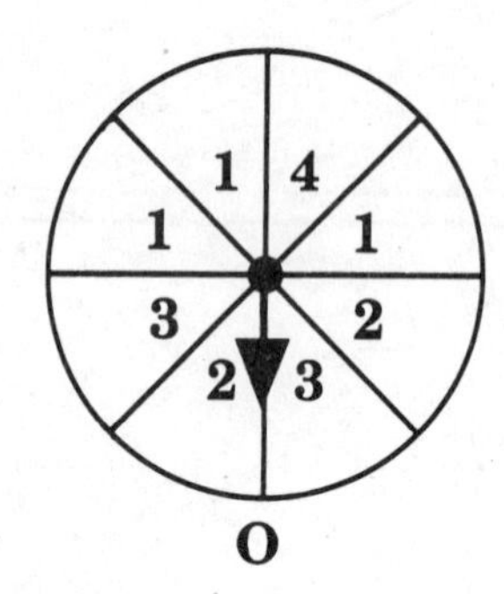

O

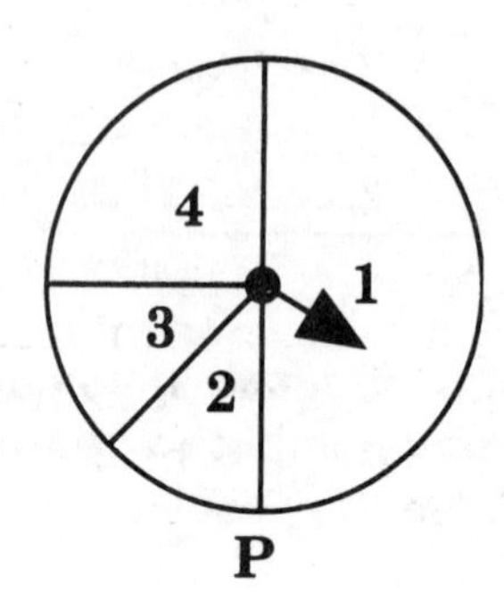

P

F M

G N

H O

J P

K You would have the same chance on all of them.

5 This chart shows the test scores for 8 students. The students are identified by their initials. What would the average score for the class be if the score of student OP increased to 96?

Students	BR	SS	OP	TR	DC	GR	LJ	JB
Scores	80	85	88	94	78	84	91	92

A 94.5

B 92

C 87.6

D 86.8

E Not Here

6 How could you find the speed at which the earth is rotating on its axis if you know the diameter of the earth is about 7900 miles?

F $\frac{7900 \times \pi}{24}$

G $\frac{3950^2 \times \pi}{24}$

H $\frac{7900 \times \pi^2}{24}$

J $\frac{3950 \times \pi}{24}$

K $\frac{7900 \times 24}{\pi}$

7 A farmer usually plants 2000 acres a year. This year, he planted 800 acres of cotton, 400 acres of sorghum, and 200 acres of soy beans. He didn't plant anything in the remaining acres because of financial problems. How can you find the percentage of planted acreage that went to cotton?

A $\frac{400}{800 + 400 + 200}$

B $\frac{2000 - 800}{2000}$

C $\frac{800}{2000}$

D $\frac{2000 - 400 - 200}{800 + 400 + 200}$

E $\frac{800}{800 + 400 + 200}$

8 There are 450 students in a school, and 234 of them are girls. If the number of students in the school increases to 525 and the percentage of girls remains the same, how many girls will be in the school?

F 216

G 273

H 274

J 286

K Not Here

STOP

Samples

Directions: Read each mathematics problem. Mark the answer you think is correct.

A Two towns are 54 miles apart. A bicyclist averaging 12 miles an hour leaves one town and rides for 3 hours. How can you find the remaining distance to the other town?

A $54 - (12 \times 3)$

B 12×3

C $54 + (12 \times 3)$

D $(54 - 12) \times 3$

E $(54 \div 3) - 12$

B Lori bought a Slurpster for $1.59 and paid with a 5-dollar bill. She asked for as many quarters as possible in her change. How many quarters did she receive?

F 16

G 15

H 14

J 13

K 12

If the answer you find is not one of the answer choices, work the problem again. Read the problem carefully, look for key words, numbers, and figures, and transfer numbers carefully to scratch paper.

Practice

1 The illustration below shows two sets of cubes. The white cubes are all the same weight, but this weight is unknown. The gray cubes each weigh 3 ounces. The groups of cubes shown below have the same total weight. What is the weight of a white cube?

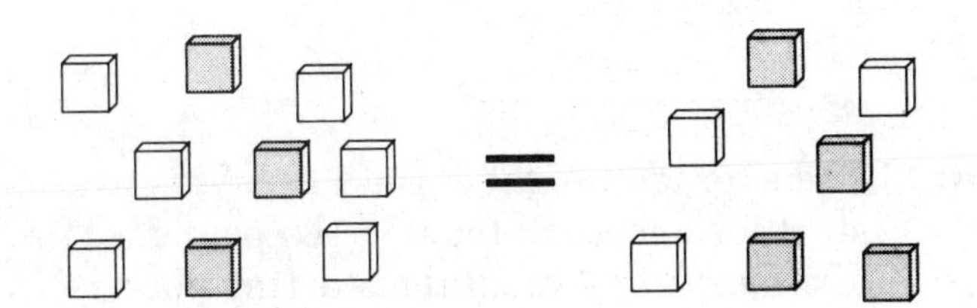

A 3.5 ounces

B 2 ounces

C 1 ounce

D 0.5 ounces

E 0.1 ounces

2 Country A is larger than country B. Country C is more than twice the size of countries A and B together. Which of these expresses this relationship among the countries?

F $C = 2(A + B)$

G $C > 2(A + B)$

H $C < A + B$

J $2C < A + B$

K $2C = A + B$

3 Anita worked 10 hours on Saturday. For 8 hours she earned $5.00 an hour, her regular rate. For 2 hours she earned 1.5 times her regular rate. How much did she earn working all day on Saturday?

A $41.50

B $43.00

C $50.50

D $51.50

E $55.00

GO

ANSWER ROWS: A Ⓐ Ⓑ Ⓒ Ⓓ Ⓔ B Ⓕ Ⓖ Ⓗ Ⓙ Ⓚ 1 Ⓐ Ⓑ Ⓒ Ⓓ Ⓔ 2 Ⓕ Ⓖ Ⓗ Ⓙ Ⓚ 3 Ⓐ Ⓑ Ⓒ Ⓓ Ⓔ

This graph shows students' scores on 5 different tests. The long vertical line shows the range of scores, the box shows the range in which two-thirds of the students' scores fall, and the horizontal bar shows the average (mean) score. Use this graph to answer questions 4 through 6.

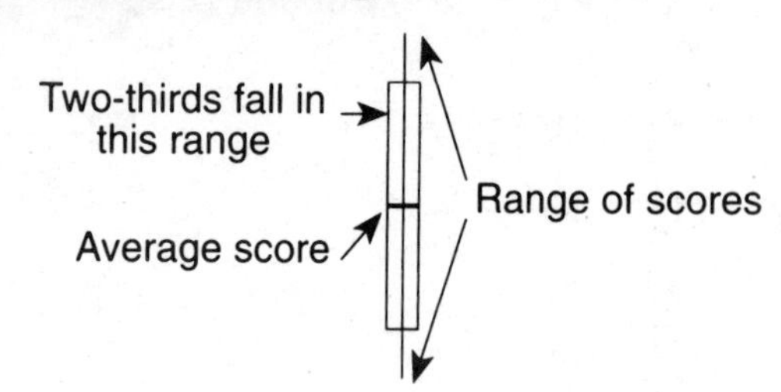

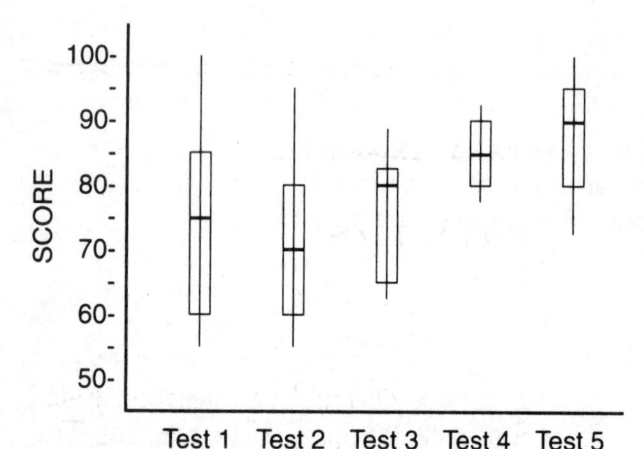

4 On which test did students' scores fall within the smallest range?

F Test 1

G Test 2

H Test 3

J Test 4

K Test 5

5 What is the difference between the lowest and highest average scores?

A 30 points

B 20 points

C 15 points

D 10 points

E 5 points

6 What is the average score for all 5 tests?

F 75

G 80

H 82.5

J 85

K 87.5

7 In the figure below, one side is 6 units and the area is 90 units². Which answer choice shows how to find the perimeter of the figure?

6 units $A = 90 \text{ units}^2$

A $(2 \times \frac{90}{6}) + (2 \times 6)$

B $(2 \times 6) + 90$

C $(2 \times 6) + (2 \times 90)$

D $2 \times (6 + \frac{6}{90})$

E $6 \times 6 \times \frac{90}{6} \times \frac{90}{6}$

8 The average weight of the 11 players who start for a football team is 185 pounds. The average weight of all the starting players except the quarterback is 188 pounds. Which sentence shows how to find Q, the weight of the quarterback?

F $Q = 10 \times 11 + (188 - 185)$

G $Q = (188 + 185) \div 2$

H $Q = (11 \times 185) - (10 \times 188)$

J $Q = (10 + 11) \times (188 - 185)$

K $Q = (188 - 11) - (185 \div 10)$

STOP

 ANSWER ROWS: 4 Ⓕ Ⓖ Ⓗ Ⓙ Ⓚ 5 Ⓐ Ⓑ Ⓒ Ⓓ Ⓔ 6 Ⓕ Ⓖ Ⓗ Ⓙ Ⓚ 7 Ⓐ Ⓑ Ⓒ Ⓓ Ⓔ 8 Ⓕ Ⓖ Ⓗ Ⓙ Ⓚ

Samples

Directions: Read each mathematics problem. Mark the answer you think is correct.

A Which of these are you least likely to find in the real world?

- **A** A car weighing 1000 kilograms
- **B** A building 100 meters high
- **C** A box with a surface area of 1 $yard^2$
- **D** A refrigerator with 12 $feet^3$ of storage
- **E** A basketball player 3 meters tall

B The distance from the earth to the moon is about 240,000 miles. A reasonable time for a round trip to the moon if you traveled at 9800 miles an hour is –

- **F** 1 week
- **G** 2 days
- **H** 1 day
- **J** 15 hours
- **K** 10 hours

Be sure to look at all the answer choices before you choose the one you think is correct.

Remember, the correct answer may not be an exact number.

Practice

1 The figure below shows a triangle and a circle. The perimeter of the circle is 314 cm, and the base of the triangle is equal to its height. A reasonable amount for the area of the triangle is —

- **A** 10,000 cm^2
- **B** 5000 cm^2
- **C** 1500 cm^2
- **D** 1000 cm^2
- **E** 500 cm^2

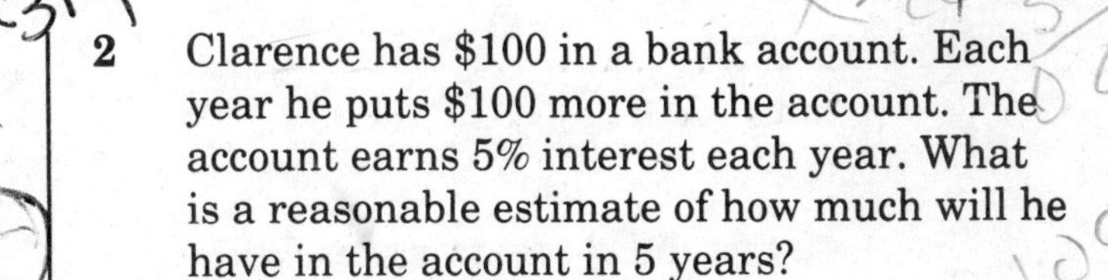

2 Clarence has $100 in a bank account. Each year he puts $100 more in the account. The account earns 5% interest each year. What is a reasonable estimate of how much will he have in the account in 5 years?

- **F** About $400
- **G** Between $400 and $500
- **H** Between $500 and $550
- **J** About $600
- **K** About $800

3 It takes a truck driver and a helper 8 hours to unload a truck. They receive $240 for their work. The driver receives 25% more than the helper. About how much does the driver make an hour?

- **A** More than $18
- **B** Between $16 and $17
- **C** About $15
- **D** Between $13 and $15
- **E** About $10

GO

4 An acre is 43,500 square feet. A football field is 100 yards long and 160 feet wide. About how many acres is a football field?

F Less than 0.4 acres

G Exactly 0.5 acres

H About 1.1 acres

J About 2.2 acres

K More than 3 acres

5 The owner of a store buys computers for $895 and sells them for $1195. Her expenses each day are $450, and the store is open 6 days a week. What is a reasonable number of computers for her to sell in a week to pay her expenses?

A 18

B 15

C 14

D 11

E 9

6 The chart below shows the salary earned by 5 sales people. Their salary is based on years of service and total sales. A reasonable salary for a person with 7 years of service whose total sales are $478,391 is —

Name	Salary	Total Sales	Years of Service
Miller	$57,000	$448,573	12
Harkins	$35,000	$321,029	3
Adams	$43,000	$329,338	10
Sligo	$48,000	$401,945	8

F more than $60,000

G about $55,000

H between $50,000 and $54,000

J about $45,000

K less than $40,000

7 The area of the figure below is 648 units^2. Side A is twice side B. A reasonable length for side A is —

Area = 648 units^2 B

A

A between 35 and 40 units

B about 32 units

C exactly 24 units

D about 18 units

E between 10 and 15 units

8 Ralph earned a 65 on his first math test. He began studying harder and improved his score by 5 points on the next test. He took 4 more math tests, and on each one, he raised his score 5 points over his previous test. What is a reasonable average score for Ralph on the 6 math tests he took?

F More than 90

G Between 85 and 90

H Between 80 and 85

J Between 75 and 80

K Less than 75

9 About how many 6 inch by 6 inch by 6 inch boxes can be put in a carton that has 12 cubic feet of space and is 3 feet long and 2 feet wide?

A More than 100

B Exactly 96

C Exactly 72

D Exactly 48

E Less than 40

STOP

ANSWER ROWS: 4 Ⓕ Ⓖ Ⓗ Ⓙ Ⓚ 6 Ⓕ Ⓖ Ⓗ Ⓙ Ⓚ 8 Ⓕ Ⓖ Ⓗ Ⓙ Ⓚ

5 Ⓐ Ⓑ Ⓒ Ⓓ Ⓔ 7 Ⓐ Ⓑ Ⓒ Ⓓ Ⓔ 9 Ⓐ Ⓑ Ⓒ Ⓓ Ⓔ

Sample A

What percentage of the larger circle shown on the right is shaded?

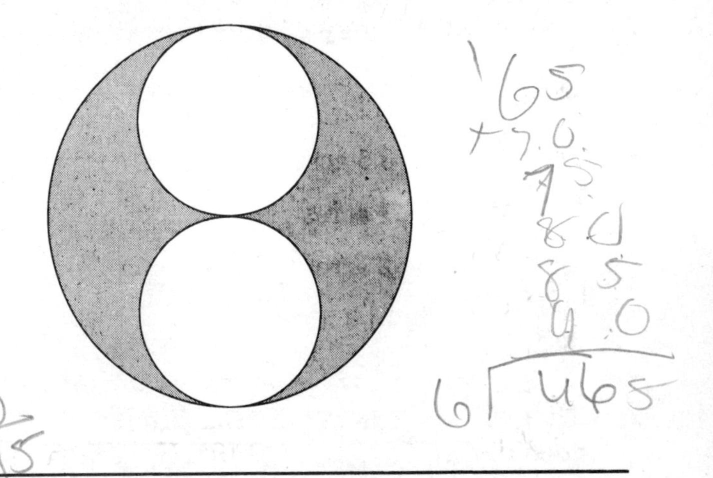

A $10\pi^2\%$

B $6\pi^2\%$

C 50%

D 45%

E 20%

---

1 A group of 10 friends is planning a ski vacation for 5 days. The round trip airfare will be $149 per person, and rooms will be $79 a night. Up to 4 people can sleep in a room. Ski rental will be $15 a day per person. Lift tickets will be $32 a day per person. About how much will it cost the group for airfare, rooms, skis, and lift tickets?

A Less than $3000

B Between $3000 and $3500

C Between $3500 and $4000

D Between $4000 and $4500

E More than $4500

2 Last year, a business paid a dividend of $2.75 for each share of stock held by the owners. This year, the business expects to increase its dividend by 15%. Suppose you had 100 shares of stock in the company. How could you calculate the total amount of your dividend check?

F ($2.75 x 0.15) x 100

G ($2.75 x 1.15) x 100

H ($2.75 + 1.15) x 100

J ($2.75 + 100) x 0.15

K ($2.75 + 0.15) x 100

3 What is the probability of getting either a 1 or a 2 by taking one turn at this spinner?

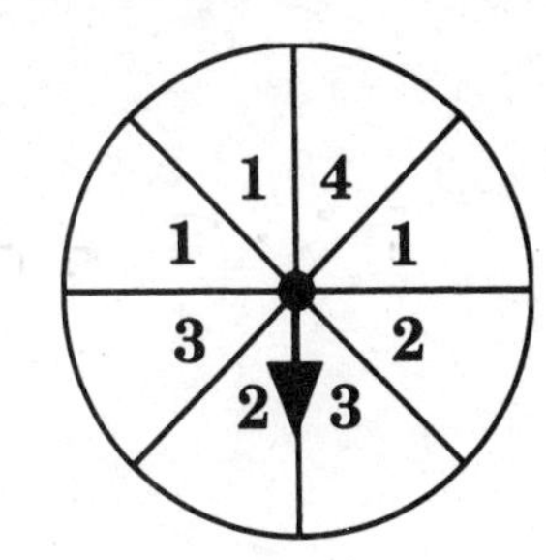

A $\frac{1}{2}$

B $\frac{3}{8}$

C $\frac{5}{16}$

D $\frac{4}{5}$

E Not Here

4 How would you find the height in cm of a person who is 6 feet tall? A cm is 0.3937 of an inch.

F (6 x 12) ÷ 0.3937

G (6 x 12) x 0.3937

H (0.3937 x 12) x 6

J (1 + 0.3937) x 12 x 6

K Not Here

GO

ANSWER ROWS: A Ⓐ Ⓑ Ⓒ Ⓓ Ⓔ 1 Ⓐ Ⓑ Ⓒ Ⓓ Ⓔ 2 Ⓕ Ⓖ Ⓗ Ⓙ Ⓚ 3 Ⓐ Ⓑ Ⓒ Ⓓ Ⓔ 4 Ⓕ Ⓖ Ⓗ Ⓙ Ⓚ

This graph shows the temperature from 8:00 in the morning to 5:00 in the afternoon. Use the graph to answer questions 5 - 7.

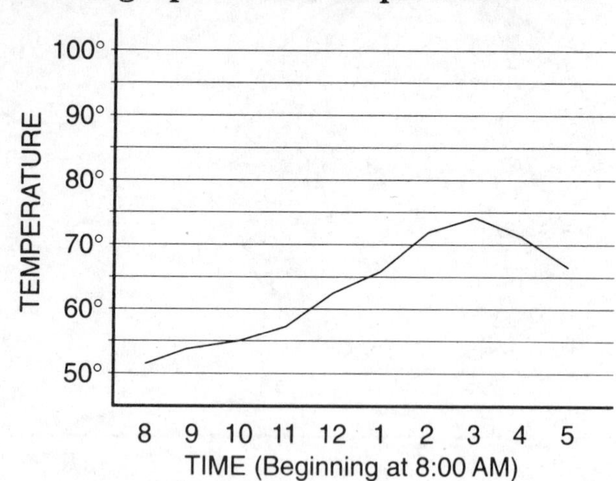

5 The temperature range for the day was —

A 14°

B 16°

C 18°

D 20°

E 22°

6 A reasonable approximation of the average temperature from 8:00 to noon is —

F less than 50°

G about 55°

H about 60°

J about 62°

K more than 62°

7 If the temperature trend continues, what will the temperature be at 7:00 PM?

A More than 65°

B Between 60° and 65°

C Between 55° and 60°

D Between 50° and 55°

E Less than 50°

8 The school year is about 180 days long. Students miss an average of 3.5 days of school a year because of illness. About how many total days will 20 students per grade miss in grades 8, 9, and 10?

F 210

G 200

H 73.5

J 70.5

K 63.5

9 Bill is 47 pounds heavier than Nick. Nick is more than 20 percent heavier than Denise. Which of these shows this relationship correctly?

A $B = (N + 47) > (1.20 \times D)$

B $B = (N + 47) > (0.20 \times D)$

C $(B - 47) = N > (1.20 \times D)$

D $(B + 47) = N < (1.20 \times D)$

E $(B + 47) = N < (1.20 \times D)$

10 There are 25 students in a class. The teacher writes each student's name on a slip of paper and puts it in a jar. At the beginning of school each day, the teacher pulls one name out of the jar and does not put it back. This student helps clean up at the end of the day. After 8 days, your name still has not been picked. What are the odds your name will be picked on day 9?

F $\frac{1}{8}$

G $\frac{1}{9}$

H $\frac{1}{17}$

J $\frac{1}{25}$

K Not Here

STOP

ANSWER ROWS: 5 Ⓐ Ⓑ Ⓒ Ⓓ Ⓔ 7 Ⓐ Ⓑ Ⓒ Ⓓ Ⓔ 9 Ⓐ Ⓑ Ⓒ Ⓓ Ⓔ
6 Ⓕ Ⓖ Ⓗ Ⓙ Ⓚ 8 Ⓕ Ⓖ Ⓗ Ⓙ Ⓚ 10 Ⓕ Ⓖ Ⓗ Ⓙ Ⓚ

Lesson 33 History and Geography

Sample

Directions: Read each question. Mark the space for the answer you think is correct.

A Which of these is America's national anthem?

A *God Bless America*
B *The Star Spangled Banner*
C *This Land Is Your Land*
D *America, The Beautiful*

Read the question carefully. If there is a map, look at it carefully. Think about what the question is asking. Then look at all the answer choices. If necessary, read the question again before choosing your answer.

Practice

1 Look at the map on the right. Which letter shows the location of the capital of this state?

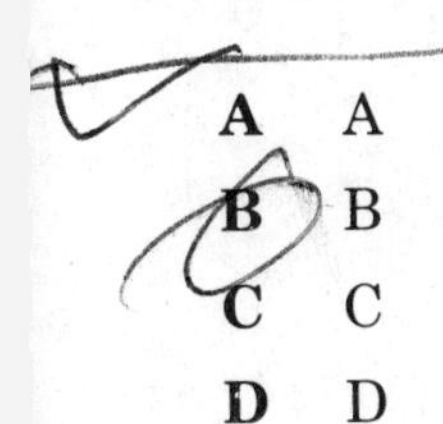

A A
B B
C C
D D

2 Look at the scale on the map. Based on the scale, about how wide is Ohio?

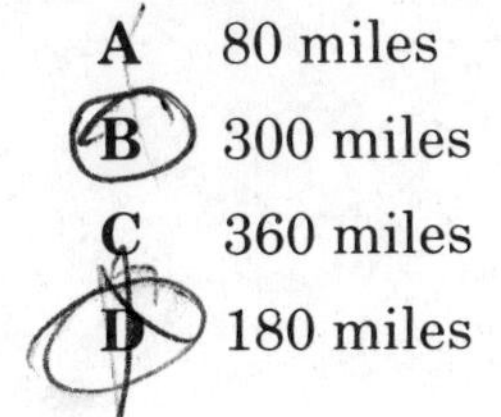

A 80 miles
B 300 miles
C 360 miles
D 180 miles

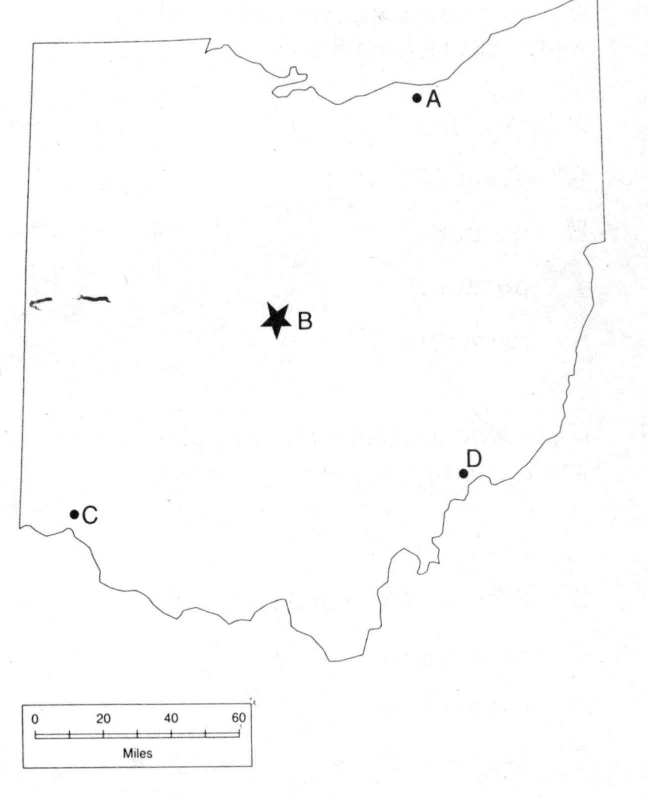

GO

ANSWER ROWS: A Ⓐ Ⓑ Ⓒ Ⓓ 1 Ⓐ Ⓑ Ⓒ Ⓓ 2 Ⓐ Ⓑ Ⓒ Ⓓ

3 Look at the map of the United States below. Which letter shows the state of Arizona?

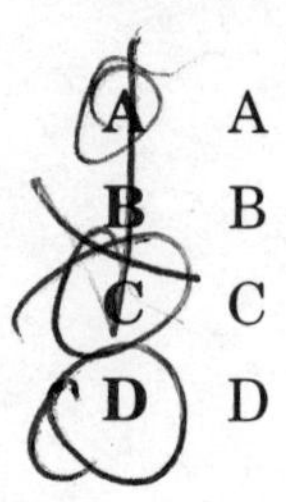

A A
B B
C C
D D

4 Look at the scale on the map. About how wide is the United States?

A 1000 miles

B 3000 miles
C 2000 miles
D 1500 miles

5 If you went from point A to point B on the map, in which direction would you be going?

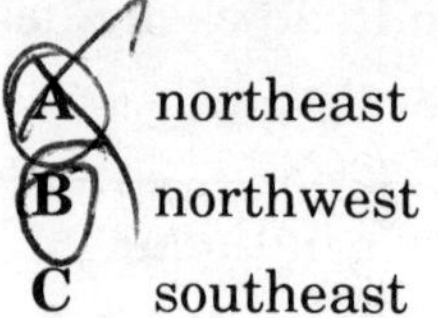

A northeast
B northwest
C southeast
D southwest

6 Which pair of points on the map is about 500 miles apart?

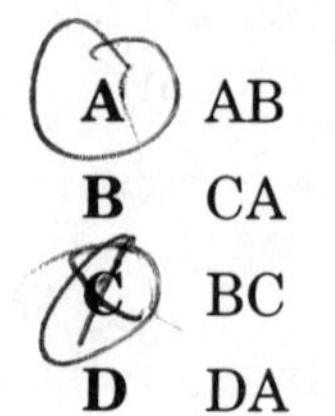

A AB
B CA
C BC
D DA

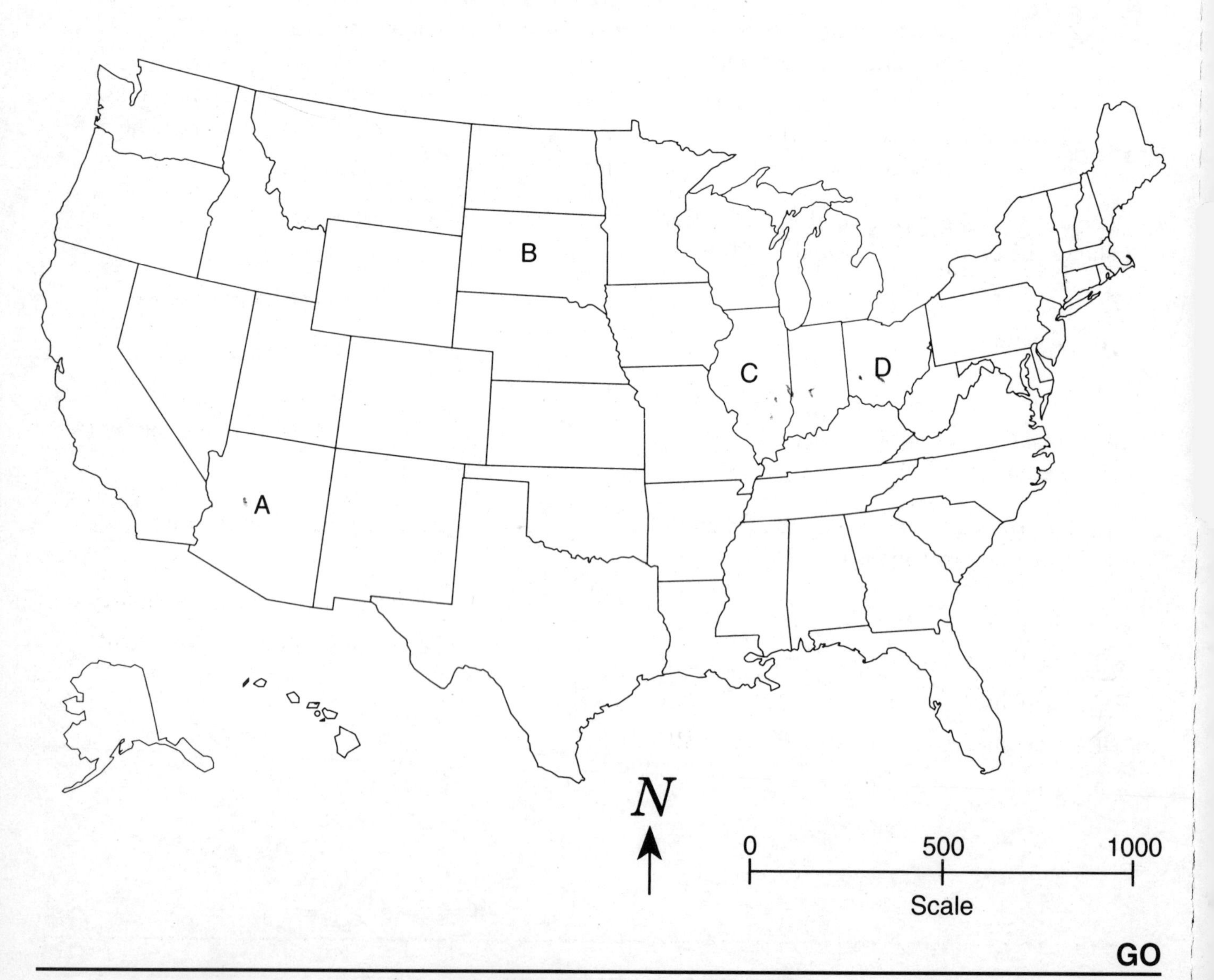

GO

 ANSWER ROWS: 3 Ⓐ Ⓑ Ⓒ Ⓓ 4 Ⓐ Ⓑ Ⓒ Ⓓ 5 Ⓐ Ⓑ Ⓒ Ⓓ 6 Ⓐ Ⓑ Ⓒ Ⓓ

7 Which of these is a major difference between Japan and the United States?

A The United States has a population made up of people from many nations, cultures, and races. Japan has a population made up of people from a single background.

B Japan has an industrial economy, while the United States has an agricultural economy.

C The United States has no seacoasts. Japan is an island nation with long coasts.

D The people of Japan vote for their leaders. The people of United States do not vote for their leaders.

8 The federal government is divided into the legislative, executive, and judicial branches. Which historic document established this division of government?

A the Federalist Papers

B the Declaration of Independence

C the Gettysburg Address

D the Constitution

9 Which of these is **NOT** included in the Declaration of Independence?

A a statement of the intention of the United States to separate from England

B the reasons why the United States wished to separate from England

C a declaration of war for independence against England

D a description of the basic rights of all people

10 The first ten amendments to the United States' Constitution are called the

A Ten Laws of the Land.

B Bill of Rights.

C Bill of Ladings.

D Monroe Document.

11 Which of these was prohibited by the Northwest Ordinance?

A slavery

B the sale of land

C statehood for Oregon

D secession from the United States

12 Alonzo is studying a document that establishes the supremacy of federal laws over state laws. Which document is he studying?

A the Bill of Rights

B the Northwest Ordinance

C the Declaration of Independence

D the Constitution

13 Which of these statements is true about the American flag?

A It has one stripe for each state.

B It has one star for each state.

C It can't be flown in a foreign country.

D It can't be flown at a sporting event.

GO

ANSWER ROWS: 7 Ⓐ Ⓑ Ⓒ Ⓓ 9 Ⓐ Ⓑ Ⓒ Ⓓ 11 Ⓐ Ⓑ Ⓒ Ⓓ 13 Ⓐ Ⓑ Ⓒ Ⓓ
8 Ⓐ Ⓑ Ⓒ Ⓓ 10 Ⓐ Ⓑ Ⓒ Ⓓ 12 Ⓐ Ⓑ Ⓒ Ⓓ Ⓐ Ⓑ Ⓒ Ⓓ

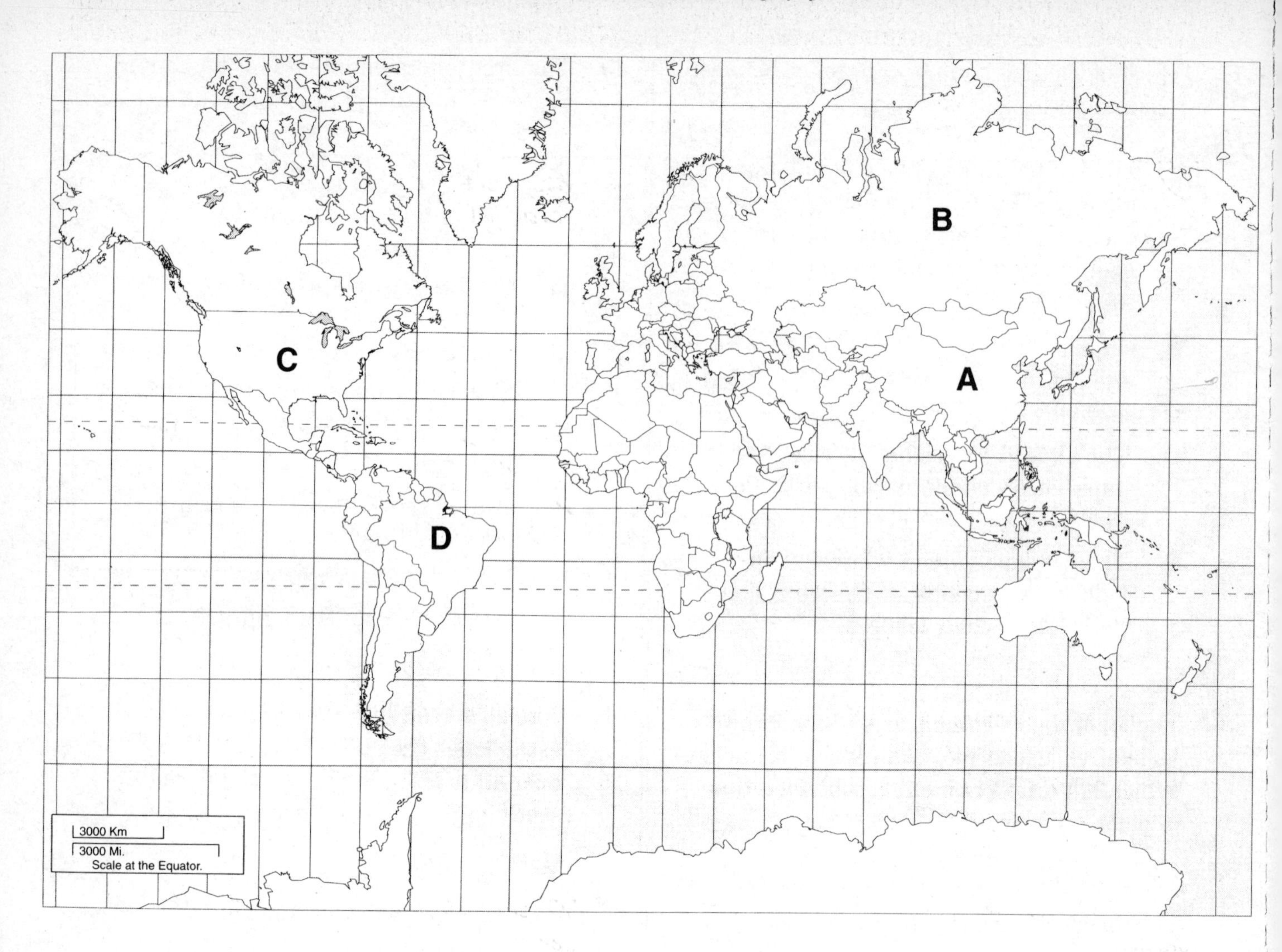

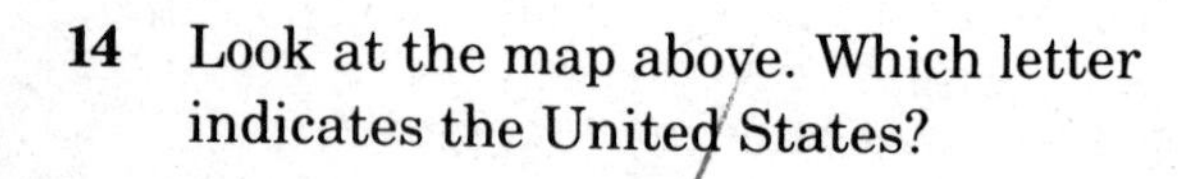

14 Look at the map above. Which letter indicates the United States?

A A

B B

C C

D D

15 Look at the map again. Find the points C and B. Now look at the scale in the bottom-left corner of the map. About how far apart are points C and B?

A 5,000 miles

B 15,000 miles

C 25,000 miles

D 100,000 miles

STOP

Samples

Directions: Read each question. Mark the space for the answer you think is correct.

A Which branch of government makes the laws?

A administrative
B executive
C judicial
D legislative

B Which of these is an example of active participation in government?

A attending a town meeting and expressing an opinion
B complaining about politicians to your friends
C going to a basketball game rather than voting
D reading the editorial page of the newspaper

Eliminate answer choices you know are wrong.

If you know which answer choice is correct, mark it and move on to the next question.

7/2 1/12

Practice

1 Who is the head of the executive branch of government?

A the President
B the chief justice of the Supreme Court
C the majority leader in the Senate
D the majority leader in the House

2 Which of these is true about a communist system of government?

A Individuals have the right to own private property.
B The government controls the production of goods and the provision of services.
C Individuals have the right to own businesses.
D Individual farmers who work the land also own it.

3 Which of these is the best explanation of the power of veto?

A A legislative body can reject a bill that has been passed by the President or governor.
B A senator or representative can introduce a bill even though the President or governor disagree with it.
C A President or governor can introduce a bill even though a senator or representative disagree with it.
D A President or governor can reject a bill that has been passed by the legislative body.

GO

ANSWER ROWS: A Ⓐ Ⓑ Ⓒ Ⓓ B Ⓐ Ⓑ Ⓒ Ⓓ 1 Ⓐ Ⓑ Ⓒ Ⓓ 2 Ⓐ Ⓑ Ⓒ Ⓓ 3 Ⓐ Ⓑ Ⓒ Ⓓ

4 Look at the graph below. It shows the results of a poll taken before an election. Candidate Sampson insists that the poll indicates that the majority of the voters support her policies. Which of these statements is the most accurate description of what the graph actually shows?

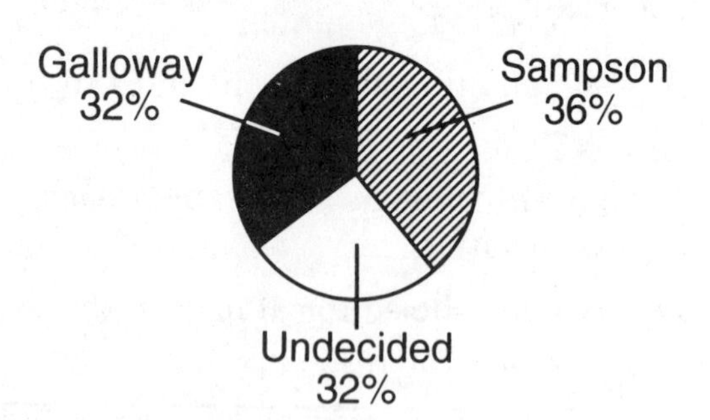

A The majority of the people polled support Sampson.

B Sampson would win the election no matter how the undecided people cast their votes.

C The majority of the people who were polled are undecided or support Galloway.

D Galloway would win the election no matter how the undecided people cast their votes.

5 The king of a small country is from the same family that has ruled the country for over 200 years. The vast majority of the people in the country love and respect him, even though he is an absolute monarch. Which of these is an advantage the king has?

A The king can have the legislature or parliament dismissed easily.

B The king can veto acts of the legislature.

C The king can be reelected by a majority of the people.

D The king can make decisions without being concerned about a legislature or parliament.

6 Which of these rights is guaranteed by the Constitution?

A A person accused of a crime has the right to a speedy and public trial.

B All Americans are entitled to a job and acceptable health care.

C All Americans are guaranteed a free, public education when they reach the age of six.

D People who pay taxes are entitled to recover the taxes when they retire.

7 Before you can vote in the United States,

A you must own valuable property such as a house or a car.

B you must be a citizen of the United States.

C you must pass a test showing you can read at the high school level.

D you must prove that you have lived in the same place for more than a year.

8 The positions taken by a political party on critical issues are called

A favoritism.

B a landscape.

C electionism.

D a platform.

9 When a law is changed, the change is called

A an amendment.

B a repeal.

C a bill.

D a veto.

GO

ANSWER ROWS: 4 Ⓐ Ⓑ Ⓒ Ⓓ 6 Ⓐ Ⓑ Ⓒ Ⓓ 8 Ⓐ Ⓑ Ⓒ Ⓓ
5 Ⓐ Ⓑ Ⓒ Ⓓ 7 Ⓐ Ⓑ Ⓒ Ⓓ 9 Ⓐ Ⓑ Ⓒ Ⓓ

10 The process by which a bill becomes a law involves a number of steps. Which of these shows the steps in the correct order?

A
1. Bill is introduced in one house by a member of that house.
2. Bill is sent to other house.
3. Bill is debated and approved.
4. Bill is studied by house committee.
5. Steps 2 and 3 are repeated.
6. When bill is approved, it is sent to President or governor.
7. Bill is signed or approved by President or governor.

B
1. Bill is introduced in one house by a member of that house.
2. Bill is debated and approved.
3. Bill is studied by house committee.
4. Bill is sent to other house.
5. Steps 2 and 3 are repeated.
6. When bill is approved, it is sent to President or governor.
7. Bill is signed or approved by President or governor.

C
1. Bill is introduced in one house by a member of that house.
2. Bill is studied by house committee.
3. Bill is debated and approved.
4. Bill is sent to other house.
5. Steps 2 and 3 are repeated.
6. When bill is approved, it is sent to President or governor.
7. Bill is signed or approved by President or governor.

D
1. Bill is introduced in one house by a member of that house.
2. Bill is studied by house committee.
3. Bill is debated and approved.
4. Steps 2 and 3 are repeated.
5. Bill is sent to other house.
6. When bill is approved, it is sent to President or governor.
7. Bill is signed or approved by President or governor.

11 Laura applied for a job as a truck driver. The manager of the trucking company said the work would be too hard for her, so he didn't hire her. Laura said she had driven the same kind of truck for several years and had recommendations to prove she had done a good job. The manager still didn't hire her. Which of these statements is probably true about this situation?

A The manager was right because Laura probably couldn't handle the job.

B It is an example of discrimination because Laura had the ability to do the job for which she applied.

C It is not an example of discrimination because the manager can refuse to hire a driver because she is a woman.

D It is an example of discrimination because Laura should not have applied for the job in the first place.

12 Which of these is an example of a legitimate activity for a political party?

A raising money to pay people to vote

B raising money to pay public officials to vote in their favor

C raising money to pay people so they won't vote for the opposition

D raising money for election campaigns

13 According to the Constitution, which of these is permitted?

A Only local governments can levy taxes.

B Only state governments can levy taxes.

C Only the federal government can declare war.

D Any state is allowed to pass a law that amends the Constitution.

GO

ANSWER ROWS: 10 Ⓐ Ⓑ Ⓒ Ⓓ 11 Ⓐ Ⓑ Ⓒ Ⓓ 12 Ⓐ Ⓑ Ⓒ Ⓓ 13 Ⓐ Ⓑ Ⓒ Ⓓ

14 Aloysius insists that the voters elect the President of the United States. Tina disagrees and argues that the Electoral College actually elects the President. What is the Electoral College?

A The Electoral College is appointed by the President. Representatives of the Electoral College actually elect senators and representatives.

B The voters choose the members of the Electoral College. Members of the Electoral College vote for senators and representatives.

C Senators and representatives vote for members of the Electoral College. The electors then vote for the President.

D The Electoral College consists of representatives from each state who actually vote for the President. The electors usually represent the popular vote in a given state.

15 Which of these is an example of how the leaders of a country make a decision based on the availability of financial resources?

A suspending the development of a space station in order to lower taxes and stimulate business growth

B raising taxes so both a space station and interstate train system can be developed

C building an interstate train system in order to stimulate business growth

D suspending the development of a space station because it has proven to be scientifically unsound

16 Fernando saved his money and started a company that manufactures small motors for satellite dishes. He makes a good profit, employs eight workers, and allows them to buy shares in the company. In which of these economic systems would this be most strongly encouraged?

A a socialist economy

B a capitalist economy

C a constitutional economy

D a communist economy

17 When Rochelle's parents wanted to buy a new house, they wanted to know how the neighborhood was zoned. Who should they contact to find this information?

A their senator in Washington

B an official in the county where they live

C their representative in Washington

D an official in the governor's office in the state where they live

STOP

ANSWER ROWS: 14 Ⓐ Ⓑ Ⓒ Ⓓ 15 Ⓐ Ⓑ Ⓒ Ⓓ 16 Ⓐ Ⓑ Ⓒ Ⓓ 17 Ⓐ Ⓑ Ⓒ Ⓓ

Samples

A Which branch of government might declare a state law to be unconstitutional?

- **A** the judicial branch
- **B** the legislative branch
- **C** the constitutional branch
- **D** the executive branch

B One of our holidays is sometimes called "Our Nation's Birthday." Which holiday is it?

- **A** Memorial Day
- **B** Thanksgiving
- **C** Independence Day
- **D** Labor Day

1 Which state was not an original colony?

- **A** New Jersey
- **B** Virginia
- **C** Tennessee
- **D** Massachusetts

2 Which of these is a legitimate reason for the federal government to impose taxes?

- **A** to punish people for being successful
- **B** to provide for the defense of the nation
- **C** to prevent people from earning too much money
- **D** to prevent citizens from exercising free speech

3 The Senate and House of Representatives are part of which branch of government?

- **A** legislative
- **B** executive
- **C** appointed
- **D** judicial

4 Many Middle-Eastern countries have large oil reserves from which they earn great profits. These same countries have almost no other natural resources, agricultural land, or manufacturing industries. Which of these strategies is a good way for them to use their oil profits?

- **A** invest their profits in countries that have large oil reserves
- **B** buy arms to defend their oil fields
- **C** invest their profits in countries with natural resources, agricultural industries, or manufacturing capabilities
- **D** buy large amounts of oil to build up their reserves

5 Which of these activities is prohibited by the Constitution?

- **A** the government's shutting down a newspaper that prints critical articles
- **B** citizens' paying taxes
- **C** the government's regulation of international trade
- **D** a state's establishment of qualifications for voting in state elections

GO

ANSWER ROWS: A Ⓐ Ⓑ Ⓒ Ⓓ 1 Ⓐ Ⓑ Ⓒ Ⓓ 3 Ⓐ Ⓑ Ⓒ Ⓓ 5 Ⓐ Ⓑ Ⓒ Ⓓ
B Ⓐ Ⓑ Ⓒ Ⓓ 2 Ⓐ Ⓑ Ⓒ Ⓓ 4 Ⓐ Ⓑ Ⓒ Ⓓ

6 Look at the map below. According to the scale, one inch on the map is equal to about

A 100 miles.

B 1 mile

C 5000 miles.

D 400 miles

7 Which letter shows the location of Washington, DC?

A A

B B

C C

D D

8 Look at the map again. About how far is it from southern Wyoming to northern Texas?

A 400 miles

B 100 miles

C 1000 miles

D 900 miles

9 What does the letter N on the map mean?

A It shows the map is NOT TO SCALE.

B It is an abbreviation for NORTH AMERICA.

C It means NORMAL VIEW.

D It shows which way NORTH is.

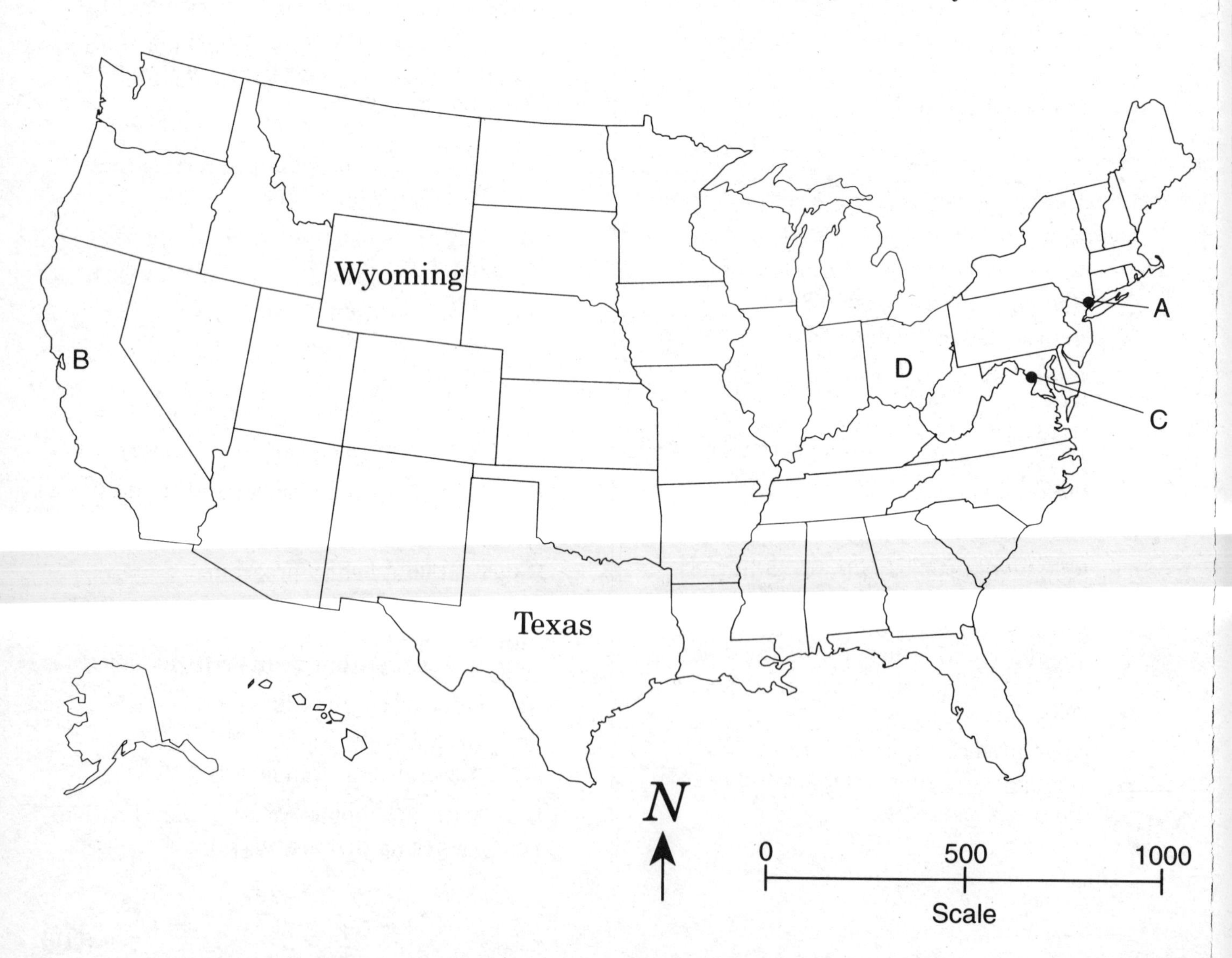

GO

10 Read the arguments below in support of a local law to require businesses to recycle 50% of the water they use. Choose the one that is supported by facts and logical argument.

- **A** Many businesses use too much water. These businesses are owned by people who live in other states and don't care about our problem. The simplest solution is to punish the businesses and fine them if they don't recycle half of their water and clean the rest before returning it to the reservoir.
- **B** Businesses are interested in only one thing, profits. The businesses in our area earned more than a billion dollars last year. They should be forced to give up these profits and buy equipment that will recycle water. It's just not fair to the rest of us for them to use so much water.
- **C** Businesses in our area use half a billion gallons of water each month. After it is used, it is returned to the river below the reservoir. At the current rate, the reservoir and the ground water supply will be emptied in ten years. If businesses recycle half of the water they use and clean the rest before returning it to the reservoir, our water problems will be solved for at least a hundred years.
- **D** Here are the facts. The workers in our area are paid less than those in other parts of the state. If businesses are not going to pay their workers, then they should pay to recycle the water they use. The people who own businesses are more interested in profits than the good of their workers. Making them pay to recycle water might cause them to treat their workers better.

11 Which of these is NOT true about voting?

- **A** People get paid to vote.
- **B** Voting is a responsibility.
- **C** Voting is a right.
- **D** People vote once each election.

12 Which of these is an example of a voluntary activity that benefits the public good?

- **A** working as a police officer
- **B** helping to clean litter from a highway
- **C** mowing your lawn
- **D** arriving for school on time

13 Which of these positions is appointed by the President and confirmed by the Senate?

- **A** vice president
- **B** federal judge
- **C** representative
- **D** governor

14 Which of these is most likely to exist in a socialist country?

- **A** a privately owned airline company
- **B** a king or queen who rules absolutely
- **C** a single person owning a railroad
- **D** a national health program

15 What is celebrated on July Fourth?

- **A** the end of the Revolutionary War
- **B** the signing of the Constitution
- **C** America's Independence
- **D** the end of the Civil War

GO

ANSWER ROWS: 10 Ⓐ Ⓑ Ⓒ Ⓓ 12 Ⓐ Ⓑ Ⓒ Ⓓ 14 Ⓐ Ⓑ Ⓒ Ⓓ
11 Ⓐ Ⓑ Ⓒ Ⓓ 13 Ⓐ Ⓑ Ⓒ Ⓓ 15 Ⓐ Ⓑ Ⓒ Ⓓ

16 A group of students was gathering information about the rise of the crime rate in America. Which of these information sources would probably give them the best idea of how crime affects Americans in general?

A read twenty newspapers taken from various areas of the country

B read the newspapers from the five largest American cities

C read the newspapers from rural areas around America

D watch the nightly news on all the television stations in their town

17 The Fifth Amendment to the Constitution declares that law enforcement officers and other officials can search a person's home only when there is "probable cause." Which of these is an example of "probable cause"?

A A victim does not recognize the person who stole her purse. She thinks it is a girl she doesn't like who lives in the neighborhood. The police have probable cause to search the house of the girl the woman doesn't like.

B A girl was caught shoplifting a month ago. Today a car was stolen in her neighborhood. The police have probable cause to search the girl's garage.

C A victim is sure she recognized the person who stole her purse, but he has never been in trouble before. The police have probable cause to search the house of the person the woman recognized.

D A man is in jail for cheating on his taxes. A bank was robbed near the man's home. The police have probable cause to search the man's house because he might have friends who would rob a bank.

18 Which of these officials is elected by the people within a single state?

A President

B Chief Justice of the Supreme Court

C Secretary of Agriculture

D Governor

19 The Supreme Court of the United States has the responsibility to decide if a new law is or is not constitutional. This responsibility is called

A legislative oversight.

B executive privilege.

C judicial review.

D parliamentary procedure.

20 Which of these is an example of a dictatorship?

A Country A has been ruled by a king for twenty years. A leader named Smith led a revolution in the country. The people of the country held a free election and voted Smith the president. He has been president for six years.

B Country B has been ruled by a king for twenty years. A leader named Smith led a revolution in the country. He made himself president and has ruled for six years.

C Country C has a king and a prime minister. The people vote for the parliament. The members of parliament appoint the prime minister. The people do not vote for king.

D Country D has a king and a prime minister. The people vote for the prime minister but not the king. They have elected the same prime minister for the past ten years.

STOP

ANSWER ROWS: 16 Ⓐ Ⓑ Ⓒ Ⓓ 18 Ⓐ Ⓑ Ⓒ Ⓓ 20 Ⓐ Ⓑ Ⓒ Ⓓ
17 Ⓐ Ⓑ Ⓒ Ⓓ 19 Ⓐ Ⓑ Ⓒ Ⓓ

NUMBER RIGHT ________

7/22/12

Sample A

Sabrina wanted to have a surprise celebration for Jordan's election as class president. She and his parents a list of people to invite. **(A)** Then she and Colette contacted them by telephone. Several of the people they called agreed to help decorate for the party.

A
- **A** She and his parents made a list. It was a list of people to invite.
- **B** She and his parents, making a list of people to invite.
- **C** She and his parents made a list of people to invite.
- **D** Making a list of people to invite, she and his parents made a list.

The farmer carefully hid the trap near the chicken coop. Tonight, he would be in for a surprise. When that thieving fox stopped by for dinner. **(1)**

Around midnight, the fox crept up to the coop. **(2)** He noticed something different about the ground near the door, so he went around to the other side. There, the fox dug a tunnel under the fence seeing no signs of danger, he crawled in. **(3)** Quick as a wink, he grabbed a hen and escaped through the tunnel.

7/2/12

1
- **A** Tonight, when that thieving fox stopped by for dinner. The fox would be in for a surprise.
- **B** When that thieving fox stopped by for dinner. Tonight, he would be in for a surprise.
- **C** Tonight, he would be in for a surprise, that thieving fox who stopped by for dinner.
- **D** Tonight, when that thieving fox stopped by for dinner, he would be in for a surprise.

2
- **F** Around midnight, the fox crept. Up to the coop he crept.
- **G** The fox crept up to the coop. Around midnight.
- **H** Around midnight at the coop, the fox crept up.
- **J** Correct as is

3
- **A** The fox dug a tunnel there under the fence seeing no signs of danger. He crawled in.
- **B** Seeing no signs of danger, he crawled under the fence. In the tunnel he dug.
- **C** There, the fox dug a tunnel under the fence. Seeing no signs of danger, he crawled in.
- **D** Correct as is

STOP

Samples

The small town of Rileyville had just purchased a new police car. Rather than sell the old one, they ___(B)___ to use it for speed control. The mayor purchased a police uniform for a department-store mannequin. She dressed ___(C)___ in the uniform and placed it in the old police car, which was parked in a spot where speeding often took place. Not surprisingly, the speeding problem in that part of town quickly disappeared.

B F decide
G will decide
H decided
J decides

C A it
B her
C him
D them

This was Jed's first year to have a garden, so he asked his grandmother for help. They prepared the soil in a small plot in the backyard and planted radishes, carrots, tomatoes, and beans. Jed weeded and ___(4)___ the garden every day, and before long, green shoots poked up through the soil.

All the vegetables did well except the beans. One day there would be a sprout, and the next day it would be gone. Jed didn't ___(5)___ what the problem was, but his grandmother had a clue. She showed Jed the small animal tracks that were visible beside the row of beans. Following the tracks, they discovered a hole in the fence around the backyard.

Jed and his grandmother nailed a board over the hole. They hoped this would solve the problem, but the next day, they found more tracks. ___(6)___ garden thief was smarter than they ___(7)___ .

4 F watered
G watering
H waters
J water

5 A not knowing
B not know
C know
D known

6 F Her
G Them
H His
J Their

7 A think
B thought
C will think
D have thought

STOP

7/23/12

Samples

The captain of a ship must often depend on sonar to dock the vessel. A sonar device, (D) sends sound waves toward the bottom of the ocean and records how long it takes for the sound to return. This (E) gives the captain an idea of the depth of the water and what type of bottom is under the ship.

D
F Spelling error
G Capitalization error
H Punctuation error
J No error

E
A Spelling error
B Capitalization error
C Punctuation error
D No error

The last thing Keith's father said to him was, "Don't forget to put (8) out the fire before you leave the cabin." Unfortunately, Keith forgot.

As he stared at the smoldering ashes that were once his familys' cabin, Keith (9) thought about what he had done. before going fishing, he had blown (10) out the lantern and locked all the windows and doors. He had even remembered to write a note on the door telling anyone who stopped by where he would be. But he had forgotten to douse the fire with a buket of water. Somehow, a spark (11) from the fire had gotten out and set the cabin ablaze.

8
F Spelling error
G Capitalization error
H Punctuation error
J No error

9
A Spelling error
B Capitalization error
C Punctuation error
D No error

10
F Spelling error
G Capitalization error
H Punctuation error
J No error

11
A Spelling error
B Capitalization error
C Punctuation error
D No error

STOP

Your town is running out of water. Two solutions have been proposed. One is to charge people more to use water, and the other is to dam up a local river and create a new water supply. The dam will flood a natural area that many people now enjoy. Write a letter to the mayor of your town in which you discuss both solutions. State your position about the issue and provide good reasons for your position.

STOP

Sample

Unwelcome Visitors

Porcupines are becoming quite a problem in Juneau, Alaska. These prickly creatures are invading homes, offices, and automobiles. Many families have discovered how creative the intruders are in finding unusual ways to enter their homes. Once inside, they munch on almost anything and leave behind a trail of telltale quills.

The porcupines have even caused extensive damage to cars. Their diet seems to include fuel lines, spark plug and ignition wires, and even tires. What's worse, when they find a good meal, they often return later for a second helping.

A From this passage, you can conclude that porcupines like to eat —

A things made of rubber

B cooked rather than raw food

C the same food as humans

D food that has been left out for them

Autumntime

I saw my first tree today. Dad finally broke down and took us to East Boston Urban Center 3 after Mom had been harping on it for the past two weeks. I think he was glad we went after all, because he was smiling quietly all during the trip back.

Dad used to tell me stories about the trees that still existed when he was a boy. There weren't very many even then, with the urbanization program in full swing, but most people had seen at least one tree by the time they started school. It wasn't like nowadays, at any rate. Oh, I've seen the plastic trees; practically every street has a few of them. But you can tell the plastic ones are artificial just from looking at the pictures in the microdot library. And now, after seeing a real tree, I can say for sure that the artificial ones aren't the same at all.

This morning when we got up, the house was all excited. Mom dialed a light breakfast of toast and synthetic milk so that we wouldn't waste time eating. And when we finished, the three of us took an elevator-bus up to the fourth level, where we caught the air track to Brooklyn. From there we took another elevator-bus down to the main level, rode the monorail to Intercity Subway Station 27, and caught the second sublevel AA train to Boston. Our expectations were so high that Dad and I didn't mind it when Mom told us again how the tree was discovered.

The O'Brien home was one of the few examples of old-style wooden structures that hadn't been demolished in Boston's urban-renewal campaign at the turn of the century. The family had been able to avoid this because of its wealth and political influence, and the house was passed on through several generations to the present. Old man O'Brien had no heirs, so when he died the family home went up for auction, and the Urban Center bought it. When local officials arrived for an appraisal, they discovered the house had a back yard, which is forbidden by zoning restrictions.

In the yard was a live tree—an oke was what Mom called it.

When the news of the tree's discovery leaked out, quite a few sightseers stopped by to have a look at it, and the local government, realizing the money-making potential, began charging admission and advertising the place. By now it had become a favorite spot for school field trips and family excursions such as ours.

When we arrived in main Boston, we rode the elevator-bus up to ground level and caught a monorail out to East Boston Urban Center 3. An air-cush taxi took us the rest of the way to the residence.

The home itself was unimpressive. It had none of the marble gloss, steely sheen of modern

GO

buildings, but rather a dull white color, with the paint peeling in places. Dad paid the admission fee, and we spent the next fifteen minutes on a dull guided tour of the house. The rooms were roped off to keep people from touching anything, but there were no windows facing the illegal back yard anyway, so it really didn't matter that I couldn't enter the rooms on that side.

My mind was on the tree, and I thought the inside tour would never end; but soon we were walking through a doorway hidden in one of the bookshelves and into the back yard. The yard was big—at least ten by twenty feet—and I was surprised to find real grass growing on the sides of the concrete walkway built for tourists. The grass didn't distract me for long, however, because I just couldn't help noticing the tree!

It was located at one end of the yard, and there was a mesh fence around it for protection. It was similar in form to the plastic trees I'd seen, but there was much more to it than that. You could see details more <u>intricate</u> than in any artificially made plant. And it was alive. Long ago someone had carved their initials in the bark, and you could see where the wound had healed. But best of all was the smell. It was a fresh, living odor, alien to the septic world outside, with all its metal, plastic, and glass. I wanted to touch the bark, but the fence prevented me from doing so. Mom and dad just breathed deeply and stared up with smiles on their faces. The three of us stood there for a moment, and then the tour guide told us to make room for the next group. I didn't want to go—in fact, I almost felt like crying.

On the way back, Mom and Dad were silent, and I read through one of the brochures that the guide had passed out. When I came to the part that said the O'Brien home would be opened only for the rest of this year, I was sad. They intend to tear down the place to make room for some kind of insurance building, and the tree will have to go, too.

For the rest of the trip I just sat still, fingering the object in my pocket that I had picked off the grass in the O'Briens' back yard. I think it's called an acorn.

A. Lentini

1 This story takes place —

A in the present

B in the past

C in the future

D on a different planet

2 There are no trees left because of —

F an urbanization program

G plant diseases

H zoning restrictions

J global warming

3 On the way to visit the tree, someone retold the story of how the tree was discovered. Who retold the story?

A Dad

B Mom

C the writer of the story

D the museum tour guide

4 In the story, it states that, "On the way back, Mom and Dad were silent." Why do you think they were silent?

F They were sad thinking that there were almost no trees left.

G They were happy that they had seen a tree.

H They didn't care one way or the other about the tree.

J They were worried that the urbanization program would end.

5 Which of these is most likely to be found in a microdot library?

A Regular newspapers

B Microscopic books and a special reader

C Regular books

D A collection of microscopic dots that look like a picture

GO

6 Which of these is the main idea of the story "Autumntime"?

F Urbanization is more important than preserving nature.

G A "tree museum" is not such a bad idea after all.

H If we are not sensible, we may lose the natural things we take for granted.

J Wealth and political influence are the best ways to preserve nature.

7 What does the word intricate mean in this story?

A artificial

B beautiful

C simple

D complicated

8 Why do you think the door to the yard with the tree was hidden in a bookcase?

F Having a back yard was forbidden by zoning restrictions.

G It made the trip to the yard more mysterious for visitors.

H There was no room for it in other parts of the room.

J The hidden door kept people from touching anything in the house.

9 The selection states that, "It was a fresh, living odor, alien to the septic world outside." What is the writer referring to?

A The sight of the tree

B The smell of the tree

C The size of the yard

D The smell of the house

The Anatomy of a Floppy Disk

The 5" floppy disk was well-known to anyone who had access to a personal computer in the 1980s. It was the most widely used means of storing information for use by a computer, and more than a billion were made since the personal computer was born in the late 1970s.

Although at first glance a floppy disk seems quite simple, it had more parts than most people realize. Each part played an important role in storing and preserving information.

The visible part of the floppy disk was the protective shell. It was usually black, although it was available in a variety of colors. The shell was made of a tough plastic outside with a softer liner on the inside. The liner let the data storage disk inside spin smoothly, provided some protection for the disk, and cleaned some contaminants from the disk.

The label area was at the top of the shell. This was where an identifying label could be

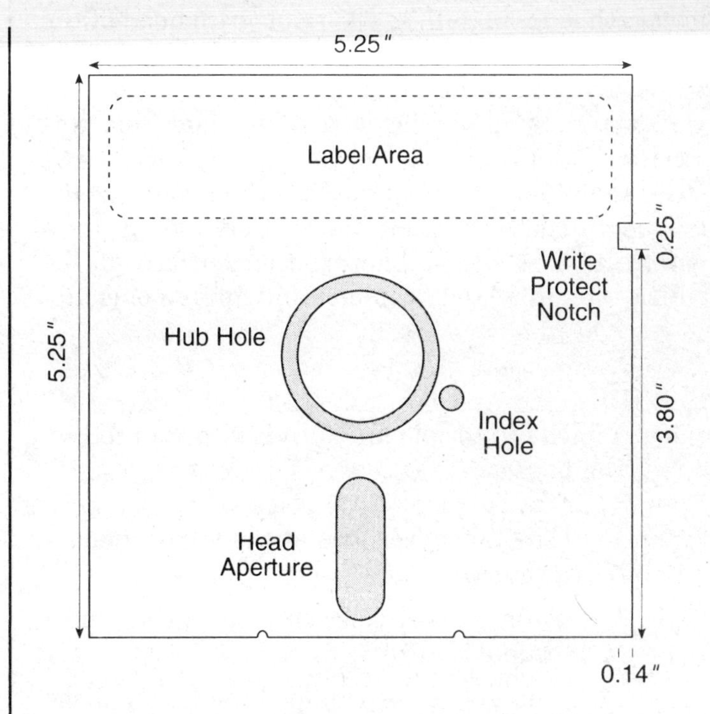

attached without harming the computer or the disk. To the right of the label area and just below it was the write protect notch. When this notch was covered by a write protect tab, information could be read from the disk, but not written on it. If this cutout was sensed by a light-sensitive switch inside the computer, data could be read from and written to the disk. Some application software came on disks without a write protect notch so that data could not be accidentally written to them. Users also attached write protect tabs to disks containing important data that should not be changed.

At the center of the disk was the hub hole. The hub of the disk drive in the computer dropped into this hole and clamped the disk in place. As you might guess, the clamping process placed considerable stress on a disk. To avoid problems this stress might cause, some manufacturers put a reinforcing hub ring in the very center of the disk to provide additional strength.

The index hole was used by some computers to identify where information was stored on the disk. Most personal computers, however, did not use the index hole. Instead, they relied on information contained on the disk to locate where data was stored.

The head aperture was an oval slot found on both sides of a disk. The read/write head of the disk drive contacted the disk at this point so information could be transferred between the disk and computer. As you might guess, it was critical to never touch the disk surface exposed by the head aperture. In addition, when you stored a floppy disk, it should have been stored in a protective sleeve so the exposed surface of the disk was protected from dirt and foreign objects.

10 Which of these is an OPINION presented in the passage?

- **F** The label area was at the top of the protective shell.
- **G** A floppy disk had more parts than most people realize.
- **H** The disk drive clamped the floppy disk in the hub hole.
- **J** A floppy disk should be stored in a protective sleeve.

11 Look at the figure on page 93. What are the dimensions of the write protect notch?

- **A** 5.25 inches x 0.25 inches
- **B** 3.80 inches x 0.25 inches
- **C** 5.25 inches x 3.80 inches
- **D** 0.25 inches x 0.14 inches

12 Which of these is implied in this passage?

- **F** The part of the disk on which data were stored was very durable.
- **G** The part of the disk on which data were stored was very delicate.
- **H** Floppy disks were actually not very floppy.
- **J** People preferred protective shells that were colors other than black.

13 Which of these is something a floppy disk user might want to do?

- **A** Remove a reinforcing hub ring to prolong the life of a disk.
- **B** Rub the part of the disk exposed by the head access aperture with a paper towel.
- **C** Cover the write protect notch with a write protect tab.
- **D** Fold a floppy disk in half so it would fit in an envelope.

14 The word <u>contaminants</u> in this passage means—

- **F** substances that might damage a disk
- **G** substances that will not affect a disk
- **H** toxic substances
- **J** substances that are electrical conductors

STOP

Sample A

The two congruent right triangles below have sides of 5 units and 8 units. The square has sides of 5 units. Imagine that you have reassembled the three figures into a trapezoid. Which statement will be true about the figure?

A The longest side will be 15 units.

B The shortest side will be 8 units.

C The perimeter will be 46 units.

D The area will be 65 units^2.

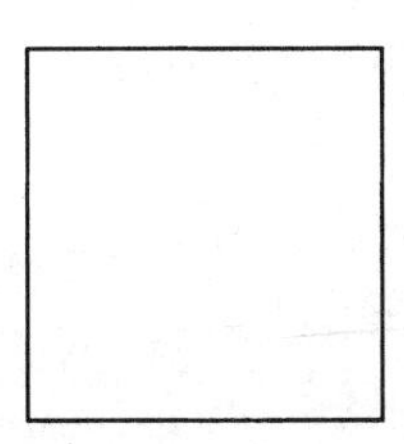

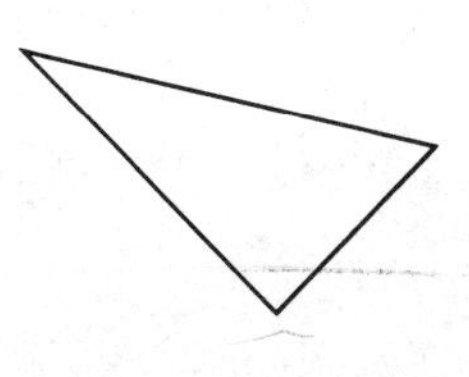

---

1 Basketball player A is 6 feet 2 inches tall. Basketball player B is 5 feet 9 inches tall. A reasonable statement about the differences in their heights is —

A A is 7 inches taller than B

B B is 1 foot taller than A

C A is 1 foot taller than B

D B is 5 inches taller than A

E A is 5 inches taller than B

2 What are the chances of getting a 2 three times in a row with this spinner?

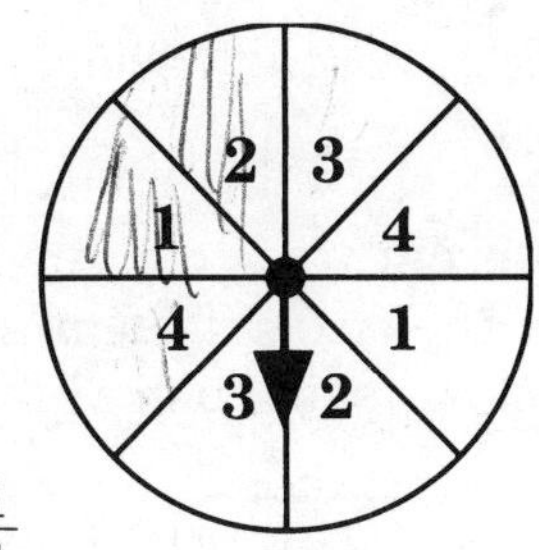

F $\frac{1}{4}$

G $\frac{1}{8}$

H $\frac{1}{64}$

J $\frac{1}{128}$

K Not here

3 The chart below shows the results of a primary election. What percentage of the total vote did the top two candidates get?

Candidate	Votes
Wujokowski	73
Miller	183
Rutledge	59
Cheng	81
Warner	102

A Between 55 and 60%

B Between 50 and 55%

C Between 45 and 50%

D Between 40 and 45%

E Less than 40%

4 Which number should come next in this pattern?

3a, 5b, 6a, 8b, 9a, ...

F 10a

G 12a

H 11b

J 12b

GO

5 A store is having a 25% off sale. How can you find the sale price of an item?

A Regular price – 0.25

B Regular price x $\frac{3}{4}$

C Regular price ÷ $\frac{3}{4}$

D Regular price ÷ 0.25

6 The average temperature in January is 4.2° lower than the average temperature in March. February's temperature is lower than either January or March. Which of these shows this relationship?

F $\text{February} < \text{January} - 4.2^\circ = \text{March}$

G $\text{February} < \text{January} = \text{March} - 4.2^\circ$

H $\text{March} < \text{January} - 4.2^\circ < \text{February}$

J $\text{March} > \text{January} - 4.2^\circ > \text{February}$

K $\text{March} - 4.2 > \text{January} > \text{February}$

7 A county had a total population of 35,000 in 1990. The graph below shows how the population was distributed. The population of Centerburg increased by 500 and the population of Jessup decreased by 200. How can you find the new percentage of the population found in Centerburg?

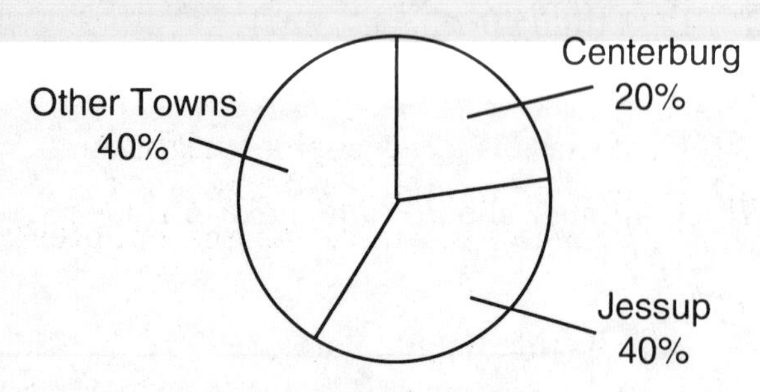

A (35,000 x 0.2) ÷ 40,000

B (7000 – 500) ÷ 42,000

C (7000 + 700) ÷ 42,000

D (7000 + 500) ÷ 42,000

E (14,000 – 200) ÷ 42,000

8 In the figure below, a plane is intersecting a cylinder. What shape is formed by the intersection?

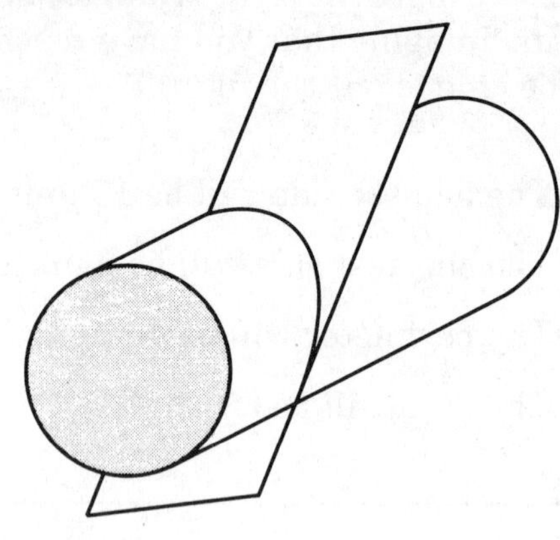

F Oval

G Circle

H Rectangle

J Square

9 A worker earns $22,500 a year. Each year for the next 4 years, the worker receives a raise of $2500. What is the worker's average salary during the five year period?

A $6500

B $24,500

C $25,000

D $27,000

E Not Here

10 How many different ways can the numbers be arranged in the boxes if the number 1 always stays in the same place?

1	2
3	4

F 24

G 16

H 6

J 4

GO

11 A customer bought 4 items at a store. He paid $3.95 for juice, $11.59 for a turkey, $9.36 for a box of laundry soap, and $6.08 for cheese from the deli. There is a sales tax on non-food items. What was the customer's total for food items?

A $19.39

B $21.62

C $24.90

D $30.98

E Not Here

12 Which answer choice shows the numbers represented on this number line from least to greatest?

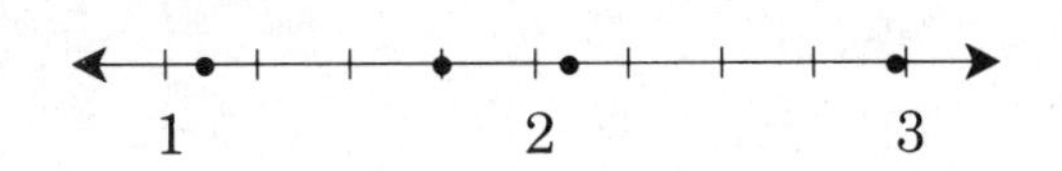

F 1.10, 1.4, 2.98, 2.09

G 1.10, 1.75, 2.9, 2.98

H 1.10, 1.75, 2.09, 2.98

J 1.10, 2.75, 2.9, 2.98

13 There are 39.37 inches in a meter. How many more inches are in a mile than a kilometer?

A 33,990 in.

B 32,990 in.

C 24,323 in.

D 24,323 in.

E 23,990 in.

14 Which of these answers is equal to 562 divided by 100,000?

F 5.62×10^{-5}

G 5.62×10^{-3}

H 5.62×10^{5}

J 5.62×10^{7}

15 Which pair of figures shows just translation?

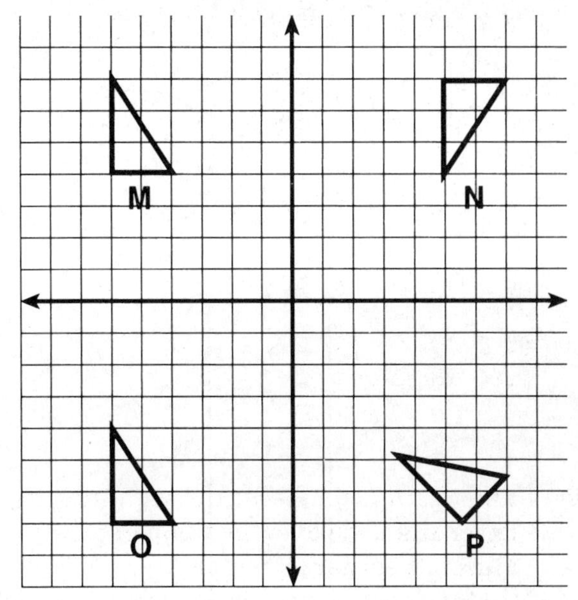

A M and O

B M and N

C N and O

D N and P

16 How much would 50 pairs of work shoes weigh if each pair weighed 1.67 pounds?

F 8.35 pounds

G 41.75 pounds

H 83.5 pounds

J 167 pounds

K Not Here

17 Which of these is a reasonable weight for 1 cubic foot of an unknown substance if 1 cubic inch of the substance weighs 2 ounces?

A 288 pounds

B 144 pounds

C 72 pounds

D 36 pounds

E 18 pounds

GO

18 What is the greatest precision that can be achieved with this scale?

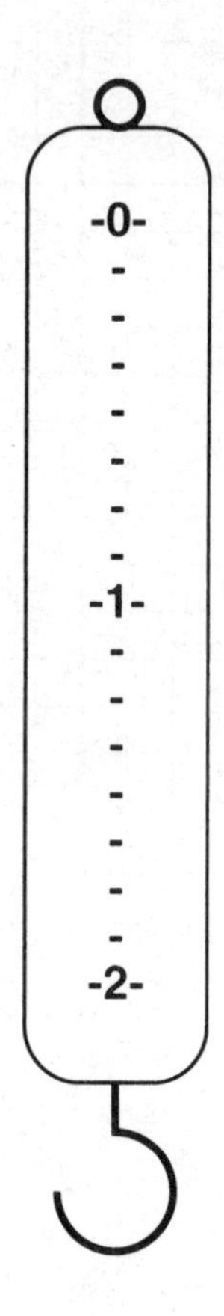

F Nearest 8 ounces

G Nearest 7 ounces

H Nearest $\frac{1}{7}$ of a pound

J Nearest $\frac{1}{8}$ of a pound

19 Sheri weighed 110.23 pounds. She lost 5.48 pounds on a diet, then gained some back. Her weight is now 3.92 pounds less than when she started the diet. How much does she weigh now?

A 114.15 pounds

B 104.75 pounds

C 106.35 pounds

D 105.31 pounds

E Not Here

20 The diameter of this circle is 7 units. The figure inside the circle is a square. What is the length of the portion of the circle going from A to B? Use $\frac{22}{7}$ for π.

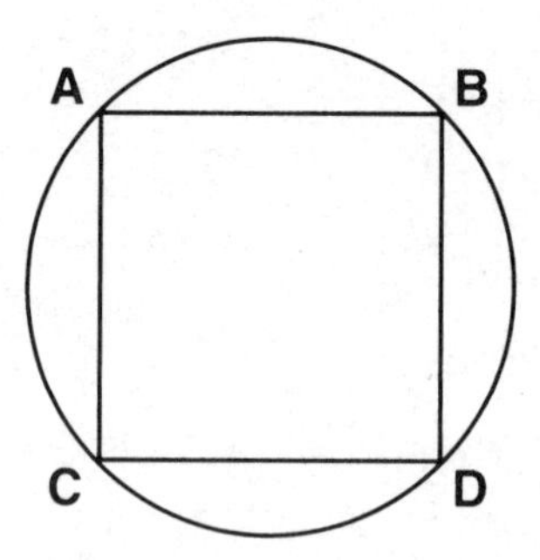

F 1.725 units

G 5.5 units

H 7 units

J 22 units

21 A piece of pipe is $8\frac{1}{2}$ feet long. A plumber must drill two holes in the pipe that are the same distance from one another and from the ends of the pipe. How far apart will she drill the holes?

A $2\frac{5}{6}$

B $3\frac{1}{2}$

C $3\frac{3}{5}$

D $4\frac{1}{4}$

22 A 1000 milliliter beaker is half full. How much will be left if you pour 150 mL out?

F 850 mL

G 500 mL

H 350 mL

J 250 mL

GO

Use this tax table for items 23 through 25.

If the amount of your income is over	But not over	Your tax is	of the amount over
0	$18,850	15%	0
18,550	44,900	$2782.50 + 28%	18,550
44,900	93,130	10,160.50 + 33%	44,900
93,130		**Use formula below**	

Tax = (Income – $26,076.40) x 40%

23 If your income is $40,000, what fraction do you use to calculate your taxes on the amount of income over $18,550?

A $\frac{1}{28}$

B $\frac{3}{20}$

C $\frac{8}{25}$

D $\frac{1}{3}$

E Not Here

24 Whitley earned $62,451 and her deductions were $9290. Her taxable income is the difference between these two numbers. How much tax does she have to pay, rounded to the nearest whole number?

F $12,887

G $12,890

H $12,900

J $17,543

K $20,609

25 How much tax would you pay on income of $113,450.67?

A $28,833.51

B $34,494.71

C $34,949.71

D $37,438.72

E $45,380.27

26 In the figure below, line AC is 23.7 units long. What is distance AB?

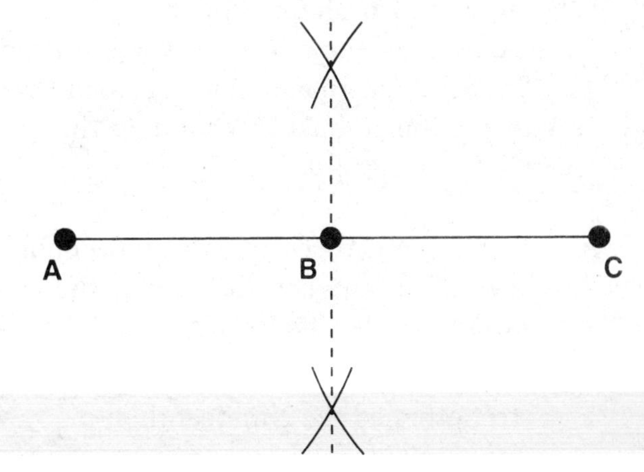

F 7.9 units

G 8.85 units

H 11.85 units

J Its length cannot be determined

27 The unit of measure called the angstrom is used to measure very small things. It is equal to one ten-millionth of a millimeter. Which of these answer choices is another way to express an angstrom unit?

A 1×10^{-6} mm

B 1×10^{-7} mm

C 0.1×10^{6} mm

D 0.1×10^{7} mm

STOP

Samples

A Which region of the United States was governed by the Northwest Ordinance?

- **A** the land north of California and west of Montana
- **B** the land gained during the Civil War
- **C** the land west of the Mississippi
- **D** the land east of the Mississippi and north of the Ohio Rivers

B A leader who rules by force is called a

- **A** constitutional monarch.
- **B** parliament.
- **C** dictator.
- **D** president pro tem.

1 The manufacture and sale of alcoholic beverages were prohibited by the Nineteenth Amendment to the Constitution. The Twenty-first Amendment repealed the Nineteenth Amendment. What does this mean?

- **A** The manufacture and sale of alcoholic beverages were permitted after the Twenty-first Amendment.
- **B** The Twenty-first Amendment strengthened the Nineteenth Amendment.
- **C** The Twenty-first Amendment repealed the first twenty amendments to the Constitution.
- **D** The manufacture and sale of alcoholic beverages were also prohibited by the Twenty-first Amendment.

2 The Pledge of Allegiance is usually made in the presence of

- **A** a copy of the Constitution.
- **B** a copy of the Declaration of Independence.
- **C** the American flag.
- **D** the *Star Spangled Banner.*

3 What makes the American system of government a democracy?

- **A** People can move from state to state.
- **B** People can own property.
- **C** Many government officials are appointed.
- **D** Many government officials are elected.

4 A tariff is a tax imposed by a country on goods imported into that country. What is the most direct effect of imposing a tariff?

- **A** The prices of imported goods will decrease.
- **B** The prices of imported goods will increase.
- **C** The prices of goods manufactured in the country will increase.
- **D** The prices of goods manufactured in the country will decrease.

5 Which of these officials is appointed by the President?

- **A** state legislator
- **B** Secretary of Education
- **C** state senator
- **D** the mayor of a major city

GO

6 Look at the map below. Which state is about 500 miles from east to west?

A Washington

B Montana

C Texas

D California

7 Look at the arrows on the map. Which shows a plane route that lands in Ohio?

A A

B B

C C

D D

8 Look at the map again. In the bottom-left corner of the map are Alaska and Hawaii. Alaska is actually much larger than Texas. Why is it shown so small on the map?

A It is distorted by the curve of the earth.

B Alaska is mostly ice and snow, not solid ground.

C Alaska is a new state and is not found on most maps of the United States.

D If it were shown to scale the map might be too large for the page.

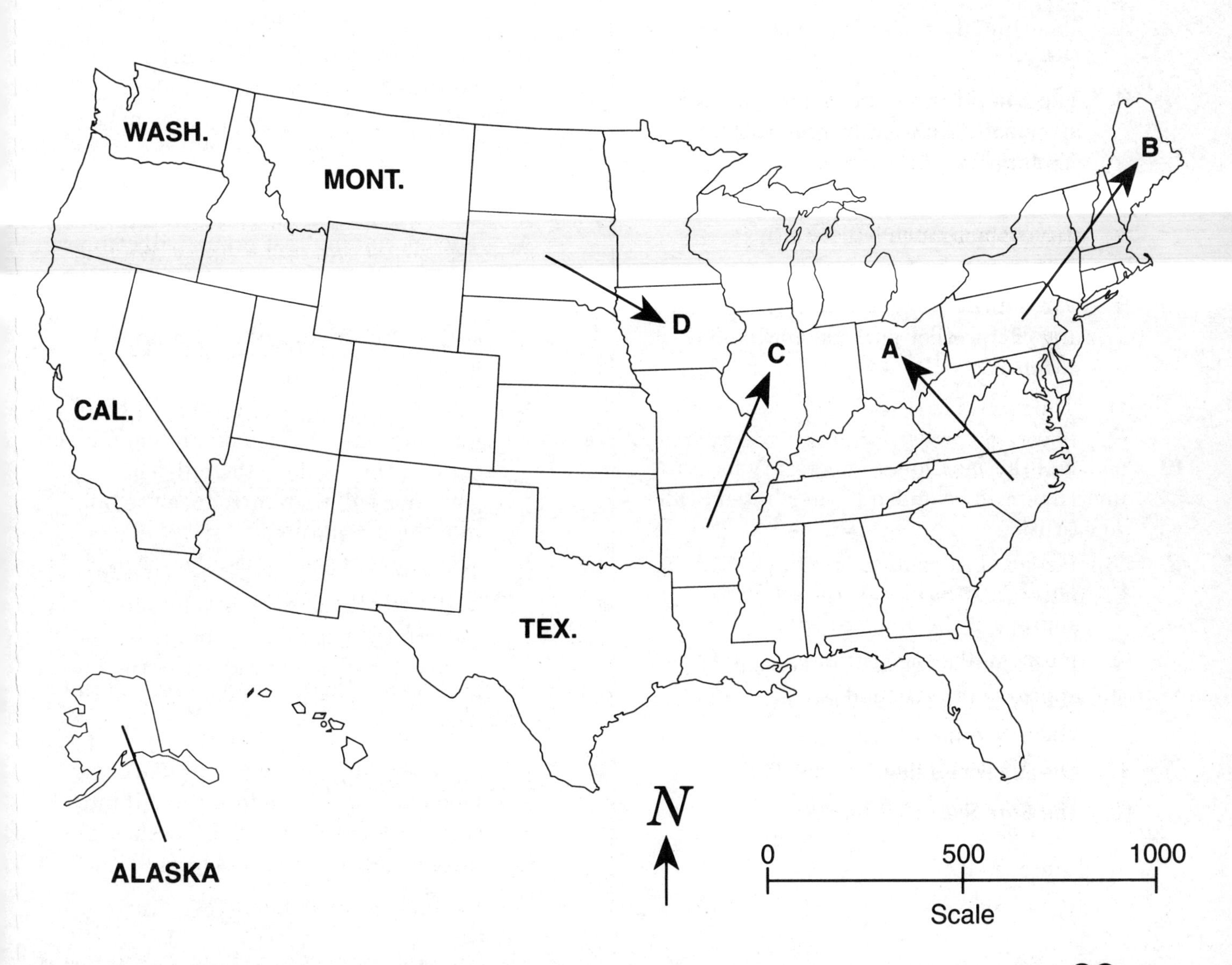

9 Look at the graph below. Which answer choice is an accurate statement about the graph?

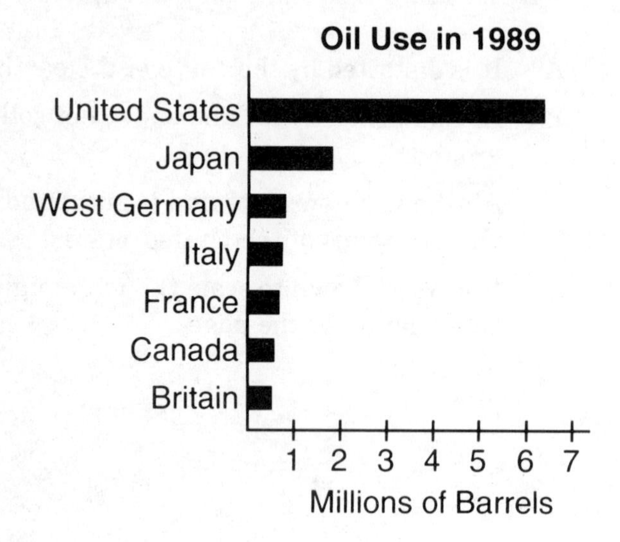

A The United States uses more oil than it should.

B The United States uses more oil than all the other nations of the world combined.

C The United States uses so much oil that there is not much left for other countries to use.

D The United States uses more oil than any of the other nations shown on the graph.

10 Which of these actions is necessary for an amendment to be added to the United States Constitution?

A Three-fourths of the states must approve of the amendment.

B Three-fourths of the Congress must approve of the amendment.

C The other amendments to the Constitution must be repealed first.

D The President must introduce the amendment as a bill that must first be approved by Congress.

11 The Ninth Amendment states that "The powers not delegated to the United States by the Constitution, nor prohibited by it to the states, are reserved to the states respectively, or to the people." Which answer choice restates the meaning of this amendment?

A No power at all is delegated to the states by the Constitution.

B The states have the right to exercise governmental powers that are not reserved for the federal government.

C Any government powers exercised by the federal government can also be exercised by the state governments.

D Power is delegated to the states according to the size of the population.

12 Special interest groups such as business associations or labor organizations may "draft" a bill for lawmakers. What does this mean?

A The special interest group will compose a preliminary version of a bill and explain the need for the bill. The group will then introduce the bill into the legislature.

B The special interest group will compose a preliminary version of a bill and explain the need for the bill. The governor will then introduce the bill into the legislature.

C The special interest group will compose a preliminary version of a bill and explain the need for the bill. A lawmaker will then introduce the bill into the legislature.

D The special interest group will compose a preliminary version of a bill. A lawmaker will introduce the bill into the legislature, and other special interest groups will vote on it.

GO

13 Which of the states below is Wisconsin?

A

B

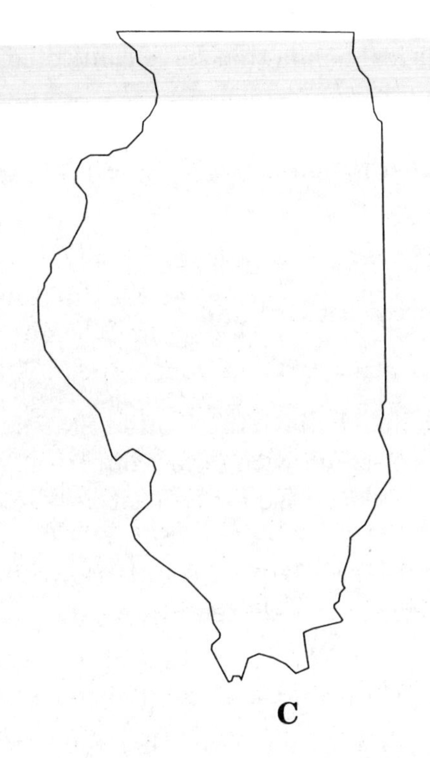

C

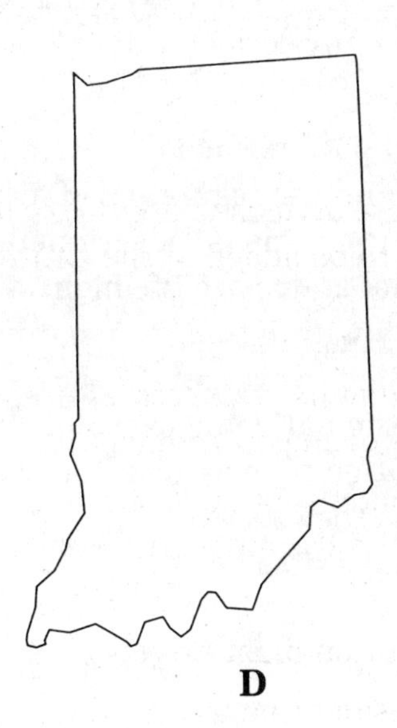

D

14 Which of these is the best description of the federal system as it has been applied in the United States?

A The constitutions of the individual states overrules the Constitution of the United States. The states exercise the greatest powers. The powers not exercised by the states are exercised by the national government. Defense, foreign trade, and other essential tasks are executed by the individual states.

B The states with large populations, like Ohio, have the greatest power. They control foreign trade, defense, and other important tasks. The smaller states exercise the powers not taken by the largest states. The remaining power is exercised by the national government. All states have the same Constitution as the United States.

C The Constitution is the highest law in the land. The states cannot have their own constitutions. The national government controls foreign trade, defense, and the law enforcement within the states. The individual states are actually symbolic, like the Queen of England, and are not expected to govern in any serious way.

D The individual states surrender certain essential powers such as national defense and the regulation of foreign trade to the national government. The individual states are the highest authority within their own borders and are entitled to exercise the powers not held by the national government. The Constitution of the United States overrules the constitutions of the individual states.

15 Which of these is an advantage of a communist economic system?

A The principal goal of the system is to meet the needs of the citizens by distributing national resources.

B The principal goal of the system is to encourage competition so that the best goods and services are offered to people at the lowest prices.

C People are encouraged to own property and to invest in the means of production and distribution of resources.

D The government decides what businesses succeed and fail so there really is no need for a free market where people can buy what they want.

16 In which of the documents below is the following quote found?

"When in the course of human events, it becomes necessary for one people to dissolve the political bonds that have connected them with another..."

A Constitution

B Bill of Rights

C Declaration of Independence

D Northwest Ordinance

17 Some people believe the United States should not trade with other countries. Why is this idea not wise for U.S. citizens?

A Trading with other countries causes prices in the United States to rise.

B The United States cannot provide all the goods and services its people need.

C When we trade with other countries, they will want to become states.

D Foreign trade is required by the Constitution.

GO

18 Nadia believes the federal and state governments should <u>not</u> have the right to tax the money earned by individuals and businesses. She argues that, "America is a free country. People work hard to earn their money and should be able to keep it all." Ernie disagrees with her. Which of these arguments in support of Ernie's position is most convincing?

A Some people earn too much money, while other people earn barely enough to live. The money that rich people pay in taxes is distributed to poor people so they can live better.

B Many people can't find a good job. By paying taxes, we can afford a large government that hires many people. These people then make a good living and spend their money, thus stimulating business.

C The federal and state governments protect us, provide a positive environment in which people can work, and perform other functions that businesses can't. Paying taxes is how we raise money for these services from which we all benefit.

D The federal and state governments are the most important institutions in the country. They tell us what to do and create jobs for many people. The more we pay in taxes, the more research the government can do to help us make wise decisions and create more jobs.

19 Which of these rights does the federal government have but not the states?

A to make laws

B to violate the Constitution

C to levy taxes

D to print money

20 Which of these activities is most likely to be carried out by a political party?

A Hosting a picnic to raise funds and introduce their candidates to the members of the party.

B Raising money to buy television time for the candidates from the opposing party.

C Drafting a bill and introducing it into the legislature.

D Creating a committee to debate a bill before introducing it into the legislature.

21 Which of these is prohibited by the Fifth Amendment to the Constitution of the United States?

A Forcing people to present evidence against themselves in a trial.

B Requiring that people be citizens before they can vote.

C Requiring that a person be at least 35 to become President.

D Forcing people to register for the draft in times of war.

22 It has been said that diversity is the strength of a nation. What does this mean?

A People in a strong nation should be as similar as possible.

B A strong nation is one that has people from many different backgrounds.

C Strong people are different from those who are not strong.

D The more different people are, the stronger will be their feelings against other countries.

STOP

Name and Answer Sheet

STUDENT'S NAME			SCHOOL
LAST	FIRST	MI	TEACHER
			FEMALE ○ MALE ○

LAST											FIRST						MI
○	○	○	○	○	○	○	○	○	○	○	○	○	○	○	○	○	○
A	A	A	A	A	A	A	A	A	A	A	A	A	A	A	A	A	A
B	B	B	B	B	B	B	B	B	B	B	B	B	B	B	B	B	B
C	C	C	C	C	C	C	C	C	C	C	C	C	C	C	C	C	C
D	D	D	D	D	D	D	D	D	D	D	D	D	D	D	D	D	D
E	E	E	E	E	E	E	E	E	E	E	E	E	E	E	E	E	E
F	F	F	F	F	F	F	F	F	F	F	F	F	F	F	F	F	F
G	G	G	G	G	G	G	G	G	G	G	G	G	G	G	G	G	G
H	H	H	H	H	H	H	H	H	H	H	H	H	H	H	H	H	H
I	I	I	I	I	I	I	I	I	I	I	I	I	I	I	I	I	I
J	J	J	J	J	J	J	J	J	J	J	J	J	J	J	J	J	J
K	K	K	K	K	K	K	K	K	K	K	K	K	K	K	K	K	K
L	L	L	L	L	L	L	L	L	L	L	L	L	L	L	L	L	L
M	M	M	M	M	M	M	M	M	M	M	M	M	M	M	M	M	M
N	N	N	N	N	N	N	N	N	N	N	N	N	N	N	N	N	N
O	O	O	O	O	O	O	O	O	O	O	O	O	O	O	O	O	O
P	P	P	P	P	P	P	P	P	P	P	P	P	P	P	P	P	P
Q	Q	Q	Q	Q	Q	Q	Q	Q	Q	Q	Q	Q	Q	Q	Q	Q	Q
R	R	R	R	R	R	R	R	R	R	R	R	R	R	R	R	R	R
S	S	S	S	S	S	S	S	S	S	S	S	S	S	S	S	S	S
T	T	T	T	T	T	T	T	T	T	T	T	T	T	T	T	T	T
U	U	U	U	U	U	U	U	U	U	U	U	U	U	U	U	U	U
V	V	V	V	V	V	V	V	V	V	V	V	V	V	V	V	V	V
W	W	W	W	W	W	W	W	W	W	W	W	W	W	W	W	W	W
X	X	X	X	X	X	X	X	X	X	X	X	X	X	X	X	X	X
Y	Y	Y	Y	Y	Y	Y	Y	Y	Y	Y	Y	Y	Y	Y	Y	Y	Y
Z	Z	Z	Z	Z	Z	Z	Z	Z	Z	Z	Z	Z	Z	Z	Z	Z	Z

BIRTH DATE

MONTH	DAY		YEAR	
JAN ○	0	0		0
FEB ○	1	1		1
MAR ○	2	2		2
APR ○	3	3		3
MAY ○		4		4
JUN ○		5	5	5
JUL ○		6	6	6
AUG ○		7	7	7
SEP ○		8	8	8
OCT ○		9	9	9
NOV ○				
DEC ○				

Test 1 Language Arts

A Ⓐ Ⓑ Ⓒ Ⓓ 3 Ⓐ Ⓑ Ⓒ Ⓓ 4 Ⓕ Ⓖ Ⓗ Ⓙ 6 Ⓕ Ⓖ Ⓗ Ⓙ D Ⓕ Ⓖ Ⓗ Ⓙ 8 Ⓕ Ⓖ Ⓗ Ⓙ 10 Ⓕ Ⓖ Ⓗ Ⓙ

1 Ⓐ Ⓑ Ⓒ Ⓓ B Ⓕ Ⓖ Ⓗ Ⓙ 5 Ⓐ Ⓑ Ⓒ Ⓓ 7 Ⓐ Ⓑ Ⓒ Ⓓ E Ⓐ Ⓑ Ⓒ Ⓓ 9 Ⓐ Ⓑ Ⓒ Ⓓ 11 Ⓐ Ⓑ Ⓒ Ⓓ

2 Ⓕ Ⓖ Ⓗ Ⓙ C Ⓐ Ⓑ Ⓒ Ⓓ

Test 2 Reading Comprehension

A Ⓐ Ⓑ Ⓒ Ⓓ 3 Ⓐ Ⓑ Ⓒ Ⓓ 5 Ⓐ Ⓑ Ⓒ Ⓓ 7 Ⓐ Ⓑ Ⓒ Ⓓ 9 Ⓐ Ⓑ Ⓒ Ⓓ 11 Ⓐ Ⓑ Ⓒ Ⓓ 13 Ⓐ Ⓑ Ⓒ Ⓓ

1 Ⓐ Ⓑ Ⓒ Ⓓ 4 Ⓕ Ⓖ Ⓗ Ⓙ 6 Ⓕ Ⓖ Ⓗ Ⓙ 8 Ⓕ Ⓖ Ⓗ Ⓙ 10 Ⓕ Ⓖ Ⓗ Ⓙ 12 Ⓕ Ⓖ Ⓗ Ⓙ 14 Ⓕ Ⓖ Ⓗ Ⓙ

2 Ⓕ Ⓖ Ⓗ Ⓙ

Test 3 Mathematics

A Ⓐ Ⓑ Ⓒ Ⓓ Ⓔ 5 Ⓐ Ⓑ Ⓒ Ⓓ Ⓔ 10 Ⓕ Ⓖ Ⓗ Ⓙ Ⓚ 15 Ⓐ Ⓑ Ⓒ Ⓓ Ⓔ 20 Ⓕ Ⓖ Ⓗ Ⓙ Ⓚ 24 Ⓕ Ⓖ Ⓗ Ⓙ Ⓚ

1 Ⓐ Ⓑ Ⓒ Ⓓ Ⓔ 6 Ⓕ Ⓖ Ⓗ Ⓙ Ⓚ 11 Ⓐ Ⓑ Ⓒ Ⓓ Ⓔ 16 Ⓕ Ⓖ Ⓗ Ⓙ Ⓚ 21 Ⓐ Ⓑ Ⓒ Ⓓ Ⓔ 25 Ⓐ Ⓑ Ⓒ Ⓓ Ⓔ

2 Ⓕ Ⓖ Ⓗ Ⓙ Ⓚ 7 Ⓐ Ⓑ Ⓒ Ⓓ Ⓔ 12 Ⓕ Ⓖ Ⓗ Ⓙ Ⓚ 17 Ⓐ Ⓑ Ⓒ Ⓓ Ⓔ 22 Ⓕ Ⓖ Ⓗ Ⓙ Ⓚ 26 Ⓕ Ⓖ Ⓗ Ⓙ Ⓚ

3 Ⓐ Ⓑ Ⓒ Ⓓ Ⓔ 8 Ⓕ Ⓖ Ⓗ Ⓙ Ⓚ 13 Ⓐ Ⓑ Ⓒ Ⓓ Ⓔ 18 Ⓕ Ⓖ Ⓗ Ⓙ Ⓚ 23 Ⓐ Ⓑ Ⓒ Ⓓ Ⓔ 27 Ⓐ Ⓑ Ⓒ Ⓓ Ⓔ

4 Ⓕ Ⓖ Ⓗ Ⓙ Ⓚ 9 Ⓐ Ⓑ Ⓒ Ⓓ Ⓔ 14 Ⓕ Ⓖ Ⓗ Ⓙ Ⓚ 19 Ⓐ Ⓑ Ⓒ Ⓓ Ⓔ

Test 4 Citizenship

A Ⓐ Ⓑ Ⓒ Ⓓ
B Ⓐ Ⓑ Ⓒ Ⓓ

1 Ⓐ Ⓑ Ⓒ Ⓓ
2 Ⓐ Ⓑ Ⓒ Ⓓ
3 Ⓐ Ⓑ Ⓒ Ⓓ
4 Ⓐ Ⓑ Ⓒ Ⓓ
5 Ⓐ Ⓑ Ⓒ Ⓓ
6 Ⓐ Ⓑ Ⓒ Ⓓ
7 Ⓐ Ⓑ Ⓒ Ⓓ
8 Ⓐ Ⓑ Ⓒ Ⓓ
9 Ⓐ Ⓑ Ⓒ Ⓓ
10 Ⓐ Ⓑ Ⓒ Ⓓ
11 Ⓐ Ⓑ Ⓒ Ⓓ
12 Ⓐ Ⓑ Ⓒ Ⓓ
13 Ⓐ Ⓑ Ⓒ Ⓓ
14 Ⓐ Ⓑ Ⓒ Ⓓ
15 Ⓐ Ⓑ Ⓒ Ⓓ
16 Ⓐ Ⓑ Ⓒ Ⓓ
17 Ⓐ Ⓑ Ⓒ Ⓓ
18 Ⓐ Ⓑ Ⓒ Ⓓ
19 Ⓐ Ⓑ Ⓒ Ⓓ
20 Ⓐ Ⓑ Ⓒ Ⓓ
21 Ⓐ Ⓑ Ⓒ Ⓓ
22 Ⓐ Ⓑ Ⓒ Ⓓ

CLOZE: READING COMPREHENSION CHALLENGE

How Cloze Works:

The word *cloze* comes from *closing*. When you see a space, your mind wants to put something there to fill and *close* the space.

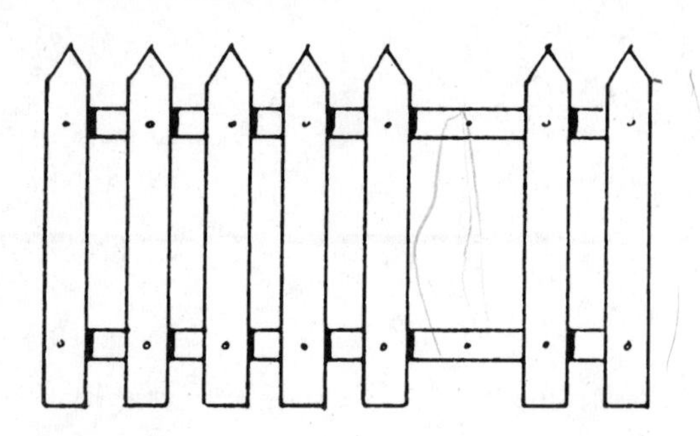

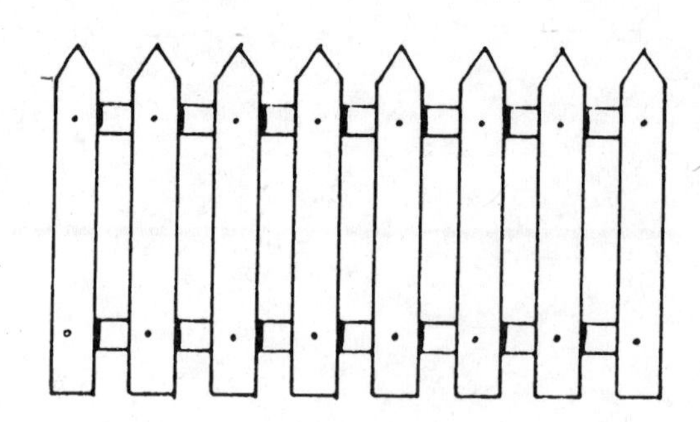

The same is true when you read. Think about this example:

The rock stars strummed their guitars. They enjoyed making ________ for their fans.

You probably said *music* almost automatically, to fill the space. You know from experience that rock stars make music.

That is how cloze works. You use clues in nearby sentences, and your own common sense, to find the best word to fill a blank.

This section contains 25 true articles for you to read. Each article has five missing words for you to determine. With most articles you will be given five choices for each missing word; you select the best one. With some articles no answer choices are given; you think of the best word on your own.

USING CLUES IN CLOZE

Do you like a good mystery story? Many people do because they enjoy finding clues to solve the mystery. In a way, each cloze item is like a mini-mystery. You have to look for clues that can help you find the missing word. Five different kinds of clues can assist you. Let's look at each kind.

1. Clues That Signal *Likeness*

A. Look for nearby words that mean **the same** or almost the same as (are *synonyms* for) the missing word.

What a messy person! Her hair and clothes were always ________.

A) attractive B) crude
C) untidy D) shiny
E) clean

Did you choose *untidy*? The word *messy* is your clue. *Messy* and *untidy* are synonyms. They are **like** each other; they mean the same thing.

You may sometimes find the missing word itself used in a nearby sentence.

Most people do not like rodents. Many are terrified of rats and mice. But some do not even like ______ that are kept as pets, such as hamsters and guinea pigs.

Rodents is in the first sentence. It is also the missing word.

B. Look for nearby words that are *something like* the missing word.

Most people want to cover their windows for privacy. Blinds can be opened or closed as needed. ______ can be, too.

A) Screens B) Drapes
C) Windows D) Doors
E) Bars

Did you choose *drapes*? *Blinds* and *too* are your clues. Drapes are **like** blinds. Both are window coverings that give privacy and can be opened or closed.

Other words that signal likeness are *like, both,* and *also*.

______ are **like** blinds. They can be opened and closed as needed.

Blinds and ______ are popular window coverings. **Both** offer privacy when it is wanted.

Blinds can give privacy and add color to a room. ______ can **also**.

C. Look for nearby words that **explain** or **tell the meaning of** the missing word.

The villain in the movie had a ______. He planned to use the weapon to stab the only witness to his crime.

A) gun B) stick
C) rope D) dagger
E) club

Did you choose *dagger*? The words *use the weapon to stab* **explain** how a dagger is used. Now think about this example:

Europe contains many ______. Most of these huge, richly decorated churches were built centuries ago.

A) cathedrals B) castles
C) restaurants D) museums
E) monuments

Did you choose *cathedrals*? *Huge, richly decorated churches* **tells the meaning of** *cathedrals*.

D. The missing word may describe what a nearby word is **like**. Look for nearby words that offer clues to the missing word.

Pony Express riders faced deadly perils from weather, accidents, and attacks as they raced to get the mail through. They were ______ people.

A) foolish B) ambitious
C) welcome D) wise
E) courageous

Courageous is the best choice. It describes what the Pony Express riders were **like**. *Faced deadly perils from weather, accidents, and attacks* are the clue words signaling that *courageous* is the best word for the blank.

Now try these examples that use *likeness* clues.

1. There were acres of corn and wheat as far as the eye could see. The _________ was rich here. Anything could grow in this soil.

   A) planting B) banking C) cooking D) farmland E) grass

2. People were shouting loudly and carrying signs demanding that their work conditions be improved This _________ was the biggest since the strike began.

   A) demonstration B) party C) audience D) program E) enterprise

3. Revolutionary War soldiers carried _________. These long, heavy guns must have been awkward in battle.

   A) tomahawks B) knives C) knapsacks D) maps E) muskets

4. From the gray skies a cold rain fell steadily. It was a typical _________ day in that land.

   A) scorching B) brilliant C) dreary D) frantic E) gusty

2. Clues That Signal *Difference*

A. Look for nearby words that mean the **opposite** (are *antonyms*) of the missing word.

One brother is rude, but his twin is nothing like him. He could not be more _________.

A) attractive B) ugly C) funny D) courteous E) stupid

Did you choose *courteous*? It is the **opposite** of *rude*. The words *but* and *nothing like* signal that what follows is **different** from what was just stated. So while one brother is rude, the other is polite, or *courteous*.

B. Look for other nearby words signaling that something **different** is coming: *other, not, yet, rather, instead, however, on the other hand*.

One brother is rude. The *other* is _________.

One brother is rude. His twin is **not** like him at all. He is _________.

Instead of being rude like his twin, the other brother tries to be _________.

One brother is rude. **However**, his twin is very _________.

One brother is quite _________. **On the other hand**, his twin is quite rude.

C. Sometimes there is no one clue word that signals a pair of opposites. But you can tell by the way the sentences are written that the missing word is **different** from or the **opposite** of a nearby word.

One brother could not be more rude. His twin could not be more _________.

Now try these examples by finding clues that signal **difference**.

1. Not all people ride horses the same way. Some always use a saddle. Others always ride __________.

   A) alone B) slowly C) confidently D) bareback E) awkwardly

2. She was full of energy, but he felt very __________. It had been a long day.

   A) angry B) fatigued C) sad D) hopeful E) bewildered

3. It is easy to make mistakes. It is often __________ to forgive other people's mistakes.

   A) odd B) hard C) easy D) cheap E) unfair

4. Many jobs are best done by machine. On the other hand, some delicate work will always need to be done __________.

   A) tenderly B) slowly C) manually D) quickly E) automatically

3. Clues That Signal *Cause* or *Effect*

A. Look for nearby words signaling a **cause, reason**, or **purpose**. They tell **why** something happened or **why** someone did something.

Jesse wanted to protect her skin against __________. So she put on plenty of lotion.

A) cold B) disease C) headache D) sunburn E) bruise

Did you choose *sunburn*? *So* in the second sentence can mean **that is why**. **Why** did Jesse put on lotion? What was the **reason (cause, purpose)** for her doing so? To protect her skin. What did she want to protect her skin against? A *sunburn*.

B. Look for other words that signal a **cause** or an **effect**: *because, why, reason, so that, therefore, thus, to, this made, this led to, this enabled, as a result.*

Jesse put on plenty of lotion. She did it **because** she did not want a __________.

Jesse wanted to protect her skin against __________. **Therefore**, she put on plenty of lotion.

Jesse put on plenty of lotion. She did this to protect her skin against __________.

Jesse wanted to protect her skin against __________. **This made** her put on plenty of lotion.

Jesse put on plenty of lotion. **As a result**, she did not get a __________.

C. Sometimes there is no **cause** or **effect** clue word, but you can still tell by the way ideas are written that they are related by cause and effect.

Jesse put on plenty of skin lotion. She did not want a __________.

Now try these examples. Find clues that signal **cause** or **effect**.

1. Michael backed the family car into a tree. So now there is a _________ in the fender.

   A) dent B) nick C) slash D) noise E) bulge

2. We are sure our team will win. As a result, we are _________ about this game.

   A) concerned B) tireless C) enthusiastic D) dejected E) flustered

3. After the crash, the survivors built a huge _________. They chose this action because they thought search planes might see the light.

   A) shelter B) sign C) storehouse D) bonfire E) enclosure

4. Some people want a reminder of the places they have visited. Therefore, tourist attractions often have a place to get _________ nearby.

   A) snacks B) maps C) information D) gas E) souvenirs

4. Clues That Signal Parts or Wholes

What **parts** make up a **whole** car? The wheels, engine, doors, headlights, and trunk, to name just a few. Apples, oranges, bananas, and pears are **parts** of a **whole** group called what? Fruits, of course. Recognizing parts and wholes can provide you with more cloze clues.

A. Look for nearby words that name **parts** of a **whole** group or object.

Knives, forks, and spoons are very common today. But centuries ago, people did not use all these _________.

A) dishes B) utensils C) tools D) metals E) comforts

Knives, forks, and spoons are kinds of eating *utensils*. They are **part** of a **whole** group called utensils.

Here is another example:

A _________ is awesome to most people. Its countless thousands of stars are hard to imagine.

A) sun B) comet C) telescope D) spaceship E) galaxy

Did you choose *galaxy*? Stars are **parts** of a **whole** galaxy.

B. Look for nearby words that name a whole thing or group. The missing word may be **part** of that whole.

It is cold enough to bring out the winter clothes. I need to buy a new pair of _________ because I lost mine last year.

A) sandals B) slippers C) gloves D) sneakers E) sunglasses

Which answer is **part** of a **whole** group called *winter clothes*? *Gloves* is the best choice.

C. To find some missing words, you may need to count the **parts** of a **whole**. Look for clue words that help you count correctly.

There were courses at the luncheon. First came the soup, then the salad, then the main dish, and last, the dessert. And each one was delicious!

A) one B) two
C) three D) four
E) five

Did you count *four*?. *First, then*, and *last* were the clues to help you count correctly.

Now try these examples that focus on **parts** and **wholes**.

1. There were many females in her family. She had five aunts and six __________.

   A) nephews B) sons
   C) nieces D) uncles
   E) grandparents

2. Young Dwight learned to play the __________. It soon became one of his favorite musical instruments.

   A) joke B) game
   C) sport D) role
   E) clarinet

3. People of that time often changed their entire wardrobes. Women, for example, would give away all their __________.

   A) money B) furniture
   C) blankets D) blouses
   E) pets

4. There are not many kings and queens left in the world today. Only a few countries have __________.

   A) monarchs B) leaders
   C) presidents D) politicians
   E) gypsies

5. Clues That Tell What is *Most Likely*

Sometimes you need to draw on your own experiences and your common sense to determine the **most likely** answer. Ask yourself *what* would most likely happen, *who* would most likely do something, *where* something would most likely occur, or *how* something would most likely be described.

A. The window was open and the television was gone. It was clear that a __________ had entered the apartment.

A) neighbor B) murderer
C) firefighter D) creature
E) burglar

Who would **most likely** come through a window and take a television? *Burglar* is the best choice.

B. Each spring, the people of that land would lead their flocks onto the mountain slopes, where the new grass was springing up fresh and green. There the herds would stay and __________ until fall arrived.

A) sleep B) graze
C) battle D) sicken
E) roar

What would the herds **most likely** do after being led into areas of fresh, green grass? They would most likely *graze* there.

C. When the war ended, millions of soldiers and sailors were released from service. They immediately rushed for the quickest transportation to their ________.

A) offices
B) camps
C) homes
D) schools
E) equipment

Where would soldiers and sailors **most likely** rush after being away in wartime service? Did you choose *homes*?

D. Think about how someone would **most likely** describe the creature in this example:

It was a ________ creature. It had long, sharp claws and a terrifying roar.

A) curious
B) dreamlike
C) gentle
D) beautiful
E) ferocious

Did you choose *ferocious*? It is the best word to describe a creature with such frightening features.

Now try these examples. Use your experience and common sense to find the **most likely** answer.

1. We took a tour of the old ________. It was strange to think of a war being fought at such a quiet place.

A) ship
B) battlefield
C) tomb
D) church
E) hideout

2. The low wail sounded through the murky mist. The ________ was sending a warning to all ships.

A) bell
B) whale
C) foghorn
D) lighthouse
E) radio

3. The bird called out to its mate in a nearby tree. In a moment came the ________.

A) thunder
B) crowd
C) reply
D) dawn
E) snake

4. The deer heard the sounds of approaching humans. The alerted animals ________ off through the woods toward the densest part of the wilderness.

A) ambled
B) crept
C) plodded
D) slinked
E) bounded

Clues of More Than One Kind

You may sometimes find more than one kind of clue to a missing word. Identifying each kind can help you double-check your answer. If the word you choose works for both types of clues, it is almost certainly correct.

Some people live in poverty. Others live in ________. These others may have big cars, big houses, and even many servants.

A) town
B) trailers
C) luxury
D) dwellings
E) disgrace

Did you choose *luxury*? It is the **opposite** of *poverty*. The words *big cars, big houses*, and *many servants* also **explain** what living in *luxury* is like.

Reading the Whole Article

Read each cloze article *completely through* before you mark or write any answers. Why? One reason is that clues often *follow* the missing word. You can see this in many of the examples on pages 108–115. Another reason is that you need to get the whole meaning of the readings. If you stop to answer each blank, you may lose the main ideas. The better you understand the articles, the more you will enjoy them-and the easier the cloze answers will be for you.

USING THIS BOOK

There are thirty articles in this section. Twenty-five of them are in Units 1–25. The other five are in five special units called "On Your Own." Each article contains five cloze blanks.

How to Do Units 1–25

Step 1: Read each article entirely through to get its whole meaning. When you reach a blank, think quickly of a word that might fit the blank. Then go on. Do not try to mark any answers now.

Step 2: Read the article again. Look at the five answers for blank 1. They are marked *A, B, C, D,* and *E*. Choose the best answer, and fill in that answer in the answer row at the bottom of the page. If you are not sure of the answer, read the paragraph again. Remember that many clues appear *after* the blanks.

Go through the rest of the article in the same way.

How to Do the "On Your Own" Units

After every five regular units there is an "On Your Own" unit. It lets you use your *own* words for the blanks. Everything is the same as in the regular units except that there are no answers to choose from. Think of the best word you know for each blank, and write that word in the blank. Here is an example:

> Many people make a hobby of collecting shells. They look for them as they walk along the ____1____. Shells can be found in the sand and at the water's edge.
>
> **1.** ______________________________

What did you think of? *Beach*? That makes sense. The clue words *shells, sand*, and *water's edge* all name **parts** of a beach. What about *shore* for your answer? That makes sense, too, since it means almost the same as *beach*. For many blanks more than one word can make sense.

Now you are ready to start the cloze activities. Enjoy the readings, think hard, and solve the mysteries of cloze.

Cloze: Reading Comprehension Challenge Checklist

UNIT 1

For Units 1–5, read each article completely. Choose the best answer and fill in your selection in the answer row at the bottom of the page.

What can go straight up or down, fly backward, forward or sideways, and even stay suspended in one spot? It also has many ___1___. These include the "flying windmill," "chopper," "whirlybird," "flying top," and "eggbeater." The answer, of course, is the helicopter. It is an aircraft that can take off or land vertically, enabling it to do jobs that other types of aircraft cannot do.

1. A) problems B) passengers C) nicknames D) critics E) admirers

The Chinese had toy helicopters over 500 years ago. About A. D. 1500, the great Italian artist and inventor Leonardo da Vinci drew pictures of a helicopter. Astonishingly, it ___2___ many of the same principles used in today's craft. It was not until 1907, however, that a helicopter capable of carrying a person was built. The first practical passenger helicopter that could stay aloft over an hour was not built until the 1930s.

2. A) employed B) restored C) mimicked D) defied E) distorted

The improvements made in helicopters in recent years have been enormous. In 1937, the farthest a helicopter could fly without refueling was less that sixty-eight miles. Today one can ___3___ well over 2,000 miles. The highest a helicopter could fly in 1937 was about 8,000 feet. Today a whirlybird may climb beyond 40,000 feet. Its speed has also increased from sixty miles per hour in the 1930s to over 200 today.

3. A) signal B) sail C) plummet D) observe E) travel

Helicopters have a variety of purposes. On farms, they spray crops. In industry, they transport equipment and materials to hard-to-reach places. These ___4___ mountain-tops or dense jungles. Helicopters are used by the armed forces for troop movements, rescue missions, and observation.

4. A) span B) avoid C) destroy D) include E) resemble

Possibly helicopters are most valuable during ___5___. They are often used to drop medicine, clothing, and food to victims of floods and earthquakes. Helicopters also rescue victims of accidents at sea, where airplanes cannot land and the nearest boats cannot reach the scene in time. The helicopter has saved many lives that would have been lost.

5. A) parades B) battles C) disasters D) festivals E) demonstrations

ANSWER ROWS: 1 Ⓐ Ⓑ Ⓒ Ⓓ Ⓔ 2 Ⓐ Ⓑ Ⓒ Ⓓ Ⓔ 3 Ⓐ Ⓑ Ⓒ Ⓓ Ⓔ 4 Ⓐ Ⓑ Ⓒ Ⓓ Ⓔ 5 Ⓐ Ⓑ Ⓒ Ⓓ Ⓔ

UNIT 2

Motorcycles have been popular for a long time. Many people use them for ____1____. They enjoy riding down highways and country trails. They may also delight in the sport of motorcycle racing. Other people travel to and from work or school on motorcycles. Police officers use these vehicles to assist in their job.

1. A) science B) recreation C) settlement D) revolution E) information

The first motorcycle-type vehicle was invented in 1885 by a German engineer named Gottlieb Daimler. Daimler fastened an engine to a wooden bicycle and connected a belt from the engine to a gear on the rear wheel. It was not until 1901, however, that the first real motorcycle, called the Thomas, was manufactured. Since then their ____2____ has grown enormously. This is evidenced by the number and variety sold.

2. A) beauty B) value C) size D) popularity E) fame

Today there are various kinds of motorcycles. *Streetbikes* are mostly for riding in cities. *Touring bikes* are fast motorcycles designed for long highway trips. *Trail bikes* are for riding through fields and climbing hills. Thus each of these kinds has its own ____3____. Smaller cycles are more like bicycles. *Mopeds* resemble bikes with motors attached. *Motor scooters* are bicycles with small wheels and little power. The one thing that all these cycles, big and small, have in common is that they are all self-propelled, two-wheeled vehicles.

3. A) purpose B) messenger C) atmosphere D) elevation E) manner

Like cars, motorcycles must be ____4____ with both hands. But unlike most cars, motorcycles require the use of both feet as well. There is a hand grip to control the speed of the vehicle. Another hand device is for the clutch. A third applies the front brakes. Two hands can control all three. One foot pedal controls the rear brake while the other shifts the gears.

4. A) polished B) repaired C) operated D) painted E) refueled

Motorcycles have both advantages and disadvantages. The great disadvantage is that riders have a high rate of serious injury in accidents. The ____5____ can make this rate even higher. Riding in snow, heavy rain, or strong wind can be particularly dangerous. Among the advantages is that motorcycles cost relatively little to buy, to repair, and especially to operate—some getting up to ninety miles per gallon of gasoline. Most devotees, though, find the biggest advantage to be that motorcycles are fun to ride.

5. A) bridge B) tolls C) luggage D) police E) weather

 ANSWER ROWS: 1 Ⓐ Ⓑ Ⓒ Ⓓ Ⓔ 2 Ⓐ Ⓑ Ⓒ Ⓓ Ⓔ 3 Ⓐ Ⓑ Ⓒ Ⓓ Ⓔ 4 Ⓐ Ⓑ Ⓒ Ⓓ Ⓔ 5 Ⓐ Ⓑ Ⓒ Ⓓ Ⓔ

UNIT 3

Leap year is a year that has 366 days instead of the usual 365. It normally occurs every four years, always on an even-numbered year. The extra day is added to our ___1___ month. That is February, which in non-leap years has 28 days, two fewer than any other month. When you see February 29 on a calendar, you know that year is a leap year.

1. A) hottest B) rainiest C) dreariest D) shortest E) lengthiest

Leap year is also called the *bissextile* year. This is its formal, or scientific ___2___. In our calendar system there is need for a leap year because the solar year (the time it takes the earth to go around the sun once) is actually slightly more than 365 days long. That extra day—February 29 every four years—helps correct the difference between our calendar and the solar calendar.

2. A) statement B) ceremony C) title D) function E) invitation

Leap year was first made part of the calendar by the ancient Roman leader Julius Caesar. His astronomers had calculated the length of the solar year to be 365 days and six hours. So Caesar declared that an extra day be added to the calendar. This is ___3___ every four years.

3. A) avoided B) done C) protested D) recited E) outlawed

Caesar's adjustment, however, was not entirely accurate because his astronomers' year exceeded the true solar year by eleven minutes and fourteen seconds. By 1582, a difference of ten days had developed between the calendar year and the true solar year. To correct this error, Pope Gregory XIII ruled that every fourth year would continue to be a leap year except for century years that could not be divided evenly by 400. By this system, century years such as 1700, 1800, and 1900 were not leap years, but the year 2000 is a leap year. This may seem ___4___, but it works.

4. A) complicated B) frivolous C) humorous D) sinister E) worrisome

Persons born on February 29 celebrate their growing up a little differently from the rest of us. They acknowledge that they get ___5___ each year. But if they go strictly by the calendar, they have only one-fourth as many birthday celebrations as most people.

5. A) wealthier B) healthier C) smarter D) taller E) older

ANSWER ROWS: 1 Ⓐ Ⓑ Ⓒ Ⓓ Ⓔ 2 Ⓐ Ⓑ Ⓒ Ⓓ Ⓔ 3 Ⓐ Ⓑ Ⓒ Ⓓ Ⓔ 4 Ⓐ Ⓑ Ⓒ Ⓓ Ⓔ 5 Ⓐ Ⓑ Ⓒ Ⓓ Ⓔ

UNIT 4

The process of photography is not as simple as it looks at the moment we press a button or flick a lever to snap a picture. However, the two basic principles that make a photograph possible are simple enough. First, light passing through a small opening ____1____ an image. Second, light darkens some substances more than others.

1. A) erases B) bypasses C) forms D) rejects E) blurs

Have you ever wondered just how a camera works? In the small opening in the front of a camera is a glass lens. When you click your camera, a shutter opens and closes in a split second. You have let light inside. This light may be from the sun or it may be artificial. The light contains the image of the scene you snapped. Inside the camera, that light strikes the film, which is coated with chemicals sensitive to light. ____2____ light makes a black patch on the film. Dimmer light results in a gray patch.

2. A) Bright B) Fluorescent C) Artificial D) Electric E) Candle

To get a finished photograph, you must have the film ____3____. The first step in this process involves passing the film through liquid chemicals until a "negative" picture appears. On the negative everything appears just the opposite of what it should be: black objects are white, and white ones black.

3. A) developed B) framed C) wound D) dried E) cleaned

The next step corrects that ____4____. The negative is placed on a special kind of paper under bright light. All shades then reverse themselves. What appears as white on the negative becomes black, and what is black becomes white, with different shades of gray in between. Then you have a photograph, the picture you took, in its natural shades. Everything and everybody appears the same as at the moment you clicked the shutter. Color photography is far more complex than black-and-white. But the ____5____ is the same.

4. A) closing B) condition C) opening D) movement E) sensation

5. A) distance B) hurdle C) lighting D) motion E) principle

Try to recall all this the next time you tell people to "watch the birdie" or "say cheese." You will have a better idea of what you are doing when you move your finger to click the camera's shutter.

 ANSWER ROWS: 1 Ⓐ Ⓑ Ⓒ Ⓓ Ⓔ 2 Ⓐ Ⓑ Ⓒ Ⓓ Ⓔ 3 Ⓐ Ⓑ Ⓒ Ⓓ Ⓔ 4 Ⓐ Ⓑ Ⓒ Ⓓ Ⓔ 5 Ⓐ Ⓑ Ⓒ Ⓓ Ⓔ

UNIT 5

"Look it up in the dictionary" is the usual comment when people are in doubt about the meaning or spelling of a word. Dictionaries are considered the final authority on these matters as well as on pronunciations and other facts about a word.

Until a few hundred years ago, however, people could not "look it up" because there were no English dictionaries. The ancient Greeks and Romans and the scholars of the Middle Ages had made lists of Latin and Greek words. But it was not until 1604 that a book of uncommon English words ____1____. The first great English dictionary listing both common and uncommon words was written by Samuel Johnson in 1755.

1. A) vanished B) failed C) tore D) burned E) appeared

In America, the most famous name in dictionary writing is that of Noah Webster. He stressed American rather than British ways of ____2____. His great dictionary, which first appeared in 1828, has been republished many times. Each time, it has been updated. The ____3____ edition is still considered "the" dictionary. It defines over 450,000 words, including *radar, television,* and others undreamed of by Webster.

2. A) driving B) acting C) irrigating D) speaking E) printing

3. A) pocket B) original C) latest D) museum E) discontinued

Dictionaries that list all kinds of words are known as general dictionaries. The huge ones that rest on stands in libraries are called *unabridged,* meaning "not shortened." They tell not only a word's meaning and spelling but also its pronunciation, origin, history, part of speech, grammatical forms, and ways of use. The smaller ones do not provide all this ____4____.

4. A) information B) clutter C) waste D) capital E) entertainment

General dictionaries are not the only kind. A bilingual dictionary, such as a Spanish-English dictionary, translates words from one language into another. A thesaurus lists other words that mean the same as each listed word. A gazetteer lists place names, and a glossary is a small dictionary in a book defining technical words in that book. There are also dictionaries of scientific terms and ones on many other special topics. There is even a dictionary of slang. Thus there are many kinds of ____5____ dictionaries. The dictionary is one of our most valuable language tools.

5. A) electronic B) special C) flimsy D) difficult E) beautiful

ANSWER ROWS: 1 Ⓐ Ⓑ Ⓒ Ⓓ Ⓔ 2 Ⓐ Ⓑ Ⓒ Ⓓ Ⓔ 3 Ⓐ Ⓑ Ⓒ Ⓓ Ⓔ 4 Ⓐ Ⓑ Ⓒ Ⓓ Ⓔ 5 Ⓐ Ⓑ Ⓒ Ⓓ Ⓔ

FIRST
ON YOUR OWN

For the First On Your Own, read each article completely. Think of the best word you know for each blank, and write that word in the blank to the right.

You have probably heard of the atmosphere and perhaps of the stratosphere, but have you ever heard of the biosphere? *Biosphere* is the name that scientists have given to the layer around the earth's surface in which all living things on our planet dwell. Above and below this layer no ___1___ is found.

1. ____________________

The biosphere begins about seven miles in the air. It extends to ___2___ of the oceans. It also includes the earth's land, from the surface to a depth of about 100 feet. In the air live not only birds but also microscopic organisms, spores, and pollen grains carried by the wind. On the land, or course, live humans and countless species of plants and animals. Beneath the land surface live worms, some insects, plant roots, and soil microbes. Even the sediment below the ocean floor contains living bacteria.

2. ____________________

Only in this thin shell of air, earth, and water do the conditions exist that enable life to survive: suitable warmth and pressure, oxygen, and water. Most living things can remain active only between 30° and 110° Fahrenheit. Most of the biosphere lies within this range of ___3___. Without the air- or water-pressure levels found in the biosphere, living things would explode or be crushed. Without the biosphere's oxygen and water, the chemical processes required to keep life going could not take place.

3. ____________________

Within the biosphere various kinds of life are dependent on one another. This dependence is called interrelationship of living things. For instance, green plants produce and give off oxygen. Animals must ___4___ this to stay alive. In turn, when animals die, their bodies decay and enrich the soil so new plants can grow.

4. ____________________

Such interrelationships mean that the biosphere exists in a delicate state of ___5___. Whatever affects one form of life may affect many others. Poisons that humans use to kill insect pests can kill helpful insects too, as well as insect-eating birds. Eventually these poisons can harm humans themselves.

5. ____________________

UNIT 6

For Units 6–10, read each article completely. Choose the best answer and fill in your selection in the answer row at the bottom of the page.

Tomatoes are vinelike plants belonging to the nightshade family and are related to the potato and the eggplant. The vine bears clusters of juicy, more-or-less round fruits. Their ___1___ varies. Some may be yellow, others orange or deep red.

1. A) size B) texture C) color D) taste E) weight

Tomatoes are grown from seeds. In temperate regions the seeds must be started in a greenhouse, hotbed, or cold frame. This prevents damage due to ___2___. The plants are not transplanted to fields until there is no danger of cold weather. They thrive in well-fertilized sandy loam but will grow in almost any fertile, well-drained soil.

2. A) theft B) frost C) humidity D) fire E) insects

The size of tomatoes can vary considerably. Some can be___3___. They may be as small as cherries. Others, called beefsteak tomatoes, may be as large as grapefruit, measuring over four inches in diameter.

3. A) baked B) broiled C) skinless D) sliced E) tiny

Tomatoes are native to the Andes Mountains and were cultivated for food in Mexico and Peru by the Indians long before the Spanish invaded South and Central America. After the Spanish explorers brought tomato seeds back to Europe, tomatoes were grown in many countries, but only as ornamental plants at first. Though they were known as "love apples," nobody ever ate them. They were thought to be ___4___. Not until late in the nineteenth century did Europeans realize that tomatoes are not only delicious but also rich in minerals and vitamins.

4. A) solidified B) healthful C) magical D) poisonous E) unattractive

In America today, 7½ million tons of tomatoes are grown each year. During the summer, they are ___5___ outdoors in every state in the Union. During the winter, tomatoes are harvested in the fields of Texas, California, and Florida, and produced in greenhouses in North Carolina and the New England states.

5. A) displayed B) consumed C) baked D) performed E) raised

ANSWER ROWS: 1 Ⓐ Ⓑ Ⓒ Ⓓ Ⓔ 2 Ⓐ Ⓑ Ⓒ Ⓓ Ⓔ 3 Ⓐ Ⓑ Ⓒ Ⓓ Ⓔ 4 Ⓐ Ⓑ Ⓒ Ⓓ Ⓔ 5 Ⓐ Ⓑ Ⓒ Ⓓ Ⓔ

UNIT 7

Works of visual art that have three dimensions, rather than being flat like a painting, are called sculptures. Their ___1___ vary greatly. They may be tiny carvings (called cameos) set into rings, or works as huge as the Statue of Liberty.

1. A) textures B) sizes C) creators D) moods E) images

Just about every civilization on earth—Asian, African, European, American, Pacific Island, Indian, Eskimo—has produced artistic sculpture, out of every available material from wood to whalebone. Examples of Stone Age carvings of animals, dating back 20,000 years, have been found in French and Spanish caves. The ancient Greeks produced such beautiful life-size statues as that of Venus de Milo. In the 1500s the Italian genius Michelangelo ___2___ dramatic figures of David, Moses, and Jesus. Twentieth-century sculpture has experimented in new directions, often shaping metal and wire into forms that represent ideas rather than persons.

2. A) described B) sought C) carved D) purchased E) painted

There are three basic kinds of sculpture. The most commonly known is freestanding, or sculpture in the round. It can be ___3___ from all sides. The Statue of Liberty is a famous free-standing sculpture. Relief sculptures are those that stand out from a flat background, such as the heads of Washington, Jefferson, Lincoln, and Theodore Roosevelt on Mount Rushmore. The third kind is sunken relief, or intaglio, in which the figure is cut into a flat background.

3. A) veiled B) polished C) rotated D) viewed E) climbed

Sculptors use a wide variety of materials and tools. Some like to mold soft substances such as clay, wax, or plaster. Others prefer the solidity of wood or stone, working with mallets and chisels. Modern sculptors often include several materials, perhaps even glass or cloth, in a single work. ___4___ are popular for making outdoor statues. Bronze is the most common of these.

4. A) Rocks B) Lavas C) Woods D) Plastics E) Metals

The world contains hundreds of famous sculptures, ancient and modern. People journey from around the world to ___5___ them. Besides those already mentioned, there are the giant stone heads on Easter Island in the Pacific, the Sphinx in Egypt, and the seated figure of Lincoln in his memorial in Washington, D.C.

5. A) admire B) acquire C) salvage D) plant E) order

 ANSWER ROWS: 1 Ⓐ Ⓑ Ⓒ Ⓓ Ⓔ 2 Ⓐ Ⓑ Ⓒ Ⓓ Ⓔ 3 Ⓐ Ⓑ Ⓒ Ⓓ Ⓔ 4 Ⓐ Ⓑ Ⓒ Ⓓ Ⓔ 5 Ⓐ Ⓑ Ⓒ Ⓓ Ⓔ

UNIT 8

In 1520 the explorer Hernan Cortez became the first European to taste vanilla. Montezuma, king of the Aztecs of Mexico, introduced both vanilla and chocolate to Cortez and his Spanish explorers. The king never realized how important these ____1____ would become to the rest of the world. Eventually, explorers returned to Europe with some precious vanilla plants, intending to grow them nearer to home.

1. A) vehicles B) sculptures C) soldiers D) fragments E) flavors

For 300 years Europeans met with complete failure while trying to ____2____ vanilla beans. Healthy vines grew, but the delicate little orchids that were supposed to produce beans blossomed and died without producing anything. Finally it was discovered that a tiny, stingless bee that lived only in Mexico was responsible for pollinating the plant. When Europeans began pollinating the vanilla plants by hand, the plants began to produce beans.

2. A) store B) cultivate C) construct D) collect E) freeze

Today, most vanilla beans come from Mexico and Madagascar, a large island off the east coast of Africa. The United States ____3____ millions of pounds each year, about fifty percent of what the world produces. Our supply, however, may change drastically from year to year because of storms and plant disease. Once vanilla plants die, the land on which they grow must rest for twenty years before it can be replanted.

3. A) exports B) wastes C) imports D) rejects E) destroys

Vanilla beans cannot just be picked and taken off to market. They require a time-consuming curing process to bring out their special flavor. The beans, about a half-inch wide and six to ten inches long, must go through two months of drying in the sun and three months of drying in a shelter. Then they are ready for ____4____. It is in this state that they are exported all over the world.

4. A) shipping B) displaying C) crushing D) picking E) planting

Though some cooks still prefer to grate vanilla beans when flavoring food, most just pour in some vanilla extract. This is a ____5____ form of the flavoring. When vanilla beans are steeped, like tea, in alcohol and water, the mixture becomes pure vanilla extract. Now, in laboratories, scientists make imitation vanilla extract. Any way it is used, vanilla is the world's most popular flavor.

5. A) rare B) delicious C) spicy D) liquid E) powdered

ANSWER ROWS: 1 Ⓐ Ⓑ Ⓒ Ⓓ Ⓔ 2 Ⓐ Ⓑ Ⓒ Ⓓ Ⓔ 3 Ⓐ Ⓑ Ⓒ Ⓓ Ⓔ 4 Ⓐ Ⓑ Ⓒ Ⓓ Ⓔ 5 Ⓐ Ⓑ Ⓒ Ⓓ Ⓔ

UNIT 9

Catacombs are systems of underground passages and rooms used centuries ago as burial places. They were cut into soft rock and extended into large networks of connecting corridors and rooms. They covered ____1____ areas. Graves were cut into the walls, with clay or marble slabs used to close some of them. The catacombs were used for funerals and for memorial services as well.

1. A) treacherous B) unsightly C) enormous D) dreary E) shallow

The most famous catacombs, on the outskirts of Rome, are a valuable source of information on every aspect of early Christianity. They were ____2____ between A. D. 200 and 400 by early Christians. Thousands of inscriptions offer evidence of how the people worshiped, and paintings on walls are examples of early Christian art, depicting such scenes as "Daniel in the Lion's Den" and "Moses Striking the Rock."

2. A) untouched B) used C) supplied D) destroyed E) manufactured

Because of a Roman law protecting grave sites, Christians took refuge in the catacombs during periods of anti-Christian activity. They did this to avoid ____3____. They also used some of the larger vaults for certain religious services. As the Christians' danger grew, they blocked old known openings. Then they made new, secret entrances and exits. They expanded the catacombs into a maze of criss-crossing tunnels lighted and ventilated by ingenious air shafts that kept the porous rock dry. Doing this preserved the ____4____ places.

3. A) strikes B) famines C) taxes D) floods E) persecution

4. A) growing B) watering C) breeding D) burial E) hunting

Catacombs have been found in other Italian cities, as well as in Malta, Egypt, and North Africa. Burial chapels in some monasteries and convents in Europe are sometimes called catacombs. But the so-called "catacombs of Paris" were not utilized for burials until 1787. They are merely abandoned stone quarries.

After the Emperor Constantine issued a proclamation in A.D. 313 giving the Christians freedom of worship, the Christians no longer needed the catacombs as a refuge. As decades passed, their ____5____ was forgotten. When accidentally uncovered in 1578, they were thought to be ruins of ancient cities.

5. A) contribution B) program C) family D) book E) existence

ANSWER ROWS: 1 Ⓐ Ⓑ Ⓒ Ⓓ Ⓔ 2 Ⓐ Ⓑ Ⓒ Ⓓ Ⓔ 3 Ⓐ Ⓑ Ⓒ Ⓓ Ⓔ 4 Ⓐ Ⓑ Ⓒ Ⓓ Ⓔ 5 Ⓐ Ⓑ Ⓒ Ⓓ Ⓔ

UNIT 10

Rice, one of the world's most important food crops, has been grown for probably thousands of years. Early records show that it was ___1___ in India as early as 326 B.C. It was introduced into Spain in A. D. 700. But it wasn't until the late 1600s that rice was finally planted in American soil.

1. A) cultivated B) conveyed C) buried D) delivered E) manufactured

Rising from two to six feet tall, rice plants look much like other grain or cereal plants. However, they need a constant supply of ___2___. Therefore, these plants must be grown in flooded fields or terraced hillsides where rainfall is heavy. Under these conditions, rice is easily raised in many types of soil.

2. A) sunshine B) oxygen C) fertilizer D) water E) heat

Rice provides us with both nourishment and by-products. A rice kernel contains eighty percent starch, twelve percent water, and eight percent protein, as well as several necessary vitamins. In some countries fermented rice makes wine, and the outer coating of the rice kernel makes livestock food, soap, and margarine. The reeds from the plant itself make good sandals, hats, and even thatched roofs. Thus rice is one of the world's most___3___ crops.

3. A) troublesome B) perishable C) useful D) hardy E) vulnerable

It is estimated that rice is a chief food for half the people in the world. In India and the rest of Asia, rice is as important as bread is to the people of North America and Europe. In America, the typical person eats seven pounds of rice a year, but in Asia the typical person ___4___ almost a pound a day.

4. A) wastes B) recycles C) dries D) consumes E) plants

Though the United States grows more than six million metric tons each year, its output is only a tiny portion of the world's supply. Asian countries grow ninety percent of the world's rice crop—but still must import from other countries. They must do so to ___5___ their more than two billion people. Without rice, there is no question that a large part of the world's population would face starvation.

5. A) manage B) rule C) protect D) employ E) nourish

ANSWER ROWS: 1 Ⓐ Ⓑ Ⓒ Ⓓ Ⓔ 2 Ⓐ Ⓑ Ⓒ Ⓓ Ⓔ 3 Ⓐ Ⓑ Ⓒ Ⓓ Ⓔ 4 Ⓐ Ⓑ Ⓒ Ⓓ Ⓔ 5 Ⓐ Ⓑ Ⓒ Ⓓ Ⓔ

SECOND
ON YOUR OWN

For the Second On Your Own, read each article completely. Think of the best word you know for each blank, and write that word in the blank to the right.

Crustaceans are those odd animals that look, to some people, like mistakes of nature. Most crustaceans seem to be a collection of knobs, knuckles, ridges, and extra legs, all cased in a hard shell. True, some other animals have shells, but a crustacean's shell is really its ____1____. It serves the purpose that bones do in other animals. It holds the body together, for the crustacean has neither bones nor a spine.

1. ____________________

There are more than 25,000 ____2____ of crustaceans. Fewer than 100 have common names, however. Crabs, shrimp, and lobsters are easily recognized, edible crustaceans. Water fleas, pill bugs, barnacles, and woodlice are less distinctive and less tasty. The kinds of crustaceans outnumber all the kinds of mammals, fish, and birds combined.

2. ____________________

Even among crustaceans there are vast ____3____ in appearance and function. A clam has no true legs, but another crustacean, the centipede, has dozens of paired legs. Most crustaceans breathe through gills, yet some smaller ones breathe through tiny pores in their feet. The pill bug curls into an armored ball when it is startled, but the scorpion, another crustacean, lashes out with its poison-barbed tail.

3. ____________________

Crustaceans have been called "the insects of the sea." Insects are found in many environments. Similarly, crustaceans ____4____ almost any body of water, from a pond to the ocean. Both insects and crustaceans have survived changes in the earth over thousands of years. Both are scavengers, feeding upon the decaying flesh of dead animals.

4. ____________________

In common with insects, too, crustaceans have compound eyes. While each human eye has but one lens, a compound eye has hundreds of lenses. Thus it can ____5____ many images at one time. Some crustaceans, oddly, do not have eyes in their heads, but at the tips of long, waving tubes, or stalks. Crustaceans are far from being nature's mistakes. Nature has equipped them to survive for millions of years.

5. ____________________

UNIT 11

For Units 11–15, read each article completely. Choose the best answer and fill in your selection in the answer row at the bottom of the page.

The Galapagos Island tortoises are probably the oldest living animals in the world. Weighing from 400 to 800 pounds at maturity, these giant, lumbering, tanklike turtles are believed to have a life span of 200 to 250 years. If this is so, then there are tortoises living on the islands today that were babies when George Washington was young.

At one time, there were as many as fifteen species of Galapagos tortoises. Today, eleven of these are ___1___. The remaining species have several characteristics in common. All have high, arched shells and are brownish-black. Being land turtles, they spend most of their lives out of water. They are also ___2___. They eat no meat but live only on grass and plants.

Of course, the best protection a Galapagos tortoise has is its thick shell. Though this tortoise cannot tightly close its top and bottom shells as many other turtles can, its front feet serve as cover and protection as it withdraws into its shell. This is how it ___3___ itself. The Galapagos tortoise has few natural enemies, however. This is why it has been able to survive for over fifteen million years.

In the 1700s and 1800s, the Galapagos Islands, lying near the equator, 650 miles off western South America, became a favorite haunt of pirates and whalers, who called them the "Enchanted Isles." In the 1800s, famished sailors landing there slaughtered an estimated 16,000 tortoises. They did this for the animals' valuable___4___. It satisfied their hunger. Civilization, then, has played a part in driving these reptiles toward extinction.

Humans directly, however, were not the primary cause of the turtles' decline in number. ___5___ proved even more deadly. Increasing numbers of rats, dogs, and pigs devoured the turtle eggs that were buried in shallow holes on the sandy beaches. As a result, the Galapagos tortoises are so near to extinction today that extreme measures have been taken to protect the few that remain.

1. A) admired B) noticeable C) popular D) extinct E) dangerous

2. A) vegetarians B) swimmers C) divers D) climbers E) champions

3. A) harms B) defends C) reproduces D) bathes E) nourishes

4. A) skins B) shells C) offspring D) teeth E) meat

5. A) Floods B) Disease C) Animals D) Pollution E) Storms

ANSWER ROWS: 1 Ⓐ Ⓑ Ⓒ Ⓓ Ⓔ 2 Ⓐ Ⓑ Ⓒ Ⓓ Ⓔ 3 Ⓐ Ⓑ Ⓒ Ⓓ Ⓔ 4 Ⓐ Ⓑ Ⓒ Ⓓ Ⓔ 5 Ⓐ Ⓑ Ⓒ Ⓓ Ⓔ

UNIT 12

A kiln is a type of oven or furnace used to cure, harden, or burn certain materials. Depending on which materials are heated in it, a kiln may be square, tunnel shaped, or beehive shaped, and is usually made of brick or stone. Its ___1___ may vary. It may be set as low as sixty-five degrees to cure grain or as high as 3,200 degrees to convert limestone to quicklime.

1. A) capacity B) weight C) utility D) color E) temperature

Kilns are used in industry and in craft-making. They have a variety of ___2___. The cement industry uses revolving kilns to heat and separate raw materials. Bricks, pottery, and china made from clay must be fired, or hardened, in kilns. Certain types of coal and timber must be kiln-dried before they can be used. Hobbyists use small kilns to fire a variety of ceramic objects.

2. A) restrictions B) parts C) regulations D) purposes E) accidents

There are two main types of kilns. A periodic kiln, used to fire certain kinds of delicate china, is raised to a high temperature and then completely cooled before its contents are removed. A continuous, or tunnel kiln contains several chambers, or zones, which heat, bake, and cool a product. Stacks of clay bricks move through a tunnel kiln on tracks. Then they ___3___, hardened and cooled.

3. A) disperse B) disintegrate C) emerge D) crack E) expand

Gas, oil, and coal are all used to heat modern kilns. Most manufacturers use whichever material is ___4___ in their area. But for special jobs, where cleanliness and careful heat are important, kilns must be heated by electricity even though it is more expensive. Small kilns used in the home or in craft shops are also heated electrically because electricity is clean and convenient.

4. A) prettiest B) cheapest C) imported D) newest E) advertised

Kilns have been in use for thousands of years. When ancient people discovered that heat hardened some materials, they were able to make durable household objects such as jugs and bowls. Today our museums display many kinds of ancient statues and art objects that have ___5___ because they had been kiln-dried. They come from lands as far apart as China and Greece.

5. A) faded B) lasted C) crumbled D) darkened E) appreciated

 ANSWER ROWS: 1 Ⓐ Ⓑ Ⓒ Ⓓ Ⓔ 2 Ⓐ Ⓑ Ⓒ Ⓓ Ⓔ 3 Ⓐ Ⓑ Ⓒ Ⓓ Ⓔ 4 Ⓐ Ⓑ Ⓒ Ⓓ Ⓔ 5 Ⓐ Ⓑ Ⓒ Ⓓ Ⓔ

UNIT 13

The bristlecone pine, sometimes called the hickory pine in the United States, is believed to be one of the world's oldest living trees. It is certainly the oldest kind of tree in America. Until recently, the giant redwood forests in California were thought to hold our oldest trees. But scientists have identified a bristlecone pine that is nearly 5,000 years old. That is even older than our most ____1____ redwood.

1. A) treasured B) healthy C) remote D) ancient E) beautiful

A bushy evergreen, the bristlecone pine usually grows from fifteen to thirty feet high. Its top limbs stand upright. Its lower limbs, however, ____2____. Its cones are thickly coated with brown-tipped scales; it is the long, curving prickles on these cones that give the bristlecone pine its name. The wood is very coarse-grained.

2. A) decay B) sparkle C) vibrate D) rise E) droop

Thousands of years ago California's White Mountains supported vast numbers of bristlecone pines. These forests remained thick and healthy as long as weather conditions were perfect. But over the ages the earth's surface underwent changes. ____3____ conditions changed. The redwood forests in the Sierra Mountains were then pushed to a higher elevation than the bristlecones in the White Mountains.

3. A) Farming B) Operating C) Traveling D) Political E) Climate

This change in elevation affected the mountain forests. Most of the rain that used to fall on the bristlecone forests was now caught in the higher Sierra Mountains. Redwoods flourished. However, most bristlecone pines died of ____4____. As time passed, the only bristlecones that could live were those at higher elevations, where they obtained moisture from the snowfields on the mountain tops.

4. A) suffocation B) thirst C) disease D) poison E) starvation

Life became so difficult for the bristlecone pines that it is a miracle even a small forest remains. Fortunately, they have the ability to adapt to a harsh existence. This is what has enabled them to ____5____ for so long. The White Mountain bristlecones exist today at an elevation of 10,000 feet, where the air is thin and winters are cold and bleak.

5. A) sway B) survive C) burn D) whistle E) float

ANSWER ROWS: 1 Ⓐ Ⓑ Ⓒ Ⓓ Ⓔ 2 Ⓐ Ⓑ Ⓒ Ⓓ Ⓔ 3 Ⓐ Ⓑ Ⓒ Ⓓ Ⓔ 4 Ⓐ Ⓑ Ⓒ Ⓓ Ⓔ 5 Ⓐ Ⓑ Ⓒ Ⓓ Ⓔ

UNIT 14

We live in a world of advertising. Advertising is any means of bringing information to the public. Its purpose is to ___1___ something. What is being presented to the public is usually a product or service, such as a car or lawnmowing. Yet it may also be an idea, as in "Vote for Jones," or an event, as in "Watch the World Series on this channel tomorrow!" Without advertising, people would have a difficult time knowing where goods could be bought or even whether certain goods or services existed.

1. A) sell B) memorize C) protect D) exchange E) regulate

Advertising began with town criers in ancient Greece, who called out the names of items available in the market. Ancient Egyptians carved ___2___ on stones. The first printed ads appeared in England in 1480, and newspaper ads began in 1648. In the twentieth century extensive new fields for advertising opened up with the invention of radio and television.

2. A) faces B) objects C) constellations D) initials E) announcements

Advertisers use whichever means, or media, they think will work best for them. For example, radio and television ads are costly. But they reach a ___3___ audience. This makes them worthwhile and cost-effective for the advertisers. Newspaper ads can feature coupons or information that can be clipped and saved. Magazines often appeal directly to special groups, such as sports fans, homemakers, or teen-agers. Other forms of advertising include direct mail, billboards, displays, calendars, giveaways, and skywriting.

3. A) youthful B) restricted C) vast D) sleepy E) sentimental

Do business owners themselves think up all those clever ads we see on TV and in the press? For the most part, they hire qualified agencies to create their advertising. An advertising agency plans a company's ads. It also does ___4___. It surveys the market and tests different approaches to determine the most effective way to sell the greatest amount of the product.

4. A) prevention B) peddling C) typing D) research E) manufacturing

How can we be sure that an ad is ___5___? Two government agencies, the Federal Trade Commission and the Food and Drug Administration, check ads against false claims. The Postal Service watches for fraudulent ads sent by mail. State and local governments also have watchdog agencies. Advertisers who deceive the public face stiff fines or other punishment.

5. A) unique B) attractive C) effective D) expensive E) accurate

 ANSWER ROWS: 1 Ⓐ Ⓑ Ⓒ Ⓓ Ⓔ 2 Ⓐ Ⓑ Ⓒ Ⓓ Ⓔ 3 Ⓐ Ⓑ Ⓒ Ⓓ Ⓔ 4 Ⓐ Ⓑ Ⓒ Ⓓ Ⓔ 5 Ⓐ Ⓑ Ⓒ Ⓓ Ⓔ

UNIT 15

Abundant energy is essential to modern civilization. Energy beyond that provided by human or animal muscles is needed for operating our factories, for heating and cooling our homes, for powering most forms of transportation, and for hundreds of other purposes. Presently, coal and oil supply the majority of our energy needs. But coal, when burned, tends to pollute the air, and oil is becoming scarcer. Other ___1___, therefore, must be developed.

1. A) structures B) machines C) territories D) mines E) sources

One alternative is solar energy. It is not a ___2___ idea. Two hundred years ago a French chemist named Lavoisier built a solar furnace that was heated to over 3000°F by the sun's collected rays. One hundred years ago solar energy was used in Chile to change salt water into fresh water. And in Egypt, in 1931, an engine powered by the sun's rays began pumping irrigation water.

2. A) better B) costly C) practical D) recent E) pleasant

Today solar batteries have been developed that can supply enough energy to operate radios and telephones. Some can even ___3___ a car. In addition, solar batteries are important parts of communication satellites now circling the earth. Such batteries, however, are presently too expensive for ordinary use.

3. A) wash B) repair C) demolish D) power E) finance

The heating and cooling of houses by solar energy has received a great amount of attention in recent years. Thousands of solar houses have been built, especially since 1974, when the United States government passed the Solar Heating and Cooling Demonstration Act. This act provided $60 million for the designing and construction of solar-energy ___4___. Most houses use devices on their roofs to collect the sun's energy and tanks to store it in the form of heated water.

4. A) battleships B) buildings C) locomotives D) tractors E) airplanes

There are many problems to be solved before the sun can become an important source of energy. A way must be found to build solar batteries inexpensively. Before houses can be heated and cooled by solar energy alone, new methods of storing the energy must be devised. ___5___ believe that these problems can and will be solved. Solar energy may be the solution to the world's quest for abundant, clean, cheap energy.

5. A) Scientists B) Farmers C) Drivers D) Educators E) Pilots

ANSWER ROWS: 1 Ⓐ Ⓑ Ⓒ Ⓓ Ⓔ 2 Ⓐ Ⓑ Ⓒ Ⓓ Ⓔ 3 Ⓐ Ⓑ Ⓒ Ⓓ Ⓔ 4 Ⓐ Ⓑ Ⓒ Ⓓ Ⓔ 5 Ⓐ Ⓑ Ⓒ Ⓓ Ⓔ

THIRD
ON YOUR OWN

For the Third On Your Own, read each article completely. Think of the best word you know for each blank, and write that word in the blank to the right.

Sand hills, camels, and a burning sun—this is probably your image of the Sahara Desert in Africa. This ____1____, however, is only partly true. In the strange Sahara you will also find huge mountains, beautiful lakes, heavy rainstorms, and even snow.

1. ____________________

The world's largest desert, the Sahara receives less than four inches of rain a year. Some portions of it are incredibly ____2____. They may go seven years without rain. Yet when rains do come, they are heavy storms that flood the empty river beds until the water disappears into the thirsty sand.

2. ____________________

Temperatures in the Sahara ____3____ greatly. Daytime readings pass 120 degrees Fahrenheit (49°C) in the summer. They drop forty degrees in an hour when the sun goes down. Once the temperature fell from 126 degrees F in the day to 26 degrees the same night!

3. ____________________

The Sahara has sand hills (called dunes), 10,000-foot mountain ranges, and vast areas of nothing but rocks or pebbles. ____4____ dust storms, called simooms, may suddenly arise. Their slashing winds, carrying vast quantities of loose sand, have been known to kill travelers and camels in ten minutes. Sometimes the mountains get snow. Much of the land is thinly covered with grass and bushes.

4. ____________________

Surprisingly, water was abundant in the Sahara thousands of years ago. Many kinds of plants and trees grew there, and many species of animals lived there. Ancient carvings of giraffes have been ____5____ on the walls of Sahara caves. Fish bones have been found beneath the sands. But today, water is difficult to find. Weary travelers must search for the water and shade of oases, those welcome areas of springs and green palm trees that are usually few and far between in the great Sahara Desert.

5. ____________________

UNIT 16

For Units 16-20, read each article completely. Choose the best answer and fill in your selection in the answer row at the bottom of the page.

The United States Coast Guard is a special naval and air force. Its primary responsibilities include combating illegal seagoing trade and aiding vessels in distress. But it also has other, weather-related and navigational ___1___. One of these is the maintaining of an ice patrol in the North Atlantic.

1. A) duties B) maps C) pictures D) charts E) equipment

Specially equipped Coast Guard planes search the North Atlantic for icebergs. Their job is to identify the dangerous ones, those which might float south into the main Atlantic shipping lanes. Once such an iceberg has been sighted and given an identification number, the International Ice Patrol Headquarters on Governor's Island, New York is notified. They are given its ___2___. Then its movement can be monitored so that it doesn't become a threat to one of the busiest shipping lanes in the world.

2. A) depth B) location C) weight D) height E) composition

Many multimillion-ton bergs drift southward from Baffin Bay each year. Luckily for the Coast Guard, most are easy to spot. Sometimes, though, an iceberg breaks away from its pack and disappears into the foggy Labrador current. Then it may ___3___ shipping for as long as three years.

3. A) record B) threaten C) observe D) guide E) supply

A renegade iceberg can do terrible things to even the largest of ships. In 1912 the liner *Titanic* sank after colliding with a berg. Fifteen hundred people died. In 1959 the Danish ship *Hans Hedtoft* smashed into one of these floating hazards and sank. Ninety-five people ___4___. All told, nineteen ships have challenged the icebergs and lost in the past seventy years.

4. A) celebrated B) failed C) perished D) fought E) marched

Each day the U. S. Coast Guard's iceberg searchers fly seven hour missions over 15,000-square mile areas. To help them locate the bergs, the crew members use radar. Nothing, however, can ___5___ these floating ice mountains. Once an iceberg was bombed, torpedoed, and blasted with five-inch (12.7 cm) naval guns, but it would not sink. Yet, if the Coast Guard cannot demolish the icebergs, it can at least keep track of them—by flying through some of the worst weather in the world every day of the year.

5. A) straighten B) pull C) block D) rival E) destroy

ANSWER ROWS: 1 Ⓐ Ⓑ Ⓒ Ⓓ Ⓔ 2 Ⓐ Ⓑ Ⓒ Ⓓ Ⓔ 3 Ⓐ Ⓑ Ⓒ Ⓓ Ⓔ 4 Ⓐ Ⓑ Ⓒ Ⓓ Ⓔ 5 Ⓐ Ⓑ Ⓒ Ⓓ Ⓔ

UNIT 17

The year is 1191 A.D., and Crusaders from the north are battering at the gates of Jerusalem. Angry ___1___ shout and scream. Arrows fly through the air. Spears find their way to human targets. For many hours the fierce struggle rages. Then, as warriors fall in exhaustion, all is quiet in the Holy Land. The battle is over: the Crusaders from Austria have won.

1. A) parents B) soldiers C) spectators D) children E) passengers

No one knew then, of course, that the death of many soldiers in battle would also mark the birth of a new flag. But when Duke Leopold V of Austria took off his bloodstained cloak, he gazed in amazement. His belt had covered one part of the cloak. Now, running directly across that bloodstained ___2___ was a band of pure white. From that moment on, a red cloth with a white stripe across the center would be the Austrian duke's personal flag. Seven hundred twenty-eight years later, in 1918, Austria chose the same design for its national flag!

2. A) weapon B) garment C) bandage D) document E) ambulance

Another old banner also has an unusual ___3___. In 1219, we are told, King Valdemar of Denmark saw a white cross in a red sky one night before a battle. Since that time, Denmark's official flag has been a white cross on a red cloth. It is the oldest flag among all the countries in the world.

3. A) pole B) fabric C) origin D) design E) color

By comparison, America's Stars and Stripes is a very young flag. It is also one that has ___4___ very often. On June 14, 1777, it flew proudly over New England with thirteen stars. As time passed, a star was added for each new state. Shortly after Hawaii became the fiftieth state in 1959, the fifty-star flag became the newest official flag of the United States. Legend tells us that Betsy Ross made the first American flag in June 1776, but there is no historical evidence to support this tale. In fact, no one knows who ___5___ the flag. Yet we do know that the first schoolhouse to fly Old Glory was on Catamount Hill in Cortain, Massachusetts. The year was 1812.

4. A) transferred B) circulated C) disappeared D) changed E) disintegrated

5. A) bought B) lost C) displayed D) found E) designed

Rarely does a nation change its flag radically, but in the 1960s Canada adopted a wholly new red-and-white banner featuring the national symbol, the maple leaf.

 ANSWER ROWS: 1 Ⓐ Ⓑ Ⓒ Ⓓ Ⓔ 2 Ⓐ Ⓑ Ⓒ Ⓓ Ⓔ 3 Ⓐ Ⓑ Ⓒ Ⓓ Ⓔ 4 Ⓐ Ⓑ Ⓒ Ⓓ Ⓔ 5 Ⓐ Ⓑ Ⓒ Ⓓ Ⓔ

UNIT 18

Depth sounding means finding the depth of water under a ship. Doing this is ____1____ for sailors. They cannot sail with assurance of safety if they do not know what is under their ship. Rocks, sandbars, or shallow water that cannot be seen from above the surface can easily cause a shipwreck. Consequently, for centuries sailors have used some kind of depth-sounding device.

1. A) enjoyable B) hazardous C) unwarranted D) foreboding E) essential

For years sailors depth-sounded with what we call the lead and line method. On the end of a long rope, a heavy piece of lead was tied. Its purpose was to ____2____ the rope down. Every six feet, or one fathom, a knot was made in the rope. If a sailor dropped the rope straight into the water and six knots went under, it meant that the water was six fathoms, or thirty-six feet, deep.

2. A) wear B) fasten C) clamp D) weigh E) flatten

When the fathometer was invented, depth sounding became easier. A fathometer is a device that sends sound signals underwater and receives their echo back. The sounds bounce off the nearest solid surface, and the echoes return to the ship. The sailors can tell how deep the water is by measuring how long it takes for an echo to return. This equipment is quite ____3____. It has been proven to give highly accurate readings.

3 A) bizarre B) reliable C) cumbersome D) inadequate E) controversial

This ____4____ makes the sailor's life much easier. In the pilot house the captain turns a switch and consults the dial on the fathomether to determine what lies under the water. Different kinds of flashes on the dial indicate that the sound waves are finding the ocean bottom, rocks, or reefs—or just a school of fish.

4. A) computer B) radio C) instrument D) flashlight E) satellite

Depth sounding has proved useful in two other ways besides navigating ships safely through the water. It ____5____ fishers and mapmakers. With the help of a fathometer, captains of fishing boats can easily locate schools of fish and increase their marketable catches. Mapmakers use fathometers to chart the mountains and valleys under the oceans.

5. A) hinders B) perplexes C) enrages D) benefits E) terrorizes

ANSWER ROWS: 1 Ⓐ Ⓑ Ⓒ Ⓓ Ⓔ 2 Ⓐ Ⓑ Ⓒ Ⓓ Ⓔ 3 Ⓐ Ⓑ Ⓒ Ⓓ Ⓔ 4 Ⓐ Ⓑ Ⓒ Ⓓ Ⓔ 5 Ⓐ Ⓑ Ⓒ Ⓓ Ⓔ

UNIT 19

If you have ever been in a school play or even made believe you were a doctor, a detective, or a space traveler, you know the enjoyment that acting brings. Almost all of us have some wish to play the part of someone—or something—else. Historical records indicate that this ___1___ is as old as civilization itself.

1. A) controversy B) occupation C) transformation D) technique E) desire

In the ancient world, acting was often associated with religious ceremonies and other special occasions. As far back as 2200 B.C. trained Chinese actors performed ceremonial dances in costume and makeup at harvest festivals. It is believed that this was the first step in the ___2___ of acting. To the dance was gradually added pantomime—the imitation of movements and gestures—as well as the wearing of masks, the singing of chants, and finally the use of dialogue (speech).

2. A) appreciation B) perception C) rediscovery D) breakdown E) development

While acting was coming into its own in the ancient Chinese classical theater, it was doing the same in the western world, in Greece. From about 500 B.C. on, acting became a highly specialized art in Greece. Greek actors, however, still wore masks, and their motions were largely fixed by custom. Consequently, they had little opportunity to demonstrate their individual ___3___.

3. A) personalities B) inventions C) fortitude D) humility E) loyalty

Modern acting, by contrast, gives the individual actor great opportunity to develop his or her personal talents for serious, comic, or musical drama. The names, faces, and styles of famous movie actors are known worldwide. Broadway and television provide other stages on which actors can display their talent. A special form of acting takes place in radio drama, which was highly popular before television. In radio drama the actors face a unique challenge. They are unseen by their ___4___. So they must rely on voice alone to make their characters real to the listeners.

4. A) peers B) directors C) audience D) musicians E) producers

Acting is not, as many people think, a quick, easy road to fame and riches. Only forty percent of Broadway actors are employed, most of them for only part of the year. Those who become stars need not only talent, but determination. They must not be easily ___5___. Otherwise, they might give up before the opportunity for stardom presents itself.

5. A) embarrassed B) discouraged C) agitated D) deceived E) recognized

 ANSWER ROWS: 1 Ⓐ Ⓑ Ⓒ Ⓓ Ⓔ 2 Ⓐ Ⓑ Ⓒ Ⓓ Ⓔ 3 Ⓐ Ⓑ Ⓒ Ⓓ Ⓔ 4 Ⓐ Ⓑ Ⓒ Ⓓ Ⓔ 5 Ⓐ Ⓑ Ⓒ Ⓓ Ⓔ

UNIT 20

Cinnamon is the dried bark of a tropical tree. We know it best as the spice that adds flavor to many baked goods. Thus it is frequently an ingredient in ___1___. Oddly enough, this sharply sweet substance, with its delightful aroma, comes from a kind of laurel tree whose flowers have a most unpleasant smell.

1. A) soda B) tea C) salad D) margarine E) cake

Southeast Asia is the source of much of the world's cinnamon. The finest of the spice is said to be that of Sri Lanka, the island nation off the coast of India. Indonesia, the West Indies, Brazil, and Egypt also produce large amounts of the pungent spice. Most of it is then ___2___. This brings those lands much needed revenue.

2. A) exported B) tested C) consumed D) sprayed E) baked

"Harvesting" and preparing cinnamon is a painstaking task. In the rainy season, when the bark of the cinnamon tree peels best, workers carefully remove thin strips of bark from the tree's lower branches. A day or so later, the workers must separate the inner bark from the outer, leaving the inner bark to dry and curl into "quills," or sticks of cinnamon. Some of it is ___3___ in this form. But most cinnamon is ground into a powder.

3. A) blended B) soaked C) twisted D) used E) sliced

Although today we can buy all the cinnamon we may want at the supermarket, obtaining the spice was not always so easy. In ancient times it was often a ___4___ luxury. It was sometimes even held sacred. It was burned as incense in King Solomon's temple and in Roman ceremonies. Wealthy Romans also scented their baths with it. In the Middle Ages, Europeans staked their fortunes—and sometimes their lives—to find new routes to the Orient so they could bring back cinnamon and other scarce spices much in demand.

4. A) taxable B) rare C) common D) forbidden E) gaudy

With such demand for cinnamon, it is not surprising that nations who produced or transported it controlled its supply tightly, to ensure themselves the highest profits. This, of course, made them ___5___. Ancient Arabs would not reveal the source of cinnamon to the Greeks. In old Sri Lanka (then called Ceylon), selling only one stick of cinnamon illegally brought a penalty of death.

5. A) unpopular B) popular C) rich D) special E) weak

ANSWER ROWS: 1 Ⓐ Ⓑ Ⓒ Ⓓ Ⓔ 2 Ⓐ Ⓑ Ⓒ Ⓓ Ⓔ 3 Ⓐ Ⓑ Ⓒ Ⓓ Ⓔ 4 Ⓐ Ⓑ Ⓒ Ⓓ Ⓔ 5 Ⓐ Ⓑ Ⓒ Ⓓ Ⓔ

FOURTH
ON YOUR OWN

For the Fourth On Your Own, read each article completely. Think of the best word you know for each blank, and write that word in the blank to the right.

The grouse is a bird that lives in the Northern Hemisphere. It has dull brown feathers and grows about as large as a chicken. Its feathers cover the main part of its body. They also ___1___ its nostrils and legs. They keep the bird from freezing in cold temperatures.

1. ________________

Grouse belong to the family of game birds that includes prairie chickens, ptarmigans, and sage hens. They never migrate from their homes, but instead during the winter they burrow into snowdrifts to keep warm. As an added safeguard against their enemies, some of their feathers may turn white during the winter. This makes the birds difficult to ___2___ in the snow.

2. ________________

Many kinds of grouse live in North America. The ruff grouse is found from Alaska to Georgia. People in the southern part of the United States often call it a partridge. The Canadian spruce grouse lives all over Alaska and Canada and as far south as New England. Hunters sometimes call spruce grouse "fool hens." The birds often become quite interested in ___3___ their hunters. As a result, they forget to escape and are very easy to shoot.

3. ________________

Grouse consume insects and berries during the summer months. In the fall they look for seed in the grain fields. All ___4___ long they survive on catkins, leaves, and buds.

4. ________________

When it is time to mate, some male grouse call to their mates by beating their wings in a kind of dance. Sometimes two males engage in a ___5___. The victor of this combat hopes to win the favor of a hen they both like. Grouse build their nests on the ground in well-hidden places, and the hens lay between ten and fifteen eggs that are tan with brown dots. The chicks leave their nest almost as soon as they hatch. If there is any danger, the mother hen gives a sharp screech that warns her chicks.

5. ________________

UNIT 21

For Units 20–25, read each article completely. Choose the best answer and fill in your selection in the answer row at the bottom of the page.

Dolphins are mammals that live all over the world, in warm ocean waters as well as in other bodies of water. Some even live in ___1___. Not only are they among the fastest of all swimmers, but they are capable of making sharp turns and sudden stops and leaping high into the air.

1. A) rivers B) deserts C) jungles D) caves E) forests

One of the two major kinds of dolphins is known as the common dolphin. These dolphins reach a length of about eight feet and an average weight of 165 pounds. Their cigar-shaped bodies are dark blue or black, with a white underside. Sometimes they change into several different colors when taken out of the ___2___.

2. A) air B) water C) dye D) soil E) chemical

The other major type of dolphin is the bottle-nosed dolphin. These creatures are considered among the smartest of all animals. Their intelligence is ranked with that of the chimpanzee. Bottle-nosed dolphins as long as twelve feet and weighing over 800 pounds have been found. However, most of the species are much ___3___. A bottle-nosed dolphin has a dark gray or blue-gray back and a white underside. Its beak, or snout, is about three inches long and contains about 200 small, sharp teeth.

3. A) smarter B) bigger C) smaller D) faster E) tamer

All dolphins have a keen sense of hearing and good eyesight and taste. But they have no sense of ___4___. Therefore they are unaware of strange odors. They are able to communicate with one another by barking, clicking, and whistling. Bottle-nosed dolphins can even imitate the sounds of human speech!

4. A) touch B) humor C) smell D) time E) thrift

Dolphins also have a natural sonar, or sound-echo system. This helps them ___5___ objects underwater. It greatly enhances their ability to find food. Each dolphin blows air through a passage that leads to a blowhole at the top of its head, and then listens for the sound to echo off whatever object it is looking for.

5. A) drop B) hide C) photograph D) bury E) locate

ANSWER ROWS: 1 Ⓐ Ⓑ Ⓒ Ⓓ Ⓔ 2 Ⓐ Ⓑ Ⓒ Ⓓ Ⓔ 3 Ⓐ Ⓑ Ⓒ Ⓓ Ⓔ 4 Ⓐ Ⓑ Ⓒ Ⓓ Ⓔ 5 Ⓐ Ⓑ Ⓒ Ⓓ Ⓔ

UNIT 22

About five percent of people are left-handed; they tend to use the left hand more often, for more purposes, than the right hand. Some parents of left-handed children worry about the condition. They think about trying to ___1___ it. But most authorities agree that left-handed children should be allowed to perform naturally. Many of the most talented people in history have been left-handed—the great artists Leonardo da Vinci and Michelangelo among them.

1. A) forget B) ignore C) explain D)change E) study

Left-handed persons find out early in life that they are living in a "right-handed society." Most of the objects they encounter are made for the convenience of right-handed people—locks, screws, doorknobs, golf clubs, and even automobiles. Left-handed people must adjust to this "right-handed" world. Most of them soon learn to ___2___ quite well. They are able to do anything that right-handed people can do.

2. A) write B) paint C) manage D) drive E) compute

No one is sure of what makes most people right-handed and a minority left-handed. But it is known that the ___3___ is not exactly the same on both sides. The left side of the face is a little different from the right. One leg is usually somewhat stronger than the other, as is one arm.

3. A) heart B) hand C) finger D) body E) foot

Scientists have even found that the right half and the left half of the brain do not function in the same way. This is still being ___4___. It is believed that in most people the left half of the brain predominates, or "rules," over the right half. The nerves from the brain cross over at the level of the neck, going to opposite sides of the body and making most people right-handed. But no one has explained why the left side of the brain dominates in most people.

4. A) studied B) preserved C) purchased D) stored E) donated

Whatever the cause, research indicates that ever since prehistoric times few humans have been left-handed. We can even see the ___5___. Ancient tools and weapons that have been unearthed were clearly made for right-handed, not left-handed, people.

5. A) logic B) dispute C) disagreement D) doubt E) evidence

 ANSWER ROWS: 1 Ⓐ Ⓑ Ⓒ Ⓓ Ⓔ 2 Ⓐ Ⓑ Ⓒ Ⓓ Ⓔ 3 Ⓐ Ⓑ Ⓒ Ⓓ Ⓔ 4 Ⓐ Ⓑ Ⓒ Ⓓ Ⓔ 5 Ⓐ Ⓑ Ⓒ Ⓓ Ⓔ

UNIT 23

At first glance, the small tailorbird of Asia is not at all remarkable. It has no flashing gold or shining red feathers. It is a dull gray-green ____1____. Its song is monotonous. About five inches long, it is similar in size to hundreds of other birds. Like many other common songbirds, it usually lays four eggs and eats insects.

1. A) bridge B) skyscraper C) color D) plant E) sea

But when it comes to nest-building, the tailorbird is unique. Its very name indicates that it is one of a kind in making nests. Long before humans invented their sewing machines, this bird was the original sewing machine! It even has a ____2____ bill.

2. A) horned B) ducklike C) short D) spoonlike E) needlelike

The tailorbird uses this bill to punch holes along the edges of two or three living leaves. Using spider webs or silk from the cocoon of the silkworm, the bird pushes these "threads" through the holes in the leaves. It draws the threads together so that the leaves form a cup or pouch. This busy worker then punches more leaves and sews them together. It adds them to the ____3____ nest. Some nests have as many as forty leaves sewn together.

3. A) straw B) unsafe C) growing D) hidden E) oldest

After the threads are all tightened, the tailorbird splits their ends, forming knots that prevent the threads from slipping through the holes. The knots are placed every half inch along the leaf edge. There are dozens of ____4____ in each nest. The bird even sews a leaf-flap over the top of the nest.

4. A) stitches B) caterpillars C) eggs D) branches E) scratches

Both the male and the female tailorbird help construct the nest. While the male puts together the sewn leaves, the female repairs any loose knots. She then fills the nest with soft grass or hair. These birds are quite ____5____. They often build their "tailor-made" nests in gardens and backyards, and even in potted plants! This is fortunate for people who enjoy watching the nest-building.

5. A) aloof B) friendly C) noisy D) vicious E) poisonous

ANSWER ROWS: 1 Ⓐ Ⓑ Ⓒ Ⓓ Ⓔ 2 Ⓐ Ⓑ Ⓒ Ⓓ Ⓔ 3 Ⓐ Ⓑ Ⓒ Ⓓ Ⓔ 4 Ⓐ Ⓑ Ⓒ Ⓓ Ⓔ 5 Ⓐ Ⓑ Ⓒ Ⓓ Ⓔ

UNIT 24

Tung oil comes from the fruit of perennial tropical trees belonging to the spurge family. It is also known as China wood oil because it has been used in China for hundreds of years to waterproof clothing, paper, and wood. It is therefore quite ____1____.

1. A) sticky B) rare C) expensive D) useful E) extravagant

There are four species of trees that produce tung oil. All of them are native to Eastern Asia and many Pacific islands. These trees, which grow to between fifteen and thirty feet, each year produce small white flowers and a capsulelike fruit that contains many seeds. The seeds are roasted, ground up, and then pressed until they yield a dark brown oil. The trees are also ____2____ in the United States and Europe.

2. A) destroyed B) attacked C) manufactured D) protected E) cultivated

Although most of the world's tung oil comes from China, about fifty million pounds of it is now produced in the United States each year. Eighty percent of the tung oil produced in America is used in the manufacture of house paints and varnishes, to increase their resistance to water. This makes them useful for ____3____ jobs.

3. A) ordinary B) outdoor C) unsightly D) small E) instant

Wood becomes protected when tung oil is rubbed into the surface with a clean rag. It is allowed to dry. Then the next coat is ____4____. Many professionals believe that tung oil provides a more desirable finish than any other material because it keeps its sheen and does not mildew or darken with age.

4. A) cleaned B) dusted C) sanded D) applied E) scraped

Tung oil solidifies when exposed to air for any length of time. This makes it difficult to ____5____. Experts recommend that if a can of tung oil is less than half full it should be poured into a smaller receptacle or the can should be filled with stones to raise the level of oil until there is no space left in the can for air.

5. A) store B) heat C) cool D) see E) moisturize

 ANSWER ROWS: 1 Ⓐ Ⓑ Ⓒ Ⓓ Ⓔ 2 Ⓐ Ⓑ Ⓒ Ⓓ Ⓔ 3 Ⓐ Ⓑ Ⓒ Ⓓ Ⓔ 4 Ⓐ Ⓑ Ⓒ Ⓓ Ⓔ 5 Ⓐ Ⓑ Ⓒ Ⓓ Ⓔ

UNIT 25

Radar is an electronic device that detects planes, ships, coastlines, landmarks, and even storm clouds. The name *radar* comes from the first letters of the words *radio direction* and *ranging*. As the human eye uses light waves to see, radar "sees" with radio waves. Without radar, planes could not land safely in bad weather and ships could not move safely in dense fog. It is therefore especially valuable to shippers and ____1____.

1. A) firefighters B) hobbyists C) athletes D) hunters E) travelers

In the 1800s it was discovered that radio waves could be reflected from objects. But scientists did not make great advances in radar research until the 1930s, when the world was threatened by war. During World War II many countries, especially Britain and the United States, used radar effectively. It has been used extensively in almost every ____2____ since then.

2. A) competition B) exhibit C) concert D) conflict E) election

Echoes make it possible for radar to work. When a beam of radio waves is sent out, it strikes an object and returns an echo. This echo is picked up by a radar antenna and recorded on a screen similar to a television screen. On the screen an observer sees a flash, or blip, that shows the direction and distance of the object. These ____3____ are now highly accurate.

3. A) routes B) programs C) flights D) targets E) measurements

Airport control towers use radar to guide planes in for safe landings. Almost all large ships depend on radar to prevent collisions with icebergs or other ships. Police track speeders in radar-equipped cars. Weather forecasters "see" the size, direction, and speed of storms on radar screens. Astronomers can even use radar to measure accurately the distance to the moon. Thus, the device has generated major ____4____.

4. A) opposition B) advancements C) publicity D) problems E) profits

Strengthening national defense is one of radar's most important functions. Huge radar antennas have been installed all over America. They guard us against possible ____5____ attacks. We have ballistic-missile warning systems that can alert us to attacks when missiles are more than 1,000 miles away. Other radar systems warn us against hostile aircraft and even spying space satellites.

5. A) mosquito B) heart C) enemy D) shark E) animal

FIFTH
ON YOUR OWN

For the Fifth On Your Own, read each article completely. Think of the best word you know for each blank, and write that word in the blank to the right.

The human ear is a special organ that sends sound waves from outside the body to the brain. It is made up of ___1___ parts. They are the outer ear, middle ear, and inner ear.

1. ________________

The outer ear is shaped like a horn so that it can collect sound waves and convey them into a tunnel, or canal, that leads to the eardrum. The canal is covered with tiny hairs and has glands that produce oil and wax to help keep dirt away from the eardrum. The eardrum itself is a thin piece of skin, like the head of a drum. It is ___2___ over the end of the canal, directly in front of the middle ear.

2. ________________

The middle ear has two parts: a tube leading to the back of the mouth and a hole about the size of a pea. The hole has three little bones that can move back and forth very rapidly. They do so whenever a ___3___ strikes the middle ear.

3. ________________

The inner ear is a curled tube shaped like a snail. It is filled with a liquid and has tiny cells covered with little hairlike nerves that go to the brain. When a sound wave strikes the eardrum, the three bones in the Middle ear move, causing the liquid in the inner ear to move also. That makes the nerve endings in the cells wiggle up and down, sending signals to the hearing centers in the brain.

The ears are very delicate and easily become infected. You should, therefore, be sure to ___4___ them. Never pinch your nostrils when you blow your nose, for germs may be pushed back into your ears. Wear ear plugs when you go swimming. Doing so will keep germs in the ___5___ from getting into your ears. Never put anything into your ear. You might break the skin in your eardrum and cause an infection. And of course, avoid prolonged exposure to loud noises.

4. ________________

5. ________________

Answer Key

Unit 1/Language Arts
Lesson 1 Sentences
Pages 12-13
A. C
1. A
2. J
3. C
4. F
5. D
6. H

Lesson 2 Usage
Pages 14-15
A. B
B. H
1. D
2. H
3. A
4. F
5. C
6. G
7. C
8. F
9. B
10. J

Lesson 3 Writing Mechanics
Pages 16-17
A. C
B. J
1. C
2. F
3. C
4. J
5. C
6. G
7. A
8. H

Lessons 4-8 Writing
(To score your child's writing see the Focused Holistic Scoring Guidelines on page 156)

Lesson 9 Test Yourself
Pages 23-25
A. C
1. B
2. J
3. A
B. J
C. A
4. J
5. B
6. F
7. C
D. H
8. J
9. C
10. G
11. C
(To score your child's writing see the Focused Holistic Scoring Guidelines on page 156)

Unit 2/Reading Comprehension
Lesson 10 Vocabulary
Pages 26-27
A. C
1. D
2. F
3. B
4. J
5. C

Lesson 11 Supporting Ideas
Pages 28-29
A. D
1. B
2. F
3. D
4. H
5. D

Lesson 12 Main Idea
Pages 30-31
A. A
1. C
2. G
3. D
4. H

Lesson 13 Relationships and Outcomes
Pages 32-33
A. C
1. B
2. J
3. A
4. H
5. D
6. G

Lesson 14 Inferences and Generalizations
Pages 34-35
A. B
1. D
2. F
3. B
4. J
5. A

Lesson 15 Evaluation
Pages 36-37
A. D
1. A
2. H
3. B
4. J
5. B

Lesson 16 Test Yourself
Pages 38-41
A. B
1. C
2. F
3. C
4. G
5. D
6. G
7. C
8. H
9. C
10. J
11. A
12. G
13. C
14. J

Unit 3/Mathematics Concepts
Lesson 17 Number Concepts
Pages 43-44
A. B
B. H
1. D
2. H
3. B
4. F
5. C
6. J
7. B
8. F

9. A
10. J
11. A

Lesson 18 Number Relations
Pages 45-46

A. D
B. F
1. A
2. J
3. B
4. H
5. B
6. H
7. A
8. H
9. B

Lesson 19 Geometry
Pages 47-48

A. A
1. C
2. J
3. B
4. F
5. B
6. H
7. B
8. J

Lesson 20 Measurement
Pages 49-50

A. A
B. H
1. D
2. F
3. B
4. J
5. D
6. H
7. A
8. H
9. B

Lesson 21 Probability and Statistics
Pages 51-52

A. D
1. B
2. J
3. B
4. G
5. D
6. F
7. C
8. H

Lesson 22 Test Yourself
Pages 53-54

A. B
1. D
2. F
3. C
4. G
5. C
6. J
7. B
8. F
9. C
10. G

Unit 4/Mathematics Operations

Lesson 23 Addition
Pages 55-45

A. E
B. F
1. D
2. G
3. A
4. J
5. E
6. K
7. B
8. H
9. B

Lesson 24 Subtraction
Pages 57-58

A. B
B. H
1. E
2. F
3. A
4. K
5. B
6. F
7. B
8. K
9. B

Lesson 25 Multiplication
Pages 59-60

A. A
B. J
1. B
2. K
3. D
4. K
5. A
6. J
7. B
8. H
9. D

Lesson 26 Division
Pages 61-62

A. D
B. K
1. B
2. K
3. E
4. G
5. B
6. H
7. E
8. F
9. E
10. J

Lesson 27 Test Yourself
Pages 63-64

A. E
B. H
1. C
2. J
3. B
4. K
5. E
6. F
7. E
8. H
9. B
10. J

Unit 5/Problem Solving

Lesson 28 Estimation
Pages 65-66

A. E
B. H
1. C
2. J
3. B
4. K
5. E
6. F

7. D
8. H
9. D
10. G

Lesson 29 Strategies
Pages 67-68

A. E
1. D
2. K
3. A
4. J
5. E
6. F
7. E
8. G

Lesson 30 Problem Solving
Pages 69-70

A. A
B. J
1. C
2. G
3. E
4. J
5. B
6. G
7. A
8. H

Lesson 31 Reasonable Answers
Pages 71-72

A. E
B. G
1. B
2. J
3. B
4. H
5. E
6. G
7. A
8. J
9. B

Lesson 32 Test Yourself
Pages 73-74

A. C
1. E
2. G
3. E
4. F
5. E
6. G
7. C
8. F
9. C
10. H

Unit 6/Citizenship
Lesson 33 History and Geography
Pages 75-78

A. B
1. B
2. D
3. A
4. B
5. A
6. C
7. A
8. D
9. C
10. B
11. A
12. D
13. B
14. C
15. B

Lesson 34 Law and Government
Pages 79-82

A. D
B. A
1. A
2. B
3. D
4. C
5. D
6. A
7. B
8. D
9. A
10. C
11. B
12. D
13. C
14. D
15. A
16. B
17. B

Lesson 35 Test Yourself
Pages 83-86

A. A
B. C
1. C
2. B
3. A
4. C
5. A
6. D
7. C
8. A
9. D
10. C
11. A
12. B
13. B
14. D
15. C
16. A
17. C
18. D
19. C
20. B

Test Practice
Test 1 Language Arts
Pages 87-90

A. C
1. D
2. J
3. C
B. H
C. A
4. F
5. C
6. J
7. B
D. H
3. D
8. J
9. C
10. G
11. A

(To score your child's writing see the Focused Holistic Scoring Guidelines on page 156)

Test 2 Reading Comprehension Pages 91-94

A. A
1. C
2. F
3. B
4. F
5. B
6. H
7. D
8. F
9. B
10. G
11. D
12. G
13. C
14. F

Test 3 Mathematics Pages 95-99

A. D
1. E
2. H
3. A
4. H
5. B
6. G
7. D
8. F
9. E
10. H
11. B
12. H
13. E
14. G
15. A
16. H
17. E
18. J
19. E
20. G
21. A
22. H
23. E
24. F
25. C
26. H
27. B

Test 4 Citizenship Pages 100-105

A. D
B. C
1. A
2. C
3. D
4. B
5. B
6. B
7. A
8. D
9. D
10. A
11. B
12. C
13. A
14. D
15. A
16. C
17. B
18. C
19. D
20. A
21. A
22. B

Cloze

(Sample answers are given for the On Your Own sections. Students may give equally acceptable synonyms.)

Unit 1, Page 117

1. C
2. A
3. E
4. D
5. C

Unit 2, Page 118

1. B
2. D
3. A
4. C
5. E

Unit 3, Page 119

1. D
2. C
3. B
4. A
5. E

Unit 4, Page 120

1. C
2. A
3. A
4. B
5. 3

Unit 5, Page 121

1. E
2. D
3. C
4. A
5. B

First On Your Own Page 122

1. life
2. bottom
3. temperatures
4. breathe
5. balance

Unit 6, Page 123

1. C
2. B
3. E
4. D
5. E

Unit 7, Page 124

1. B
2. C
3. D
4. E
5. A

Unit 8, Page 125

1. E
2. B
3. C
4. A
5. D

Unit 9, Page 126

1. C
2. B
3. E
4. D
5. E

Unit 10, Page 127

1. A
2. D
3. C

4. D
5. E

Second On Your Own Page 128

1. skeleton
2. types
3. differences
4. inhabit
5. see

Unit 11, Page 129

1. D
2. A
3. B
4. E
5. C

Unit 12, Page 130

1. E
2. D
3. C
4. B
5. B

Unit 13, Page 131

1. D
2. E
3. E
4. B
5. B

Unit 14, Page 132

1. A
2. E
3. C
4. D
5. E

Unit 15, Page 133

1. E
2. D
3. D
4. B
5. A

Third On Your Own Page 134

1. picture
2. dry
3. vary
4. dangerous
5. discovered

Unit 16, Page 135

1. A
2. B
3. B
4. C
5. E

Unit 17, Page 136

1. B
2. B
3. C
4. D
5. E

Unit 18, Page 137

1. E
2. D
3. B
4. C
5. D

Unit 19, Page 138

1. E
2. E
3. A
4. C
5. B

Unit 20, Page 139

1. E
2. A
3. D
4. B
5. C

Fourth On Your Own Page 140

1. protect
2. locate
3. observing
4. winter
5. fight

Unit 21, Page 141

1. A
2. B
3. C
4. C
5. E

Unit 22, Page 142

1. D
2. C
3. D
4. A
5. E

Unit 23, Page 143

1. C
2. E
3. C
4. A
5. B

Unit 24, Page 144

1. D
2. E
3. B
4. D
5. A

Unit 25, Page 145

1. E
2. D
3. E
4. B
5. C

Fifth On Your Own Page 146

1. three
2. stretched
3. sound
4. protect
5. water

Unit 1: Language Arts
Record of Scores

Page	Lesson	Lesson Name	My Score	Total Possible Score
12	1	Sentences		6
14	2	Usage		10
16	3	Writing Mechanics		8
18	4	Descriptive Writing*		60
19	5	Informative Writing*		60
20	6	Classificatory Writing*		60
21	7	Persuasive Writing*		60
22	8	Comparative Writing*		60
23	9	Test Yourself		11
		Total Scores		**335**

*See page 156 for Focused Holistic Scoring Guidelines

Unit 2: Reading
Record of Scores

Page	Lesson	Lesson Name	My Score	Total Possible Score
26	10	Vocabulary		5
28	11	Supporting Ideas		5
30	12	Main Idea		4
32	13	Relationships and Outcomes		6
34	14	Inferences and Generalizations		5
36	15	Evaluation		5
38	16	Test Yourself		14
		Total Scores		**44**

Unit 3: Mathematics Concepts
Record of Scores

Page	Lesson	Lesson Name	My Score	Total Possible Score
43	17	Number Concepts		11
45	18	Number Relations		9
47	19	Geometry		8
49	20	Measurement		9
51	21	Probability and Statistics		8
53	22	Test Yourself		10
		Total Scores		**55**

Unit 4: Mathematics Operations
Record of Scores

Page	Lesson	Lesson Name	My Score	Total Possible Score
55	23	Addition		9
57	24	Subtraction		9
59	25	Multiplication		9
61	26	Division		10
63	27	Test Yourself		10
		Total Scores		**47**

Unit 5: Problem Solving
Record of Scores

Page	Lesson	Lesson Name	My Score	Total Possible Score
65	28	Estimation		10
67	29	Strategies		8
69	30	Problem Solving		8
71	31	Reasonable Answers		9
73	32	Test Yourself		10
		Total Scores		**45**

Unit 6: Citizenship
Record of Scores

Page	Lesson	Lesson Name	My Score	Total Possible Score
75	33	History and Geography		15
79	34	Law and Government		17
83	35	Test Yourself		20
		Total Scores		**52**

Test Practice
Record of Scores

Page	Test	Lesson Name	My Score	Total Possible Score
87	1	Language Arts		11
91	2	Reading Comprehension		14
95	3	Mathematics		27
100	4	Citizenship		22
		Total Scores		**74**

Special Section
Cloze: Reading Comprehension Challenge
Record of Scores

Pages	Section	My Score	Total Possible Score
117-121	Units1-5		25
122	First On Your Own		5
	Total Scores		**30**
123-127	Units 6-10		25
128	Second On Your Own		5
	Total Scores		**30**
129-133	Units 11-15		25
134	Third On Your Own		5
	Total Scores		**30**
135-139	Units 16-20		25
140	Fourth On Your Own		5
	Total Scores		**30**
141-145	Units 21-25		25
146	Fifth On Your Own		5
	Total Scores		**30**

Focused Holistic Scoring Guidelines for Writing

Criterion	0	1 – 2	3 – 4
Purpose	No writing has been done	Purpose of writing is vague	Purpose of writing is correct
Audience	Addressed wrong audience	Little sense of audience	Strong sense of audience
Topic	Completely off topic	Topic is difficult to understand	Topic is clear and consistent
Mode	Not enough text to score	Wrong mode	Mode is obvious and correct
Organization	Too illegible to read	Organization is weak	Organization is consistent
Sequence	Wandering	Sequence is difficult to follow	Clear sense of order
Word Choice	Not enough text to score	Rudimentary vocabulary	Varied word choice
Logic	No position stated	Position too difficult to understand	Position is well defined
Elaboration	Student copies prompt	Few details presented	Effective use of details
Sentence Structure	Single words	Mostly fragments	Lively sentences
Paragraph Structure	Unstructured	Paragraphs have no topic	Topic is clear and supported
Story Structure	Confused	Structure is difficult to grasp	Flow of writing is consistent
Development of Ideas	No ideas are present	Ideas are minimally developed	Ideas are fully developed
Language Control	Foreign language	Lacks language control	Rich and diverse language
Mechanics	Too incoherent to read	So many errors as to be distracting	Few or no errors

Each criterion is scored on the scale: 0   1 ------------------ 2 ------------------ 3 ------------------ 4

NOTES

NOTES

NOTES

NOTES